Second Workshop on Text Simplification, Accessibility and Readability (TSAR 2023)

Varna, Bulgaria
7 September 2023

ISBN: 978-1-7138-9064-5

Printed from e-media with permission by:

Curran Associates, Inc.
57 Morehouse Lane
Red Hook, NY 12571

Printed with permission by Curran Associates, Inc. (2025)

Association for Computational Linguistics
209 N. Eighth Street
Stroudsburg, Pennsylvania 18360

Phone: 1-570-476-8006
Fax: 1-570-476-0860

acl@aclweb.org

Additional copies of this publication are available from:

Curran Associates, Inc.
57 Morehouse Lane
Red Hook, NY 12571 USA
Phone: 845-758-0400
Fax: 845-758-2633
Email: curran@proceedings.com
Web: www.proceedings.com

TSAR 2023

Second Workshop on Text Simplification, Accessibility and Readability

associated with

The 14th International Conference on Recent Advances in Natural Language Processing'2023

Proceedings of the Workshop

September 7th, 2023
Varna, Bulgaria

Workshop on Text Simplification,
Accessibility and Readability
Associated with the International Conference
Recent Advances in Natural Language Processing'2023

PROCEEDINGS

Varna, Bulgaria
7th September 2023

Designed by INCOMA Ltd.
Shoumen, BULGARIA

Preface

Welcome to the proceedings of the 2nd edition of the Workshop on Text Simplification, Accessibility and Readability (TSAR), hosted at the 14th Conference on Recent Advances in Natural Language Processing (RANLP 2023), in Varna, Bulgaria.

This year, we received 24 submissions to the workshop. These submissions covered a variety of current topics of interest to the TSAR community. Three papers examined the area of lexical simplification, considering context-awareness, lexical deletion and the fine-tuning of large language models (LLMs). Five papers considered simplification at the whole-text level, considering cognitive disabilities, the capacity of LLMs to adapt to genre-specific simplification, operations for simplification, coherence in document level simplification and tools for simplification of texts. Additionally, research was presented on accessibility and readability, covering easy-language translation, mediation and evaluation. The research was linguistically diverse, proposing solutions for English, Spanish, Swedish and French.

All submissions were peer-reviewed by the members of the program committee which includes distinguished specialists in text simplification, accessibility, and readability. Out of the 24 submissions to the workshop, 10 were rejected, 11 were accepted and 3 were accepted subject to improvements in line with reviewer feedback. Out of 14 accepted papers, 6 were selected to be presented orally and 8 as posters, which were presented during a lightning-talk session.

The workshop is held in-person, with online attendance for authors who were unable to attend due to constraints beyond the organisers control. The program encompasses: a keynote speech by Dr. Victoria Yaneva, National Board of Medical Examiners, USA; two oral sessions, comprising six presentations; a round of lightning talks to introduce the poster presentations; and a hosted discussion session on current issues and trends in text simplification, accessibility and readability research.

We would like to thank the members of the program committee for their timely help in reviewing the submissions and all the authors for submitting their papers to the workshop. We also thank the organisers of RANLP for hosting the workshop and their kind support in producing these proceedings.

TSAR Organizing Committee

Sanja Štajner, Matthew Shardlow, Fernando Alva-Manchego, Horacio Saggion

Organizing Committee

- Sanja Štajner, Independent Researcher
- Matthew Shardlow, Manchester Metropolitan University
- Fernando Alva-Manchego, Cardiff University
- Horacio Saggion, Universitat Pompeu Fabra

Programme Committee

- Bruce W. Lee (University of Pennsylvania)
- Christina Niklaus (University of St. Gallen)
- Giulia Venturi (Institute of Computational Linguistics "Antonio Zampolli" (ILC-CNR))
- Jaap Kamps (University of Amsterdam)
- Jasper Degraeuwe (Ghent University)
- Jipeng Qiang (Yangzhou University)
- Kim Cheng Sheang (Universitat Pompeu Fabra)
- Laura Vásquez-Rodríguez (University of Manchester)
- Liana Ermakova (HCTI EA-4249, Université de Bretagne Occidentale)
- Maja Popović (ADAPT, Dublin City University)
- Mounica Maddela (Georgia Institute of Technology)
- Natalia Grabar (CNRS STL UMR8163, Université de Lille)
- Oliver Alonzo (Rochester Institute of Technology)
- Philippe Laban (Salesforce Research)
- Piotr Przybyła (Universitat Pompeu Fabra)
- Regina Stodden (Heinrich Heine University Düsseldorf)
- Rémi Cardon (CENTAL, ILC, Université Catholique de Louvain)
- Sarah Ebling (University of Zurich)
- Susana Bautista (Universidad Francisco de Vitoria)
- Sweta Agrawal (University of Maryland)
- Tadashi Nomoto (National Institute of Japanese Literature)
- Tannon Kew (University of Zurich)

Table of Contents

Using ChatGPT as a CAT tool in Easy Language translation

Silvana Deilen **Sergio Hernández Garrido,**
Ekaterina Lapshinova-Koltunski **Christiane Maaß**

University of Hildesheim
{deilen,hernandezs,lapshinovakoltun,maassc}@uni-hildesheim.de

Abstract

This study sets out to investigate the feasibility of using ChatGPT to translate citizen-oriented administrative texts into German Easy Language, a simplified, controlled language variety that is adapted to the needs of people with reading impairments. We use ChatGPT to translate selected texts from websites of German public authorities using two strategies, i.e. linguistic and holistic. We analyse the quality of the generated texts based on different criteria, such as correctness, readability, and syntactic complexity. The results indicated that the generated texts are easier than the standard texts, but that they still do not fully meet the established Easy Language standards. Additionally, the content is not always rendered correctly.

1 Introduction

Generative Pre-trained Transformer (GPT) models show remarkable advances not only in natural language generation (Brown et al., 2020), but also in automated translation (Hendy et al., 2023). However, their performance in specific machine translation tasks has not been yet extensively explored. While the online ChatGPT is also known for its ability to translate texts from one language to another (so-called interlingual translation), so far very little is known about its ability to translate texts from standard language into a complexity-reduced language variety of the same language (so-called intralingual translation). In this study, we investigate the feasibility of using ChatGPT to translate citizen-oriented administrative texts from public agencies into Easy Language for people with reading impairments. The aim of our study is twofold: first, to answer the question of whether and to what extent large language models like ChatGPT are able to generate translations from standard German into Easy Language and second, to determine whether a holistic or a text-based approach leads to a more comprehensible output.

In our study, we aim to test whether ChatGPT is fit to be used as a tool for translating texts into German Easy Language. We selected a number of texts and ordered the tool to perform several translation tasks with two different strategies: linguistic level dependent and holistic. In this paper, we present the results of the qualitative and quantitative data from the analysis and on their basis, we draw the first conclusions on the usability of ChatGPT as an Easy Language CAT[1] tool.

The remainder of this paper is structured as follows. In Section 2, we outline the relevance of the demand for the current situation with Easy Language in Germany. In Section 3, we summarize the existing related work. In Section 4, we describe the data used in this study and outline our research design. In Section 5, we present our main results and lastly, in Section 6, we discuss our main findings and suggest promising directions for future research.

2 Easy Language in Germany

In Germany, the Federal Act on Equal Opportunities of Persons with Disabilities (Behindertengleichstellungsgesetz [BGG] 2016/2018) states that public authorities must on request explain official notices, general rulings, public-law contracts and forms in Easy Language to individuals with intellectual or psychological disabilities. However, since many German public authorities still do not provide sufficient information in Easy Language, these rights to information in Easy Language are often disregarded. One of the main reasons for the lack of information in Easy Language is that translating texts into Easy Language is very time-consuming and costly and requires professional training (cf. Maaß 2020, Hansen-Schirra et al. 2020).

Consequently, the problem is twofold: On the

[1] Computer-aided translation

Proceedings of the Second Workshop on Text Simplification, Accessibility and Readability associated with RANLP-2023, pages 1–10,
held in Varna Bulgaria, Sept 7, 2023.
https://doi.org/10.26615/978-954-452-086-1_001

one hand there is an increasing demand for texts in Easy Language and, due to the legal situation, a significantly rising text volume to be translated (Rink, 2019), and on the other hand, people who are responsible for translating texts into Easy Language often lack sufficient translation experience and expertise (Maaß, 2020). At the moment, Easy Language translations are not always carried out by academically trained translators but also often by persons without academic translation training, such as employees of public authorities or organizations or social education workers, who have access to the Easy Language target groups but who do not have "the necessary text expertise and adequate formal training in intralingual translation" (Hansen-Schirra et al. 2020, p. 121). This lack of professional academic training leads to a heterogeneous and often very poor text quality. This is problematic for several reasons: Firstly, texts in Easy Language are only functional when they are of high quality. This is especially true for target groups with special communication needs who may not be able to understand poorly written texts (for an overview of the Easy Language target groups see Bredel and Maaß 2016). In addition, poorly written texts can also negatively affect the public image of Easy Language and may even stigmatize its users (cf. Maaß 2020). Furthermore, texts of poor quality are detrimental to the development of machine translation systems for Easy Language, because the successful training of such systems requires a large corpus of rule-consistent high quality Easy Language translations (cf. Hansen-Schirra et al. 2020). Thus, texts of poor quality hinder the compilation of such a corpus and therefore slow down the advancement of automatic text simplification systems that can be used for intralingual translation.

However, due to the significantly rising text volume and the lack of professional translators, the need for technological assistance is obvious. As texts in Easy Language are based on defined rules on the word, sentence and text level, Easy Language is often treated as a controlled language (cf. Hansen-Schirra et al. 2020). This in turn means that, seen from a theoretical perspective, they offer a high automation potential. Yet, due to the above-mentioned reasons, texts in Easy Language are mostly translated manually.

As large language models (LLMs) like ChatGPT are trained on large amounts of data from the internet and use this data to generate new content, it is conceivable that LLMs like ChatGPT are able to reduce the complexity of a text by applying strategies of lexical and syntactic simplification. Seen from a theoretical perspective, it therefore seems plausible that LLMs have the potential to convert a source text into a text version that is easier to read and understand. However, at this time we are not aware of any studies that evaluate the feasibility of such systems for intralingual translation.

3 Related work

3.1 Easy German

Easy German has become a subject of scientific research since 2014 (Maaß et al., 2014) with rapidly growing output of publications in the following years for German and other national Easy varieties. The studies point in two basic directions: studies on text qualities and possible barriers in various forms of communication on the on the one side (see, for example, Rink 2019 for legal communication in Easy Language) and studies on comprehensibility and recall by different target groups on the other (see, for example, Gutermuth 2020 and Deilen 2021). For an overview on the situation of Easy Languages in Europe see Lindholm and Vanhatalo 2021 and, specifically, the chapter on Easy German Maaß et al. 2021).

3.2 Automatic text simplification for Easy and Plain Language

Even though there are many previous studies on automatic text simplification methods that aim to automatically convert a text into another text that is easier to understand but ideally conveys the same message as the source text (cf. Saggion 2017), the role of automation and CAT tools for Easy Language translation is still a major research desideratum. Easy and Plain language display different grades of comprehensibility and address differing target groups that need accessible communication to participate in various fields of society (Bredel and Maaß, 2016). Maaß et al. (2014) were the first to discuss the potentials of computer-aided translation tools for Easy Language translation. In their 2020 paper, Hansen-Schirra et al. (2020) reconsidered and extended these potentials and published them for an international scientific community. Both papers show that intralingual terminology management comes with some challenges because, in contrast to interlingual translation, in Easy Language translation the description, explanation and definition of a concept has to be made explicit in the text and cannot be hidden in the termbase. Furthermore, when it comes to intralingual sentence alignment, there is usually no 1:1 correspondence between source text and target text. This is due to sentence compression or splitting strategies, additional explanations, or the shifting of the order of information in the source text. This in turn means that the alignment process has to be done or corrected manually by the translator, which increases the workload. With regard to the use of translation memories, they suggest lowering the threshold value for fuzzy matches, because in intralingual translation also matches below 70% (which is the common threshold in interlingual translation) can be used as a template and can therefore be useful for the translator. As a consequence, they conclude that intralingual terminology management is feasible, but requires specific adaptations of the best practices. Likewise, Welch and Sauberer (2019) conclude that the structure of common interlingual terminology systems is too restrictive to be used in Easy Language translation. After listing the requirements for an intralingual termbase they therefore propose a theoretical set-up, additional fields and features that would be needed in an Easy Language terminology tool. However, to our knowledge such a tool still does not exist.

Although existing studies in automatic text simplification operating with deep learning methods (see e.g. Sheang and Saggion 2021; Maddela et al. 2021; Martin et al. 2020 amongst others) also aim at textual accessibility, most of them do not consider the needs of target audience. Scarton and Specia (2018) did present an approach for automatic text simplification that makes use of the Newsela corpus[2]. This corpus was built for various target audiences with each corpus article being labeled with a grade level and having also various simplified versions. The authors showed that using such target audience oriented data helped to build better models than general purpose ones. However, such models do not necessarily reflect the specificities of Easy Language.

To our knowledge, Säuberli et al. (2020) were the first to adapt neural models to the features of German Easy Language. Their models were able to implement some specificities of Easy Language, such as choosing basic words or shortening sentences. However, despite these achievements, they also showed that in most cases the content was not preserved or contained wrong details. As their analysis also revealed that in most cases, the sentences were not significantly easier than the original sentences, they conclude that a larger parallel corpus is needed to successfully train an automatic text simplification system for German Easy Language.

Spring et al. (2021) expanded the corpus used by Säuberli et al. (2020) and developed a sentence-based machine translation approach to automatically simplify standard German into different simplification levels of the Common European Framework of References for Languages (CEFR). To tackle the above-mentioned alignment problems, they used the Sentence Alignment Tools Evaluation Framework (SATEF), which allows for n:m alignments, meaning that one alignment segment can consist of a varying number of sentences in the source and target text. Alignment issues were also addressed by Kopp et al. (2023) who developed a translation memory for non-professional intralingual translators in the field of public administration. Its main functionality lies in the assistance in the creation of alignment corpora in standard language and Easy Language by using automatic alignment algorithms. This translation memory serves in the short term as a database with aligned text passages that support the translation process into Easy Language. In the long term, the created corpora can serve as high quality data to train AI for intralingual machine translation purposes.

However, both Säuberli et al. (2020) and Spring et al. (2021) showed that existing models tend to copy the source segments. The latter were able to reduce the copying behavior of the text simplification models by applying different pretraining and fine-tuning strategies and by adding copy labels. As their simplification models mostly outperformed the baseline models in terms of the BLEU score (Papineni et al., 2002) and SARI (Xu et al., 2016), their study showed that pretrained and fine-tuning NMT models is a promising approach to German automatic text simplification. Anschütz et al. (2023) also used fine-tuning for five pre-trained language models for German Easy Language. They found that both in terms of models' perplexities and readability of the output the fine-tuned models showed better conformity to the linguistic features and structure of German Easy Language than the original versions of the models.

[2]https://newsela.com/data

Therefore, their study revealed that it is possible to train models to adapt to the style of German Easy Language. They conclude that even though the generated output might not be used by the target groups directly, it might serve as a draft for professional German Easy Language translators and might thus, similarly to post-editing in interlingual translation, reduce their workload.

Although the above mentioned studies show advances in applying neural models to Easy Language, none of them evaluated the outcome generated by an already existing, non-self-trained model.

3.3 LLMs / ChatGPT for translation tasks

As already mentioned in Section 1 above, GPT models have been successfully tested for automated translation in various tasks. For instance, Hendy et al. (2023) analysed performance of three GPT models (including ChatGPT) for different translation directions showing that such models achieved competitive translation quality for high resource languages. Kocmi and Federmann (2023) used GPT models to test if these can be applied for automatic translation quality assessment. The authors showed that their quality assessment scheme correlates with larger models only. Interestingly, their method for translation quality assessment only works with GPT 3.5 and larger models. They also showed that the least constrained template achieved the best performance in this analysis.

Apart from overall translation tasks, ChatGPT has been tested for handling specific linguistic phenomena, e.g. translation of coreference chains, ellipsis, terminology and other lexical issues and especially ambiguous constructions (Castilho et al., 2023). ChatGPT turned to deal better with context-related issues than other MT engines under analysis and also suggest creative translation solutions.

To our knowledge, none of the existing studies has addressed the performance of ChatGPT for intralingual translation tasks, specifically for German Easy Language. The only study known to us that addresses readability, which is one of the features we analyse, is Pu and Demberg (2023). The authors compare reading difficulty of the ChatGPT outputs with human-written texts. Their results show that although ChatGPT-generated sentences for experts showed greater complexity than for layperson, the magnitude of the difference in the reading difficulty scores between the two types of texts (for experts vs. layperson) was much smaller than that observed in human-generated texts.

4 Research Design

4.1 Data collection

To test the chatbot ChatGPT[3] for intralingual translation into German Easy Language, we used twenty texts from three different websites of German public authorities. Each text contained between 179 and 672 words. The texts contained information about different citizen-oriented topics, such as how to report lost and found items, how to take parental leave, or how to obtain a criminal record certificate.

In our study, we tested two different approaches: As human translators usually follow a holistic approach when translating a text, our first approach corresponds to a natural translation strategy. However, as German Easy Language is a controlled language that is characterized by specific rules on text, sentence, and word level, it is also conceivable that simplifying the linguistic levels separately improves the machine generated output. In our second approach, the so-called linguistic level dependent approach, we therefore adapted our prompts to the text, sentence and word level respectively.

Starting with the holistic approach, we first asked the tool to translate the following text into German Easy Language. However, when looking at the generated output, it quickly became clear that the texts did not follow the common German Easy Language rules and were still too complex. For example, the independent clause-only principle was violated and the texts still contained complex nominal phrases. Therefore, in a second step we requested ChatGPT to make the text easier. This request was formulated twice.

Afterwards, we tested the second approach. In this approach, we tried to simplify the source texts step by step, according to the strategies that are applied in Easy Language translation. We differentiated between simplifying strategies on text level, sentence level and word level. Starting from the text level, we first asked ChatGPT to reformulate the text but to leave out unimportant information. In a second step, we requested the tool to reformulate the text without compound sentences and with simple syntactic structures. In a third step, we requested ChatGPT to add explanations of difficult words in the text. In our analysis, we only

[3]Our study was conducted in April 2023, i.e., the results are based on GPT-3.5, the latest free version of ChatGPT available at the time of writing.

considered the final outputs of the two approaches, i.e., the version the tool generated after each of the respective last query. Table 1 provides an overview of the resulting subcorpora under analysis[4]. They include source texts (S), texts generated with the holistic approach (H), and the texts generated with the linguistic approach (L).

subcorpus	tok
source (S)	8.919
holistic (H)	2.707
linguistic (L)	5.950
total	**17.576**

Table 1: Corpus statistics in tokens (tok)

Then, we compared the three supcorpora using three different criteria: The first criterion was the correctness of the content (see 4.2.1) applied to the H and L subcorpora only, the second criterion was the readability of the generated output (see 4.2.2), and the third criterion was the syntactic complexity of the texts (see 4.2.3).

4.2 Data analysis

4.2.1 Correctness

In our analysis, we first evaluated whether the content of the generated texts is correct. The evaluation was done according to the four-eyes principle, e.g., the correctness of each text was evaluated independently by two people. In case of discrepancies, the respective text was reviewed and discussed in plenary until a unanimous decision was reached. As we know that like other LLMs, ChatGPT suffers from hallucination issues in the context of logical reasoning (Bang et al., 2023), we expect to find some incorrect contents in the H and L subcorpora.

4.2.2 Readability

Secondly, we compared the comprehensibility of the different approaches. The comprehensibility was assessed by TextLab, a software that determines text-comprehensibility based on the Hohenheim Comprehensibility Index (HIX). The HIX is a meta index that calculates the readability of a text taking into account the four major readability formulas common in German Easy Language Research (Bredel and Maaß, 2016, p. 61ff). They include the Amstad index, the simple measure of gobbledygook (G-SMOG) index, the Vienna nonfictional text formula (W-STX) and the readability index (LIX), with an index of 0 indicating an extremely low comprehensibility and an index of 20 an extremely high comprehensibility (for further details see: `https://klartext.uni-hohenheim.de/hix`). To evaluate whether a text can be classified as a German Easy Language text, we used a predefined benchmark for German Easy Language, according to which Easy Language texts should have a HIX of at least 18 points (cf. Rink 2019, p. 77).

4.2.3 Syntactic complexity

We operationalise syntactic complexity as a distribution of specific syntactic relations, i.e. specific clauses. We automatically identify syntactic relations using dependency parsing that we obtained with the Stanford NLP Python Library Stanza (v1.2.1)[5] with all the models pre-trained on the Universal Dependencies v2.5 datasets. Our list of selected structural categories include the following: acl (adnominal clause or clausal modifier of noun), advcl (adverbial clause modifier), ccomp (clausal component), csubj (clausal subject), xcomp (open clausal element) and parataxis (parataxis relation). They are all listed under the clause dependents[6] in the Universal Dependency (see De Marneffe et al. 2021for more details) definition. The occurrence of these categories is collected and analysed across the three subcorpora under analysis. We assume that the higher the number of these dependency relations in the corpus, the more complex the texts contained in these subcorpora are.

5 Results

5.1 Correctness

Analyzing the correctness of the content revealed that, altogether, 37.5% of the generated texts were content-wise correct. In 62.5% however, the text contained at least one incorrect piece of information. When looking at the two approaches separately, we found that from the holistic output, 80% of the texts were marked as incorrect, whereas from the linguistic level dependent output, 45% of the texts were classified as incorrect. An example of an incorrect translation is illustrated in (1).

[4]The analysed data is available under `https://github.com/katjakaterina/chatgpt4easylang`.

[5]`https://stanfordnlp.github.io/stanza/index.html`

[6]`https://universaldependencies.org/u/dep/`

1a. *Bis zum 18. Lebensjahr ist auch der gesetzliche Vertreter antragsbefugt. [Up to the age of 18, the legal representative is also authorised to file the application]* (16S)

1b. *Wenn man unter 18 ist, kann es nur von einem gesetzlichen Vertreter beantragt werden. [If you are under 18, it can only be filed by a legal representative]* (16H)

While the source sentence in (1a) means that both a person under 18 and her/his legal representative are authorised to file the application, the translation output in (1b) means that only the representative can do so.

5.2 Readability

Comparing the comprehensibility of the different approaches revealed that the holistic approach had the highest comprehensibility, with a mean HIX value of 15.3 (SD: 3.53). The linguistic-level based approach yielded a mean HIX value of 9.53 (SD: 2.96), whereby the source text had a mean HIX value of 6.04 (SD: 2.84) (see Figure 1). As mentioned in Section 4, the benchmark for a text to be classified as a German Easy Language text is set at 18 points. Therefore, we can conclude that none of the texts that were generated with the linguistic level approach can be classified as German Easy Language texts. In comparison, the holistic approach yielded four texts with a HIX value of at least 18, so that – according to this criterion – 20% of the texts could indeed be classified as being easy to understand.

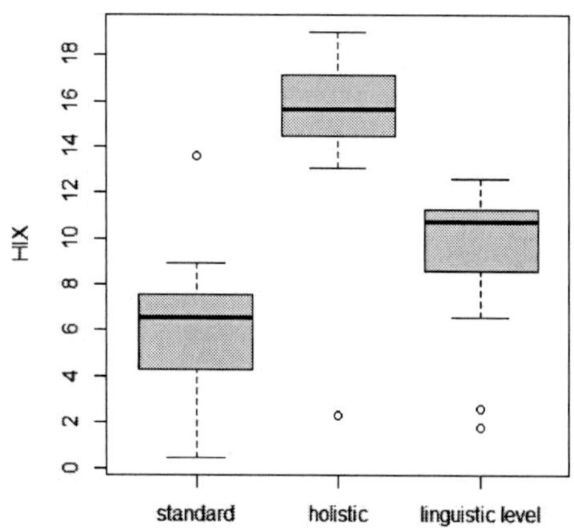

Figure 1: HIX values of the source text and the two simplified variants under analysis.

5.3 Syntactic complexity

In the next step, we analyse the distribution of the dependency relations across the three subcorpora under analysis. We summarise the results (frequencies normalised per 1000) in Figure 2.

Overall, both simplified text versions seem to have a higher number of complex syntactic relations than the source text. For the latter, we observe higher number for parataxis relations only. Clausal subjects (`csubj`), clausal complements of verbs and adjectives (`ccomp`), as well clauses modifying verbs and adjectives (`advcl`) predominate in the holistic version, whereas subjectless clausal complements (`xcomp`) and clauses modifying nouns (`acl`) prevail in the text version simplified with a linguistic approach. Clauses modifying verbs and adjectives that are in general most frequent amongst all the relations under analysis often include temporal and locative clauses, and clauses that express manner, reason, consequence, alternative or condition. The sentence in the text version simplified with a holistic approach illustrated in example 2a contains two causes of this type: one starting with *wenn* (*if*, condition), and the second with *um* (*so that*, consequence). Both the source text and the text simplified with a linguistic approach are identical (2b) and contain only one `advc` relation expressing condition.

2a. *Eltern bekommen auch einen Bonus, wenn sie sich abwechseln, um auf das Baby aufzupassen. [Parents also get a bonus when they take turns taking care of the baby]* (10H)

2b. *Zwei Partnermonate werden zusätzlich als Bonus gewährt, wenn der jeweils andere Elternteil in dieser Zeit seine Erwerbstätigkeit zugunsten der Kindererziehung zeitlich einschränkt oder aussetzt. [Two additional months of parental leave are granted as a bonus when the other parent reduces or suspends their employment during this time for the purpose of child care.]* (10S, 10L)

An example of the other frequent syntactic relation, i.e. clauses modifying nouns (`acl`), is illustrated in (3). Here we observe a relative clause in the text version simplified with a linguistic approach (3a) and a conditional clause instead in the version simplified with a holistic approach (3b).

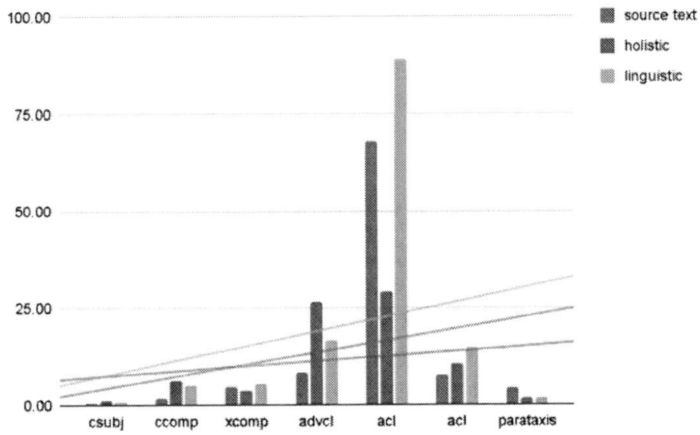

Figure 2: Distribution of syntactically complex dependency relations in the source text and the two simplified variants under analysis.

> 3a. *Eltern, die vor der Geburt ihres Kindes nicht erwerbstätig waren, erhalten ein Mindestelterngeld von 300 Euro monatlich. [Parents, who were not employed before the birth of their child, receive a minimum parental allowance of 300 euros per month]* (10L)
>
> 3b. *Wenn Eltern vor dem Baby nicht arbeiteten, bekommen sie mindestens 300 Euro im Monat. [If parents did not work before the baby, they get at least 300 euros per month.]* (10H).

Another syntactic construction which is least frequent in the holistic output is `xcomp` (subjectless clauses) in (4).

> 4a. *Falls mehrere Termine gebucht werden, behält sich der Fachdienst das Recht vor, zusätzliche Termine zu löschen, um anderen Bürgern zeitnahe Terminreservierungen zu ermöglichen. [If multiple appointments have been booked, the authority reserves the right to cancel additional appointments to allow other citizens to book appointments in a timely manner.]* (18L).
>
> 4b. *Sollten mehrere Termine gebucht werden, behält sich der Fachdienst vor, die weiteren Termine zu löschen, um Terminkapazitäten nicht einzuschränken und anderen Bürgerinnen und Bürgern ebenfalls zeitnahe Terminreservierungen zu ermöglichen. [If multiple appointments have been booked, the authority reserves the right to cancel the additional appointments so as not to restrict appointments capacities and to allow other citizens to book appointments in a timely manner.]* (18S).

In summary, simplified texts turned out to contain less complex syntactic constructions for certain relations only.

6 Summary and Discussion

The present paper focused on the feasibility of using ChatGPT for intralingual translation, i.e. translation of administrative texts into German Easy Language. Our results show that in terms of readability, the generated texts are easier than the source texts, however, most of the texts still do not meet the Easy Language standards. In other words, the texts are easier, but not easy enough. Furthermore, the content of the texts was not always correct. However, in terms of correctness, it should be noted that classifying a text as "incorrect" does not mean that the entire content was incorrect. In most texts that were labelled as incorrect, most of the content was transferred correctly and only one small piece of information was incorrect, or some crucial information was missing, which in turn led to the fact that the message differed from the source text.

All in all, our results allow us to conclude that so far, ChatGPT might be used as a template for professional translators rather than a standalone Easy

Language translation tool. The conclusion that in Easy Language translation, human translators are still indispensable is also due to the fact that only parts of the translation can be performed by adhering to simplification rules. Even when all rules are applied, there are still some tasks that require the translator's specialized knowledge, creativity and understanding and awareness of the target group.

Therefore, in addition to the text perspective, a functional Easy Language translation also has to focus on the reader and has to be adapted to the reader's prior knowledge. This for example means that the translator, on the one hand, has to select and prioritize the information for its users and, on the other hand, has to add paraphrases, examples and explanations. As information is processed and retained more easily if presented in a multimodal and multicodal way, the translator also has to include images to reflect, clarify, or exemplify the subject-related information and to highlight core concepts and associations. This shows that even though in Easy Language translation there clearly is a potential for automation, the translation task consists of much more than applying text-based rules. Thus, if translators use ChatGPT to translate texts into German Easy Language, they need to have professional post-editing competences for intralingual translation, such as error detection, research, and correction skills.

However, the more we engaged with the topic, the more we learnt how to get more precise and tailored outputs, i.e., we learnt that other - more appropriate - prompts can improve the comprehensibility of the generated texts. One way to improve the quality of the answers is to assign ChatGPT a role. For example, when telling the tool that it is a translator for Easy Language before asking it to translate a text into Easy Language, it seems that the output is less complex than without the previous role assignment. ChatGPT seems also to deliver more appropriate outcomes if a context is set before asking for a translation. For instance, it may be helpful to ask ChatGPT about German Easy Language rules and then ask for a translation into German Easy Language. A set contextual framework may deliver more appropriate results. Still, the extent to which the versions differ from each other still has to be investigated in a larger-scale study.

Considering that there are no prompting instructions when opening ChatGPT, we expect that the average user is not aware of these techniques i.e., they do not know that assigning a role or setting a context improves the quality of the output. This highlights the paramount importance of professional competences when using these kind of tools in intralingual Easy Language translation.

In our future work, we will extend the evaluation techniques applied, as we have focused on those commonly used in German Easy Language research so far. We will also include further automated evaluation and quality estimation methods derived from automatic text simplification. Moreover, we would like to more closely look into different cases of partial correctness mentioned above, where only piece of information was incorrect or missing.

7 Lay Summary

This study sets out to investigate whether ChatGPT is fit to be used as a tool for translating texts into German Easy Language. For this purpose, we selected 20 citizen-oriented administrative texts and asked the tool for a translation into German Easy Langauge, a a rule-based variety that is adapted to the needs of people with reading impairments. In our study we tested two different approaches. The first approach was a so-called holistic approach, which means that we simply asked the tool to translate the entire text into German Easy Language. In our second approach, the so-called linguistic level dependent approach we asked the tool to carry out the translation step by step and to first apply rules on text level, then on sentence level and afterwards on word level. We compared the final output based on three criteria: the correctness of the content, the readability of the text, and the complexity of the sentence structure. Our results indicate that the texts generated by ChatGPT are easier than the standard texts, but that most of them are still not easy enough for the intended target groups of German Easy Language. In addition we found that the content was not always rendered correctly.

References

Miriam Anschütz, Joshua Oehms, Thomas Wimmer, Bartłomiej Jezierski, and Georg Groh. 2023. Language Models for German Text Simplification: Overcoming Parallel Data Scarcity through Style-specific Pre-training. *arXiv preprint arXiv:2305.12908*.

Yejin Bang, Samuel Cahyawijaya, Nayeon Lee, Wenliang Dai, Dan Su, Bryan Wilie, Holy Lovenia, Ziwei

Ji, Tiezheng Yu, Willy Chung, Quyet V. Do, Yan Xu, and Pascale Fung. 2023. A Multitask, Multilingual, Multimodal Evaluation of ChatGPT on Reasoning, Hallucination, and Interactivity.

Ursula Bredel and Christiane Maaß. 2016. *Leichte Sprache: Theoretische Grundlagen, Orientierung für die Praxis*. Dudenverlag.

Tom Brown, Benjamin Mann, Nick Ryder, Melanie Subbiah, Jared D Kaplan, Prafulla Dhariwal, Arvind Neelakantan, Pranav Shyam, Girish Sastry, Amanda Askell, Sandhini Agarwal, Ariel Herbert-Voss, Gretchen Krueger, Tom Henighan, Rewon Child, Aditya Ramesh, Daniel Ziegler, Jeffrey Wu, Clemens Winter, Chris Hesse, Mark Chen, Eric Sigler, Mateusz Litwin, Scott Gray, Benjamin Chess, Jack Clark, Christopher Berner, Sam McCandlish, Alec Radford, Ilya Sutskever, and Dario Amodei. 2020. Language models are few-shot learners. In *Advances in Neural Information Processing Systems*, volume 33, pages 1877–1901. Curran Associates, Inc.

Sheila Castilho, Clodagh Quinn Mallon, Rahel Meister, and Shengya Yue. 2023. Do online Machine Translation Systems Care for Context? What About a GPT Model? In *Proceedings of the 24th Annual Conference of the European Association for Machine Translation*, pages 393–417, Tampere, Finland.

Marie-Catherine De Marneffe, Christopher D Manning, Joakim Nivre, and Daniel Zeman. 2021. Universal dependencies. *Computational linguistics*, 47(2):255–308.

Silvana Deilen. 2021. *Optische Gliederung von Komposita in Leichter Sprache. Blickbewegungsstudien zum Einfluss visueller, morphologischer und semantischer Faktoren auf die Verarbeitung deutscher Substantivkomposita*. Frank & Timme.

Silke Gutermuth. 2020. *Leichte Sprache für alle?: eine zielgruppenorientierte Rezeptionsstudie zu Leichter und Einfacher Sprache*, volume 5. Frank & Timme GmbH.

Silvia Hansen-Schirra, Jean Nitzke, Silke Gutermuth, Christiane Maaß, and Isabel Rink. 2020. Technologies for translation of specialised texts into easy language. *Easy Language Research: Text and User Perspectives. Berlin: Frank & Timme*, pages 99–127.

Amr Hendy, Mohamed Gomaa Abdelrehim, Amr Sharaf, Vikas Raunak, Mohamed Gabr, Hitokazu Matsushita, Young Jin Kim, Mohamed Afify, and Hany Hassan Awadalla. 2023. How Good Are GPT Models at Machine Translation? A Comprehensive Evaluation. *ArXiv*, abs/2302.09210.

Tom Kocmi and Christian Federmann. 2023. Large language models are state-of-the-art evaluators of translation quality. *ArXiv*, abs/2302.14520.

Tobias Kopp, Amelie Rempel, Andres P. Schmidt, and Miriam Spieß. 2023. Towards machine translation into easy language in public administrations: Algorithmic alignment suggestions for building a translation memory. In Silvana Deilen, Silvia Hansen-Schirra, Sergio Hernández Garrido, Christiane Maaß, and Anke Tardel, editors, *Emerging Fields in Easy Language and Accessible Communication Research*, pages 371–406. Frank & Timme, Berlin.

Camilla Lindholm and Ulla Vanhatalo. 2021. *Handbook of easy languages in Europe*. Frank & Timme.

Christiane Maaß. 2020. *Easy Language–Plain Language–Easy Language Plus: Balancing Comprehensibility and Acceptability*. Frank & Timme.

Christiane Maaß, Isabel Rink, Silvia Hansen-Schirra, Camilla Lindholm, and Ulla Vanhatalo. 2021. Easy Language in Germany. *Handbook of Easy Languages in Europe*, 8:191.

Christiane Maaß, Isabel Rink, and Christiane Zehrer. 2014. Leichte sprache in der sprach-und übersetzungswissenschaft. *Sprache barrierefrei gestalten. Perspektiven aus der Angewandten Linguistik. Berlin: Frank & Timme*, pages 53–85.

Mounica Maddela, Fernando Alva-Manchego, and Wei Xu. 2021. Controllable text simplification with explicit paraphrasing. In *Proceedings of the 2021 Conference of the North American Chapter of the Association for Computational Linguistics: Human Language Technologies*, pages 3536–3553, Online. Association for Computational Linguistics.

Louis Martin, Éric de la Clergerie, Benoît Sagot, and Antoine Bordes. 2020. Controllable sentence simplification. In *Proceedings of the Twelfth Language Resources and Evaluation Conference*, pages 4689–4698, Marseille, France. European Language Resources Association.

Kishore Papineni, Salim Roukos, Todd Ward, and Wei-Jing Zhu. 2002. BLEU: a method for automatic evaluation of machine translation. In *Proceedings of the 40th Annual Meeting of the Association for Computational Linguistics*, pages 311–318, Philadelphia, Pennsylvania, USA. Association for Computational Linguistics.

Dongqi Pu and Vera Demberg. 2023. ChatGPT vs human-authored text: Insights into controllable text summarization and sentence style transfer. In *Proceedings of the 61st Annual Meeting of the Association for Computational Linguistics (Volume 4: Student Research Workshop)*, pages 1–18, Toronto, Canada. Association for Computational Linguistics.

Isabel Rink. 2019. *Rechtskommunikation und Barrierefreiheit: Zur Übersetzung juristischer Informationsund Interaktionstexte in Leichte Sprache*. Frank & Timme.

Horacio Saggion. 2017. Applications of automatic text simplification. In *Automatic Text Simplification*, pages 71–77. Springer.

Andreas Säuberli, Sarah Ebling, and Martin Volk. 2020. Benchmarking data-driven automatic text simplification for German. In *Proceedings of the 1st workshop on tools and resources to empower people with reading dIfficulties (READI)*, pages 41–48.

Carolina Scarton and Lucia Specia. 2018. Learning simplifications for specific target audiences. In *Proceedings of the 56th Annual Meeting of the Association for Computational Linguistics (Volume 2: Short Papers)*, pages 712–718, Melbourne, Australia. Association for Computational Linguistics.

Kim Cheng Sheang and Horacio Saggion. 2021. Controllable sentence simplification with a unified text-to-text transfer transformer. In *Proceedings of the 14th International Conference on Natural Language Generation*, pages 341–352, Aberdeen, Scotland, UK. Association for Computational Linguistics.

Nicolas Spring, Annette Rios, and Sarah Ebling. 2021. Exploring German multi-level text simplification. In *Proceedings of the International Conference on Recent Advances in Natural Language Processing (RANLP 2021)*, pages 1339–1349, Held Online. INCOMA Ltd.

Birgit Welch and Gabriele Sauberer. 2019. Easy-to-read language and terminology: New needs, new rules, new software? In *Systems, Software and Services Process Improvement: 26th European Conference, EuroSPI 2019, Edinburgh, UK, September 18–20, 2019, Proceedings 26*, pages 647–658. Springer.

Wei Xu, Courtney Napoles, Ellie Pavlick, Quanze Chen, and Chris Callison-Burch. 2016. Optimizing statistical machine translation for text simplification. *Transactions of the Association for Computational Linguistics*, 4:401–415.

Context-aware Swedish Lexical Simplification

Emil Graichen
Department of Computer and Information Science
Linköping University
Linköping, Sweden
emigr679@student.liu.se

Arne Jönsson
Department of Computer and Information Science
Linköping University
Linköping, Sweden
arne.jonsson@liu.se

Abstract

We present results from the development and evaluation of context-aware Lexical simplification (LS) systems for the Swedish language. Three versions of LS models, `LäsBERT`, `LäsBERT-baseline`, and `LäsGPT`, were created and evaluated on a newly constructed Swedish LS evaluation dataset. The LS systems demonstrated promising potential in aiding audiences with reading difficulties by providing context-aware word replacements. While there were areas for improvement, particularly in complex word identification, the systems showed agreement with human annotators on word replacements.

1 Introduction

Lexical simplification (LS) is the task of replacing complex words with easier ones. The approaches to this task usually involve replacing words with simpler synonyms found in a linguistic database (Devlin, 1998; Gooding and Kochmar, 2019; Rennes, 2022), implementing rules to "translate" linguistic units into easier ones (Zhu et al., 2010; Coster and Kauchak, 2011), or using word embeddings to generate similar substitution candidates (Glavaš and Štajner, 2015; Gooding and Kochmar, 2019). As mentioned in Qiang et al. (2021) these methods usually fail to take the context of the target word into account, resulting in nonsensical substitutions.

Recently, with the introduction of large-scale pre-trained transformer language models such as BERT (Devlin et al., 2018) and GPT-3 (Brown et al., 2020) a new chapter in the field of Natural Language Processing (NLP) has begun. GPT-3 and BERT perform well on a broad set of downstream NLP tasks (Brown et al., 2020; Devlin et al., 2018). BERT has already been implemented in LS systems for English (Qiang et al., 2021; Li et al., 2022), Portuguese (North et al., 2022), Spanish, and German (Pimienta Castillo, 2021). The benefit of using these models, trained on vast amounts of text, over conventional methods is that these models can generate more contextually appropriate substitutions for complex words, which is reflected in the high performance of these systems (Li et al., 2022; Qiang et al., 2021; Saggion et al., 2022). The TSAR-2022 Shared Task (Saggion et al., 2022) demonstrated that BERT-based LS systems were surpassed only by a GPT-3 based method (Aumiller and Gertz, 2022), highlighting the effectiveness of large-scale pre-trained transformers in the realm of Lexical simplification.

In this paper, three versions of a Swedish LS system are presented: two versions of an LS system (called `LäsBERT`) inspired by the approach by Qiang et al. (2021) using two Swedish BERT models for substitution generation. One version uses a BERT model fine-tuned on easy-to-read-text and one uses an out-of-the-box model to investigate how fine-tuning the BERT model affects the end-to-end performance of the LS system. Furthermore, a GPT-3 based LS system (called `LäsGPT`) was developed which uses OpenAI:s GPT-3 for generating substitutes. These three systems are evaluated on a newly collected evaluation dataset.

2 Lexical Simplification

Shardlow (2014) and Paetzold and Specia (2016) described the general pipeline of Lexical Simplification: *Complex Word Identification* (CWI) which aims to find candidates in need of simplification and *Substitution Generation* (SG) which describes the process of generating alternative words to the identified complex words. The most synonymous generated alternatives are selected in the next step conveniently named *Substitution Selection*. Finally, in the *Substitution ranking* task, the remaining words are ranked according to simplicity, where

Proceedings of the Second Workshop on Text Simplification, Accessibility and Readability associated with RANLP-2023, pages 11–20,
held in Varna Bulgaria, Sept 7, 2023.
https://doi.org/10.26615/978-954-452-086-1_002

the simplest word is chosen as the final word substitute.

2.1 Complex Word Identification

Shardlow (2013) showed that the performance of an overall LS system is dependent on the performance of the CWI component. If too many words are identified as complex, the system ends up making unnecessary substitutions which might alter the meaning of the sentences too much. If too few words are selected, the output text is not simplified enough.

Smolenska (2018) developed and evaluated systems for Swedish CWI, along with a dataset for training models on this task. It was found that a Random Forest Classifier (RFC) (Breiman, 2001) trained on fifteen (15) features concerning the frequency and syntactic function of the word performed best at the task of classifying complex words. It was concluded that using only the frequency features in the training of the classifier could maintain the scores of the classifier.

2.2 Substitution Generation

There are several approaches to SG present in the literature. The goal is to generate suitable substitutes for the input complex word. The words generated should preserve the meaning of the text and if possible be substitutes that simplify the text.

Keskisärkkä (2012), Abrahamsson et al. (2014), and Abrahamsson (2011) used the Swedish synonym dictionary SynLex (Kann and Rosell, 2006) to find appropriate synonyms for target words. This approach is based on using established dictionaries to generate alternatives and is also commonly found in the literature for English LS (Gooding and Kochmar, 2019; Devlin, 1998; De Belder and Moens, 2010). A more recent method to generating alternative words to an input word is by comparing the word embeddings of the input to other semantically similar words (Rennes, 2022; Glavaš and Štajner, 2015; Paetzold and Specia, 2016). Both these methods usually operate on a word level when generating substitution candidates. The possible drawback of analyzing words without their context is that it might result in generating synonyms that aren't synonyms in the specific context in which they are found.

Using pre-trained encoders such as BERT to reformulate SG into a Masked Language Modelling (MLM) task has been done to avoid the problem of disregarding context in LS tasks (Qiang et al., 2021; Pimienta Castillo, 2021; North et al., 2022). The method works by obscuring the complex words in an input text with `[MASK]` tokens and letting the BERT model generate a probability distribution over suitable alternatives that fit into the slot of the obscured word. These words are then treated as replacement candidates for the complex word (Qiang et al., 2021).

SG has also been reformulated as a language generation task (Lee et al., 2021; Aumiller and Gertz, 2022). To generate suitable alternatives to specific words in a short paragraph they utilised the in-context learning abilities of GPT-3 (Brown et al., 2020) to generate suitable substitutions.

2.3 Substitution Selection and Ranking

Gooding and Kochmar (2019) filtered and ranked the generated substitutes based on three factors: contextual simplicity, contextual semantic equivalence, and grammaticality. Contextual simplicity was calculated by reusing the sequential CWI model used earlier in their pipeline to check if a given substitution generated a simpler sentence than the original word. Contextual semantic equivalence utilised ELMo embeddings (Peters et al., 2018) to encode the sentences and to calculate the cosine distance between the substitutes and the original word in the context of the sentence that was to be simplified. To check whether or not a generated word was grammatical in a sentence, the occurrence of bigrams in a corpus was evaluated. If the replacement word together with its right or left neighbour formed a bigram that didn't occur once in the corpus it was assumed that the bigram was ungrammatical, and thus removed (Gooding and Kochmar, 2019).

Others have used the probability distribution of words that BERT returns in the MLM task to determine the likelihood of a generated substitution being a "relevant" substitute (Qiang et al., 2021). Frequency features of words are usually one component of the ranking system, where words that are more frequent are preferred over less frequent words (Qiang et al., 2021; Keskisärkkä, 2012). Ranking synonyms exclusively based on the number of characters in a word has also been proposed, but this approach has some considerable limitations (Abrahamsson, 2011).

3 Data used in our studies

Various data sources were used to train the Random Forest Classifier (RFC) for Complex Word Identification, fine-tune BERT to generate easier substitutes, and construct the first evaluation dataset for the Swedish LS systems.

3.1 Linguistic Resources for RFC training

The following resources were used to train the RFC for CWI:

The Stockholm-Umeå Corpus (SUC) is a balanced corpus collected in the nineties with annotated POS tags, morphological features, and lemmas. The corpus' token frequencies, were used to train the RFC for CWI. The version used in this paper is SUCX 3.0[1] which is free to use without a license (Ejerhed et al., 2006).

Språkbanken hosts corpora from blogs[2] and Twitter[3]. The blogs were selected from the top lists of *bloggportalen.se*[4] a Swedish homepage hosting blogs on various topics, and the Twitter posts were sourced from a selection of Swedish Twitter users. The statistics data sheets for both the BloggMix and the TwitterMix corpora were also used, which included token frequency, lemma, and POS tags for each token. Smolenska (2018) determined that word frequencies in blog corpora are highly informative for predicting complex words. Therefore, the BloggMix corpus served as the main source of word frequencies for training the RFC. However, it was also used to construct the evaluation dataset.

Smolenska (2018) collected a dataset of 4,238 words derived from Rivstart dictionaries (Natur och Kultur), a series of textbooks designed for second-language learners of Swedish. The dataset was collected to train and evaluate CWI systems. The books in this series are structured along the progression of *Common European Framework of Reference for Language* (CEFR) scores. These scores, taking the values **A1** (novice)**, A2, B1, B2, C1**, and **C2** (proficient), correspond to language proficiency levels (Volodina and Kokkinakis, 2012). These six categories, **A1** to **C2**, of sourced words, were grouped into three, and a fourth group was added containing the most complex words. The words in the fourth group were sourced from Ordtestet[5], a website that targets native Swedish speakers, where users can test their understanding of difficult words.

3.2 Linguistic Resources used for fine-tuning

Two corpora containing easy-to-read text were used to fine-tune the BERT model in one of the `LäsBERT` versions. 8sidor is a Swedish newspaper with easy-to-read texts targeting audiences with different reading difficulties. The newspaper is produced by the Swedish Agency for Accessible Media and is published weekly (Myndigheten för tillgängliga medier). The 8sidor corpus contains over 420 000 sentences and over 4.5 million tokens[6]. LäSBarT is a corpus containing easy-to-read texts sourced from children's books. The corpus contains a little over 100,000 sentences and 1 million tokens (Mühlenbock, 2008)[7].

3.3 Linguistic Resources used for the evaluation dataset

The Kelly Swedish List (Volodina and Kokkinakis, 2012; Kilgarriff et al., 2014) is a lexical resource with over 8,000 Swedish word lemmas annotated with Word frequencies, word classes, and CEFR scores. All **C1** and **C2** words in the Swedish Kelly list[8], i.e. words that were assumed to be complex, were sourced for the evaluation dataset.

SynLex (Kann and Rosell, 2006) was constructed by querying users of the Lexin translation service about the perceived level of synonymy between two words. The 82,000 word pairs of the lexicon were annotated with a synonymy score between 0-5 by a distributed user group. 0 represents no synonymy at all, and 5 represents two perfect synonyms. In the dataset used in this project[9] only synonyms that were rated at the synonymy level of 3 or higher were included which amounted to 38,000 word-pairs.

SALDO is a Swedish lexical-semantic resource developed by Borin et al. (2013) containing word relations and their senses. The resource includes a lexicon where the words in SALDO are put into

[1] `https://spraakbanken.gu.se/resurser/sucx3`

[2] `https://spraakbanken.gu.se/resurser/bloggmix`

[3] `https://spraakbanken.gu.se/resurser/twitter`

[4] `https://www.bloggportalen.se`

[5] `https://ord.relaynode.info/`

[6] `https://spraakbanken.gu.se/resurser/attasidor`

[7] `https://spraakbanken.gu.se/resurser/lasbart`

[8] `https://spraakbanken.gu.se/resurser/kelly`

[9] `http://folkets-lexikon.csc.kth.se/lexikon/synpairs.xml`

an example sentence[10]. These example sentences, the complex words from the Kelly Swedish List, and the SynLex synonyms were used to create the evaluation dataset.

4 Creating the evaluation dataset

The evaluation dataset was collected automatically and evaluated manually. The collection process began with retrieving all **C1** and **C2** level words in the Kelly Swedish list. These words represent words that are used by proficient users and were therefore assumed to be complex words. The corpus frequency of these words in the BloggMix corpus was retrieved. Following this, all available synonyms to the retrieved words were saved from the SynLex dictionary. The corpus frequencies of these synonyms were also saved. The final step was to find an example sentence in SALDO where the complex word occurred, resulting in 185 quadruples consisting of a complex word, its corpus frequency, a dictionary of suitable synonyms, and an example sentence. After a manual annotation process, nonsensical quadruples were removed, leaving a total of 150 quadruples.

Three native Swedish student annotators were enlisted to evaluate the dataset. The annotators assessed the *quality, coverage*, and *complexity* of the dataset. *Quality* refers to if the alternatives were synonymous with the complex word in the context of the example sentence. *Coverage* refers to if all possible synonyms were listed in the dataset. *Complexity* refers to the perceived complexity of the complex word. Student annotators from Linköping University's Cognitive Science Bachelors program were recruited. Two online versions of the Swedish academic aptitude test, *Högskoleprovet*, (Universitets och högskolerådet, 2023) were used to assess their word knowledge. The combined maximum score was 40 and the annotators scored 37, 33, and 35 respectively, indicating their strong lexical proficiency.

Each annotator got 50 separate quadruples to evaluate to ensure that all of the 150 quadruples in the dataset were human-annotated once. The annotators answered three questions regarding the *quality*, *coverage*, and *complexity* with "True" or "False" for each quadruple.

The results (see Table 1) show that the annotators in general agree that the synonyms proposed in the dataset fit in the context of the example sentence (86.6% of the quadruples). For 72% of the quadruples, the annotators thought that there were no omitted synonyms that could replace the complex word in the sentence. However, as discussed by Lee et al. (2021), humans generally don't recall all possible substitutions for a given word when working from memory. The *perceived* coverage of the dataset is therefore probably higher than the *actual* coverage. This has the possible effect of artificially limiting the score that a Lexical Simplification system can achieve on the dataset since valid substitutions could be missing in the set of correct alternatives. The annotators did generally not think that the words sourced from the Kelly Swedish List were complex, with only 28,6% of quadruples being annotated as complex. However, since the annotators were native Swedish speakers with a university education, the perception of what constitutes a complex word might not generalise well to audiences with reading difficulties. The dataset is freely available at `https://github.com/emilgraichen/SwedishLSdataset`.

TRUE	Quality	Coverage	Complexity
%	86.6%	72 %	28.6%
#	130/150	108/150	43/150

Table 1: Percent of quadruples annotated with "True" in response to the statements regarding *Quality, Coverage*, and *Complexity*.

5 Method

In this section, we will describe the implementation and evaluation of three LS systems, each varying only in the substitution generation subtask. The developed systems are two BERT-based versions of an LS system called `LäsBERT`, and one version of a GPT-3 based LS system called `LäsGPT`. The structure of this section is based on the general pipeline of other LS systems described in Section 2.

5.1 Complex Word Identification

As described in Section 2.1, frequency features can be treated as the main predictor for word complexity. Constructing a Random Forest Classifier (RFC) (Breiman, 2001) to classify word complexity only using frequency features can be built and generate good results (Smolenska, 2018). An RFC was trained using the `ensemble` module in the Python library Scikit-Learn (Pedregosa et al., 2011) utilising the Swedish complex word dataset developed

[10] `https://spraakbanken.gu.se/resurser/saldoe`

by Smolenska (2018). The RFC was trained on a dataset containing four (4) word features and outputs a word complexity score between 1-4. In this implementation, the features that the RFC used were the word's corpus frequency in the BloggMix, TwitterMix, and SUCX 3.0 corpora together with the length of the word. The corpus frequencies were normalised by computing the common logarithm of the absolute frequency. This normalisation method yielded the best results in earlier work (Smolenska, 2018). The RFC training dataset was split into 90% training data and 10% test data (see Table 3 for the classifier performance).

Informativeness was the basis for using the frequency datasets of the BloggMix, TwitterMix, and SUCX 3.0 corpora. According to Smolenska (2018), the selected corpora were amongst the most informative for predicting word complexity, which is why the corpora were suitable for this implementation. Earlier work has also established a relationship between word length and its complexity (Bingel and Bjerva, 2018). The number of characters in each word was therefore used as the last feature for Complex Word Identification (CWI).

To implement the trained RFC in the LS pipeline the first step involved splitting the input sentence into individual words, because the RFC operates on a word-by-word basis. All non-alphanumerical characters in the sentence were also removed. To avoid classifying words without semantic content, i.e. stopwords, all Swedish stopwords included in the NLTK resource `nltk.stopwords` (Bird et al., 2009) were removed from the input sentence.

Every word in the input sentence was then classified by the trained RFC from "1" to "4". Words scored with "1" or "2" were treated as non-complex and scores of "3" or "4" were sent further down the pipeline for simplification.

5.2 Substitute Generation

Two versions of `LäsBERT` were developed. The first version used a fine-tuned KB-BERT model[11], developed by the Royal Library of Sweden (Malmsten et al., 2020). It was fine-tuned on easy-to-read texts and used to generate substitutes for the identified complex words. The second version of `LäsBERT` uses the original version of KB-BERT without any fine-tuning. By developing two versions of the LS system, it is possible to investigate whether fine-tuning has any effect on the final performance of the overall LS system.

The idea to reformulate the substitution generation subtask as an MLM task was developed by (Qiang et al., 2021) for English and was in this paper adapted for Swedish. The idea involves obscuring a complex word with a `[MASK]` token and letting the BERT model predict the obscured word. The prediction consists of words that hopefully can be used as substitutes for the complex word.

To generate substitutes for a complex word the target sentence to be simplified was cloned into a sentence pair "{S, S'}". The second sentence S' had the identified complex words replaced with a `[MASK]` token and fed into the model. The rationale behind feeding the original sentence into the model twice is that it forces the model to consider the meaning of the complex word when generating substitutes. A probability distribution was returned with substitutes and their corresponding probability, in this case, the BERT models generated 20 alternatives. These alternatives are generated based on the left and right context of the masked-out word. This should handle the problem that some of the conventional approaches face; that words generated are not synonyms in all contexts.

The out-of-the-box KB-BERT model is trained on text data from different sources and time periods to be representative of the Swedish language. This is, however, not necessarily desirable in the context of LS. The aim is to get the model to generate the easiest words possible to aid tasks downstream in the pipeline. The model should preferably have a bias towards easier words and suppress more difficult words when predicting masked-out complex words. To accomplish this the KB-BERT model was fine-tuned on the LäsBarT and 8sidor corpora which contain easy-to-read texts. The huggingface tutorial[12] (Huggingface) to adapt masked language models to domain-specific data was adapted to the easy-to-read corpora and the KB-BERT model.

The fine-tuning of the BERT model in one of the `LäsBERT` versions began with creating a fine-tuning dataset with the words from the 8sidor and LäSBarT corpora and concatenating them into sentences. These sentences were written to a text file and a random split into training and test sets was performed. 10% of the dataset was used for testing and 90% for training. The test set was used to

[11] `https://huggingface.co/KBLab/bert-base-swedish-cased`

[12] `https://huggingface.co/learn/nlp-course/chapter7/3?fw=tf`

test the perplexity of the model, which is a measure of the model's (un)certainty in predicting a masked-out word. This in turn reflects the model's estimated word error rate when predicting a word (Chen et al., 1998).

The perplexity of the models on unseen easy-to-read text can be found in Table 2, indicating a significant decrease in perplexity and improved performance of the language model.

	Fine-tuned KBLab/BERT	**Not Fine-tuned** KBLab/BERT
Perplexity	**4.58**	18.88

Table 2: The perplexity of the models on unseen part of the fine-tuning dataset.

`LäsGPT` utilised OpenAI:s GPT 3.5 `text-davinci-003` model[13] to generate substitutes as a language generation task. To generate substitutes for the complex word reliably and in a predictable format the model needed to be prompted in an appropriate way. Brown et al. (2020) showed that conditioning the model with several examples of the task, i.e. few-shot learning, generally yielded the best results for several tasks. The prompt format and parameters used by Lee et al. (2021) to generate substitutes for English complex words were used but with an adaptation for Swedish. Except for the max_token parameter, the same parameters used in Lee et al. (2021) were used in this implementation. GPT-3 was prompted to generate around six alternatives for each word.

5.3 Substitute Filtering and Selection

The generated words for all LS systems needed to be filtered to remove substitutions that were not appropriate. A basic criterion for synonymy is that two words have the same Part-of-speech (POS) tag. Therefore, the POS tag for both the generated alternatives and the complex word was retrieved from the SUCX 3.0 corpus. If the POS tags did not match, the alternative was removed. If the generated token was empty or incomplete, it was removed as well.

The KB-SENTENCE-BERT model maps sentences to a 768-dimensional vector space (Rekathati, 2021), in contrast to the KB-BERT models which work on a word level. This facilitates comparison between sentences by calculating the cosine distance between their vector representations. To select which of the generated substitutes preserve the meaning of the sentence as much as possible, new sentences were constructed replacing the complex word with each of the generated and filtered substitutes in the original sentence. By examining the similarity of sentences rather than comparing individual words using a thesaurus or word embeddings, the meaning-preserving effect on the bigger linguistic unit is taken into account, thus minimising the likelihood of substitutions that are inappropriate in the context.

The alternative sentences were encoded using the SENTENCE-BERT model and the cosine distance between the sentence vector representations of the original sentence and the alternative sentences were calculated. The five substitutes that created the most similar sentences were selected as the most meaning-preserving substitutes.

5.4 Substitute Ranking

The five substitutes selected in the substitution selection task were words that preserve the meaning of the original sentence as much as possible. Assumptions regarding these words are that they are synonymous to the original word and that they fit into the context of the original sentence. The next step is to rank the selected substitutes according to simplicity to simplify the text as much as possible.

Word features were generated for the selected substitutes and the original complex word. The RFC used in the CWI subtask was used to rate the complexity of the selected substitutes and the original word. The easiest word was used as a replacement for the complex word. If the complex word was easier than all generated alternatives, no substitution was made. This step is important to minimise substitutions that replace the complex word with more difficult words. Replacing a complex word with a word with the same difficulty should be avoided. The more words that are replaced in a sentence, the more the meaning of the sentence is altered. If there is no obvious increase in readability when replacing a word with another, a simplification algorithm should be designed to be conservative, which is the case for this implementation. The baseline version of `LäsBERT` is available at `https://github.com/emilgraichen/SwedishLexicalSimplifier`.

[13] `https://platform.openai.com/docs/models/gpt-3-5`

6 Results

The performance of the Random Forest Classifier is presented in Table 3. The RFC used for Complex word identification (CWI) and substitution ranking was tested on 424 out of 4238 words in the CWI dataset.

Class	Precision	Recall	F1-score	Support
1	0.63	0.73	0.67	154
2	0.35	0.28	0.31	107
3	0.59	0.65	0.62	103
4	0.54	0.42	0.47	60
Weighted Avg:	0.54	0.55	0.54	$\Sigma =$ 424

Table 3: The precision, recall, and F1-score of the RFC used for CWI. The support column represents the distribution of classes in the test set.

Accuracy is the proportion of all correctly classified classes in the dataset, which in the case of this classifier was 0.55.

	LäsBERT (baseline)	**LäsBERT** (fine-tuned)	**LäsGPT**
Recall	**53/150 (35.3%)**	**53/150 (35.3%)**	49/150 (32.7%)

Table 4: Number of complex words substituted for any word. Bold font highlights the best performance.

Table 4 shows that the `LäsBERT` baseline system that had not been fine-tuned found and exchanged as many complex words as the fine-tuned `LäsBERT` system (35.3% of the complex words). They both found and replaced slightly more complex words than the `LäsGPT` system (32.7% of the complex words).

Synonymous replacements	**LäsBERT** (baseline)	**LäsBERT** (fine-tuned)	**LäsGPT**
<u>total</u> complex words	14/150 (9.33%)	12/150 (8%)	**16/150 (10.6%)**
<u>replaced</u> complex words	14/53 (26.4%)	12/53 (22.6%)	**16/49 (32.7%)**

Table 5: Replacements that resulted in the complex word being exchanged for a synonym in the dataset. Bold font highlights the best performance.

Table 5 shows that the `LäsBERT` baseline system that had not been fine-tuned replaced complex words with words that were found in the dataset 9,33% of the time. The fine-tuned `LäsBERT` system replaced 8% of the complex words with a synonym included in a dataset. The `LäsGPT` system replaced 10.6% of the complex words with a synonym included in the dataset.

Replacements	**LäsBERT** (baseline)	**LäsBERT** (fine-tuned)	**LäsGPT**
<u>total</u> complex words replaced with a synonymous *and* more frequent word	13/150 (8.7%)	11/150 (7.33%)	**15/150 (10%)**
<u>synonymous</u> that resulted in a more frequent word	13/14 (92.9%)	11/12 (91.7%)	**15/16 (93.8%)**

Table 6: Replacements that exchanged the complex word with a synonymous *and* more frequent word. Bold font highlights the best performance.

Table 6 shows that the `LäsBERT` baseline system replaced complex words with synonyms found in the dataset that also were more frequent than the complex word 8.7% of the time. The fine-tuned `LäsBERT` system replaced 7.33% of the complex words with a more frequent synonym. The `LäsGPT` system replaced 10% of the complex words with a synonym in the dataset that was more frequent than the original word.

	LäsBERT (baseline)	**LäsBERT** (fine-tuned)	**LäsGPT**
True Positive (annotated as complex *and* replaced)	**26/43 (60.5%)**	**26/43 (60.5%)**	22/43 (51.2%)
True Negative (annotated as non-complex *and* **not** replaced)	**80/107 (74.7%)**	79/107 (73.4%)	**80/107 (74.7%)**
Total agreement	**106/150 (70.1%)**	105/150 (70%)	102/150 (68%)

Table 7: The proportion of words that the LS systems and the annotators marked as complex. Bold font highlights the best performance.

The results in Table 7, reflect the system-annotator agreement. If a complex word in the dataset evaluation, see Section 4, was regarded as complex by the annotators *and* replaced by an LS system at test time it counted towards the True Positive score. If annotators marked the words as non-complex *and* the LS systems didn't replace the word with anything it counted towards the True Negative score.

Both `LäsBERT` versions replaced 60.5% of the words that were annotated as complex by the humans. `LäsGPT` scored lower and replaced 51.2%

of the words annotated by humans as complex. LäsGPT and the baseline version of LäsBERT both agreed with the annotators on 74.4% of the words that were annotated as non-complex. The baseline version of LäsBERT had the highest overall agreement with the human annotators with 70.1% of the words being aligned with the human annotators.

7 Discussion

The results revealed that both the LäsBERT and LäsGPT systems had relatively low recall rates, replacing only about one-third of the complex words in the evaluation dataset. This indicates the need for improvement in the systems' ability to identify and replace complex words accurately. The CWI component of the LS pipeline was highlighted as an area for future improvement. Regarding system-annotator agreement, the LS systems showed agreement with human annotators between 68% (LäsGPT) and 70.1% (LäsBERT baseline) of the time. The LäsBERT versions performed slightly better, with an agreement of 60.5% for true positives, indicating that the systems and human annotators generally agreed on which words needed to be replaced.

When it comes to synonymous replacements, LäsGPT performed the best, with a rate of 10.6% of complex words replaced by synonyms. However, when considering only the replaced complex words, the synonymous replacement rate improved to 32.7% for LäsGPT. The LäsBERT models demonstrated lower percentages of synonymous substitutions.

Furthermore, almost all synonymous replacements resulted in words with higher corpus frequencies, indicating a simplification effect. LäsGPT had a slightly bigger impact on text simplification, with 10% of the words resulting in a word with higher corpus frequency. While there is still potential for improvement, the relatively low perceived complexity of the complex words in the dataset and the more promising system-annotator agreement suggests that some issues are attributable to the dataset itself rather than to the LS systems.

The effects of fine-tuning the language model for substitution generation did not affect the number of words replaced by the model on this evaluation dataset. Both versions performed similarly, identifying and replacing 35.3% of complex words and agreeing with human annotators 70.1% and 70% of the time, respectively. This lack of difference is assumed to be attributed to the small size of the evaluation dataset, limiting the expression of subtle effects. The evaluation also revealed that both versions had a very similar number of synonymous replacements, with next to all of these replacements also resulting in words with higher corpus frequency. Interestingly, the baseline version tended to make more synonymous and simpler replacements than the fine-tuned version. This indicates that it's not worth the effort to fine-tune the language model since it seems to have a detrimental rather than beneficial effect on the end-to-end performance. The reason behind the reduced performance of the fine-tuned version remains unclear. A possible explanation is that fine-tuning had an adverse impact on the model's overall language comprehension.

8 Conclusion

The lexical simplifiers presented in this paper do not differ substantially in their performance from each other. The LäsBERT versions have a slightly higher recall, whilst LäsGPT performs slightly more synonymous replacements that also have a higher corpus frequency. The absolute percentage of the number of substitutions is not very high with around just a third of the complex words in the dataset being replaced by the LS systems. However, the agreement between the systems and annotators on which words should be substituted is relatively high (68% to 70.1%).

There is room for improvement of the evaluation dataset. A higher proportion of perceived complex words is needed to more accurately reflect which words need to be simplified.

The fine-tuning process did not have a noteworthy impact on the number of words replaced by the model. Both the fine-tuned and non-fine-tuned versions identified and replaced approximately 35.3% of complex words and had a similar agreement with human annotators. However, the evaluation revealed that the baseline version tended to make slightly more synonymous and simpler replacements compared to the fine-tuned version. This suggests that fine-tuning the model may not be beneficial and could potentially have a detrimental effect on the system's performance. The exact reason for the reduced performance of the fine-tuned version remains unclear, but it may be that the fine-tuning process have negatively affected the model's overall language comprehension.

Lay Summary

Lexical simplification is the task of replacing complex words with easier ones. The approaches to this task usually involve replacing words with simpler synonyms found in a linguistic database, implementing rules to "translate" linguistic units into easier ones, or using language models to generate similar substitution candidates. These methods usually fail to take the context of the target word into account, resulting in nonsensical substitutions.

We present results from the development and evaluation of context-aware Lexical simplification systems for the Swedish language. Three versions of lexical simplification models were created and evaluated on a newly constructed Swedish evaluation dataset. The simplification systems demonstrated promising potential in aiding audiences with reading difficulties by providing context-aware word replacements. While there were areas for improvement, particularly in complex word identification, the systems showed agreement with human annotators on word replacements.

References

Emil Abrahamsson, Timothy Forni, Maria Skeppstedt, and Maria Kvist. 2014. Medical text simplification using synonym replacement: Adapting assessment of word difficulty to a compounding language. In *Proceedings of the 3rd Workshop on Predicting and Improving Text Readability for Target Reader Populations (PITR)*, pages 57–65.

Peder Abrahamsson. 2011. Mer lättläst: Påbyggnad av ett automatiskt omskrivningsverktyg till lätt svenska. Bachelor's thesis, linköpings universitet, Linköping University.

Dennis Aumiller and Michael Gertz. 2022. UniHD at TSAR-2022 shared task: Is compute all we need for lexical simplification? In *Proceedings of the Workshop on Text Simplification, Accessibility, and Readability (TSAR-2022)*, pages 251–258, Abu Dhabi, United Arab Emirates (Virtual). Association for Computational Linguistics.

Joachim Bingel and Johannes Bjerva. 2018. Cross-lingual complex word identification with multitask learning. In *Proceedings of the thirteenth workshop on innovative use of NLP for building educational applications*, pages 166–174.

Steven Bird, Ewan Klein, and Edward Loper. 2009. *Natural language processing with Python: analyzing text with the natural language toolkit.* " O'Reilly Media, Inc.".

Lars Borin, Markus Forsberg, and Lennart Lönngren. 2013. Saldo: a touch of yin to wordnet's yang. *Language resources and evaluation*, 47(4):1191–1211.

Leo Breiman. 2001. Random forests. *Machine learning*, 45:5–32.

Tom Brown, Benjamin Mann, Nick Ryder, Melanie Subbiah, Jared D Kaplan, Prafulla Dhariwal, Arvind Neelakantan, Pranav Shyam, Girish Sastry, Amanda Askell, et al. 2020. Language models are few-shot learners. *Advances in neural information processing systems*, 33:1877–1901.

Stanley F Chen, Douglas Beeferman, and Roni Rosenfeld. 1998. Evaluation metrics for language models.

Will Coster and David Kauchak. 2011. Learning to simplify sentences using Wikipedia. In *Proceedings of the Workshop on Monolingual Text-To-Text Generation*, pages 1–9, Portland, Oregon. Association for Computational Linguistics.

Jan De Belder and Marie-Francine Moens. 2010. Text simplification for children. In *Prroceedings of the SIGIR workshop on accessible search systems*, pages 19–26. ACM; New York.

Jacob Devlin, Ming-Wei Chang, Kenton Lee, and Kristina Toutanova. 2018. Bert: Pre-training of deep bidirectional transformers for language understanding. *arXiv preprint arXiv:1810.04805*.

Siobhan Devlin. 1998. The use of a psycholinguistic database in the simplification of text for aphasic readers. *Linguistic databases*.

Eva Ejerhed, Gunnel Källgren, and Benny Brodda. 2006. Stockholm-umeå corpus version 2.0. *Stockholm University, Dep. of Linguistics and Umeå University, Dep. of Linguistics*.

Goran Glavaš and Sanja Štajner. 2015. Simplifying lexical simplification: Do we need simplified corpora? In *Proceedings of the 53rd Annual Meeting of the Association for Computational Linguistics and the 7th International Joint Conference on Natural Language Processing (Volume 2: Short Papers)*, pages 63–68.

Sian Gooding and Ekaterina Kochmar. 2019. Recursive context-aware lexical simplification. In *Proceedings of the 2019 Conference on Empirical Methods in Natural Language Processing and the 9th International Joint Conference on Natural Language Processing (EMNLP-IJCNLP)*, pages 4853–4863.

Huggingface. Fine-tuning a masked manguage model. `https://huggingface.co/learn/nlp-course/chapter7/3?fw=tf`. Accessed: 2023-04-24 from `https://huggingface.co/learn/nlp-course/chapter7/3?fw=tf`.

Viggo Kann and Magnus Rosell. 2006. Free construction of a free swedish dictionary of synonyms. In *Proceedings of the 15th Nordic Conference of Computational Linguistics (NODALIDA 2005)*, pages 105–110.

Robin Keskisärkkä. 2012. Automatic text simplification via synonym replacement. Bachelor's thesis, linköpings universitet, Linköping University.

Adam Kilgarriff, Frieda Charalabopoulou, Maria Gavrilidou, Janne Bondi Johannessen, Saussan Khalil, Sofie Johansson Kokkinakis, Robert Lew, Serge Sharoff, Ravikiran Vadlapudi, and Elena Volodina. 2014. Corpus-based vocabulary lists for language learners for nine languages. *Language resources and evaluation*, 48:121–163.

Mina Lee, Chris Donahue, Robin Jia, Alexander Iyabor, and Percy Liang. 2021. Swords: A benchmark for lexical substitution with improved data coverage and quality. *arXiv preprint arXiv:2106.04102*.

Xiaofei Li, Daniel Wiechmann, Yu Qiao, and Elma Kerz. 2022. Mantis at tsar-2022 shared task: Improved unsupervised lexical simplification with pretrained encoders. *arXiv preprint arXiv:2212.09855*.

Martin Malmsten, Love Börjeson, and Chris Haffenden. 2020. Playing with Words at the National Library of Sweden – Making a Swedish BERT. *arXiv preprint arXiv:2007.01658*.

Katarina Mühlenbock. 2008. Readable, legible or plain words–presentation of an easy-to-read swedish corpus. In *Multilingualism: Proceedings of the 23rd Scandinavian Conference of Linguistics*, volume 8, pages 327–329. Acta Universitatis Upsaliensis Uppsala, Sweden.

Myndigheten för tillgängliga medier. Lättläst. `https://www.mtm.se/var-verksamhet/lattlast/`. Accessed: 2023-04-21, `https://www.mtm.se/var-verksamhet/lattlast/`.

Natur och Kultur. Rivstart. `https://www.nok.se/laromedel/serier/Rivstart/`. Accessed: 2023-04-21 from `https://www.nok.se/laromedel/serier/Rivstart/`.

Kai North, Marcos Zampieri, and Tharindu Ranasinghe. 2022. Alexsis-pt: A new resource for portuguese lexical simplification. *arXiv preprint arXiv:2209.09034*.

Gustavo Paetzold and Lucia Specia. 2016. Unsupervised lexical simplification for non-native speakers. In *Proceedings of the AAAI Conference on Artificial Intelligence*, volume 30.

F. Pedregosa, G. Varoquaux, A. Gramfort, V. Michel, B. Thirion, O. Grisel, M. Blondel, P. Prettenhofer, R. Weiss, V. Dubourg, J. Vanderplas, A. Passos, D. Cournapeau, M. Brucher, M. Perrot, and E. Duchesnay. 2011. Scikit-learn: Machine learning in Python. *Journal of Machine Learning Research*, 12:2825–2830.

Matthew E. Peters, Mark Neumann, Mohit Iyyer, Matt Gardner, Christopher Clark, Kenton Lee, and Luke Zettlemoyer. 2018. Deep contextualized word representations. In *Proceedings of the 2018 Conference of the North American Chapter of the Association for Computational Linguistics: Human Language Technologies, Volume 1 (Long Papers)*, pages 2227–2237, New Orleans, Louisiana. Association for Computational Linguistics.

Jorge S Pimienta Castillo. 2021. Multilingual lexical simplification. Master's thesis, Universitat Pompeu Fabra.

Jipeng Qiang, Yun Li, Yi Zhu, Yunhao Yuan, Yang Shi, and Xindong Wu. 2021. Lsbert: Lexical simplification based on bert. *IEEE/ACM Transactions on Audio, Speech, and Language Processing*, 29:3064–3076.

Faton Rekathati. 2021. The kblab blog: Introducing a swedish sentence transformer.

Evelina Rennes. 2022. *Automatic Adaptation of Swedish Text for Increased Inclusion*. Ph.D. thesis, Linköping University Electronic Press.

Horacio Saggion, Sanja Štajner, Daniel Ferrés, Kim Cheng Sheang, Matthew Shardlow, Kai North, and Marcos Zampieri. 2022. Findings of the TSAR-2022 shared task on multilingual lexical simplification. In *Proceedings of the Workshop on Text Simplification, Accessibility, and Readability (TSAR-2022)*, pages 271–283, Abu Dhabi, United Arab Emirates (Virtual). Association for Computational Linguistics.

Matthew Shardlow. 2013. A comparison of techniques to automatically identify complex words. In *51st annual meeting of the association for computational linguistics proceedings of the student research workshop*, pages 103–109.

Matthew Shardlow. 2014. Out in the open: Finding and categorising errors in the lexical simplification pipeline. In *LREC*, pages 1583–1590.

Greta Smolenska. 2018. Complex word identification for swedish. Master's thesis, Uppsala Universitet.

Universitets och högskolerådet. 2023. Öva på gamla högskoleprov. `https://www.studera.nu/hogskoleprov/infor-hogskoleprovet/ova-pa-gamla-hogskoleprov/`. Accessed: 2023-04-27 from `https://www.studera.nu/hogskoleprov/infor-hogskoleprovet/ova-pa-gamla-hogskoleprov/`.

Elena Volodina and Sofie Johansson Kokkinakis. 2012. Introducing the swedish kelly-list, a new lexical e-resource for swedish. In *LREC*, pages 1040–1046.

Zhemin Zhu, Delphine Bernhard, and Iryna Gurevych. 2010. A monolingual tree-based translation model for sentence simplification. In *Proceedings of the 23rd International Conference on Computational Linguistics (Coling 2010)*, pages 1353–1361, Beijing, China. Coling 2010 Organizing Committee.

TextSimplifier: A Modular, Extensible, and Context Sensitive Simplification Framework for Improved Natural Language Understanding

Sandaru Seneviratne[1], **Elena Daskalaki**[1], **Hanna Suominen**[1,2]
[1]The Australian National University (ANU) / Canberra, ACT, Australia
[2]University of Turku / Turku, Finland
{sandaru.seneviratne, eleni.daskalaki, hanna.suominen}@anu.edu.au

Abstract

Natural language understanding is fundamental to knowledge acquisition in today's information society. However, natural language is often ambiguous with frequent occurrences of complex terms, acronyms, and abbreviations that require substitution and disambiguation, for example, by "translation" from complex to simpler text for better understanding. These tasks are usually difficult for people with limited reading skills, second language learners, and non-native speakers. Hence, the development of text simplification systems that are capable of simplifying complex text is of paramount importance. Thus, we conducted a user study to identify which components are essential in a text simplification system. Based on our findings, we proposed an improved text simplification framework, covering a broader range of aspects related to lexical simplification — from complexity identification to lexical substitution and disambiguation — while supplementing the simplified outputs with additional information for better understandability. Based on the improved framework, we developed TextSimplifier, a modularised, context-sensitive, end-to-end simplification framework, and engineered its web implementation. This system targets lexical simplification that identifies complex terms and acronyms followed by their simplification through substitution and disambiguation for better understanding of complex language.

1 Introduction

Limited reading or comprehension skills can hinder managing and maintaining a comfortable lifestyle in today's information society. Regardless of acquiring skills related to reading and comprehension over many years, sometimes understanding text can be challenging for, for example, people with limited reading skills, cognitive conditions like aphasia or dyslexia (Saggion et al., 2022), limited knowledge of technical domains, non-native speakers, and children (Kajiwara et al., 2013). Therefore, different methods have been introduced to assist with reading and comprehension of language, ranging from i) manual efforts of "translating" text to more understandable formats to ii) automated simplification methods (see Section 2).

Text simplification aims to modify the content and structure of complex text to output simpler text while preserving meaning. Commonly, the two main concepts associated with simplification are identified as readability and understandability. Even though these two concepts seem highly coupled, they address two different aspects of simplification (Shardlow, 2014): Readability focuses on how complex text can be converted to simple text to make it easier to read. In contrast, understandability is related to how much information a user can grasp from the text. Depending on the context and audience for which the text simplification is intended, the focus on improving the readability or understandability may differ.

Consequently, being sensitive to the different intents, researchers have introduced various methods for simplification (see Section 2): If the aim of the simplification is readability improvement, different methods focusing on the simplification of the syntactical structure have been proposed. These methods achieve simplification primarily by deleting, reordering, and splitting sentences to convert them to syntactically simpler formats so that the text is easier to read (Chandrasekar and Srinivas, 1997; Siddharthan, 2006). On the other hand, for understandability improvement, most methods focus on generating alternative substitutes for target complex words in text, focusing on the lexical simplicity of the text (Seneviratne et al., 2022c).

Improving the understandability of text benefits many audiences. For example, these understandability-focused simplification methods are helpful for non-native speakers and second-

Proceedings of the Second Workshop on Text Simplification, Accessibility and Readability associated with RANLP-2023, pages 21–32,
held in Varna Bulgaria, Sept 7, 2023.
https://doi.org/10.26615/978-954-452-086-1_003

language learners to learn about new languages. Moreover, these methods can be helpful for students learning about new technical content or anyone who is not an expert in a specific technical domain. For example, domains like medical and scientific domains contain technical content, which is quite difficult for lay people to understand. Hence, extensive research has been done on the improved understandability of complex text (see Section 2).

Text simplification systems focusing on improved understandability of text explore different aspects related to simplification. For example, some methods investigate the complexities in text , (Pouran Ben Veyseh et al., 2021; Orlando et al., 2021), whereas others investigate the generation of alternatives for complex words (Azab et al., 2015; Paetzold and Specia, 2016) . Recent methods of text simplification rely on machine translation-based Sequence-to-Sequence (Seq2Seq) models for text simplification (Zhang and Lapata, 2017; Nisioi et al., 2017; Zhao et al., 2018; Maddela et al., 2021), which tackle both lexical and syntactic simplification of text. One of the limitations of Seq2Seq models is that they achieve simplification mainly by reducing the length of the sentences through the deletion of tokens which results in improved readability, however, at the cost of understandability (Maddela et al., 2021). Hence, when focusing on the understandability aspect of the text, modular approaches which tackle one subtask at a time may yield better outputs.

Generally, most practical simplification methods targetting lexical simplicity or understandability follow a modular approach with a pipeline proposed by Shardlow (2014). This pipeline comprises complex word identification, substitution generation, selection, and ranking methods for improved understandability. However, even though this pipeline has been adopted for many functional simplification systems, they only focus on complex words or phrases and simplification of them. For better understandability identifying other aspects that contribute to the complexity is essential. For example, in technical domains like medical or scientific, technical shorthand (i.e., acronyms or abbreviations for technical terms) are often used for ease of use and to avoid repetitions (Suominen et al., 2018). Hence, in such instances, shorthand identification and disambiguation of them is crucial for better understandability. Moreover, considering the complexities in text, in some instances, generating an alternative word or phrase may not be enough for accurate comprehension, thus requiring additional information.

The existing practical lexical simplification systems typically focus on one aspect of simplification, like addressing the complexity by acronyms (Pouran Ben Veyseh et al., 2021) or the ambiguity by the polysemic words (Orlando et al., 2021). In contrast, some systems rely on the pipeline by Shardlow (2014) and incorporate several components together (Bingel et al., 2018). Nevertheless, there are systems, which focus on both lexical and syntactic simplifications (Saggion et al., 2015; Ferrés et al., 2016). However, practical systems for lexical simplification at present have a limited coverage of components, thus requiring more comprehensive systems for practical lexical simplification.

In this paper, we present an improved text simplification framework targeting lexical simplification, extending the pipeline proposed by Shardlow (2014). It consists of the following four components: complex word identification, substitution generation, selection, and ranking. We report on a preliminary user study that we conducted to identify additional components required to enhance the simplification output for better understandability. Based on the user study, we have investigated and incorporated different components into the pipeline: i) an acronym identification module to address the complexities of shorthand, specifically acronyms, ii) an acronym disambiguation module to tackle the existence of multiple expansions for an acronym, and iii) an information module to supplement the outputs with more information for better understandability, together with iv) the conventional components. We have combined them as a pipeline to form both an improved framework and its implementation as a web-based system for lexical simplification, focusing on understandability. The proposed simplification system mainly addresses general-language and specialised (scientific/medical) text, due to the availability of resources and models.

2 Related Work

The earliest attempt to develop a text simplification system for practical use was made by Devlin and Unthank (2006), who introduced HAPPI — Helping Aphasic People Process Information, a web-based system to assist people with aphasia in reading online information. The system achieved this by providing alternative words for complex words obtained through a database. The database consisted of psycholinguistic information about words like frequency and the familiarity of words used in the simplification process.

Text simplification systems for improved comprehension targeting lexical simplicity advanced in mid-2010s. Azab et al. (2015) introduced a text simplification system targeting second-language learners of the English language, with an interactive web interface for the users. The simplification was achieved by providing synonyms for complex words. Glavaš and Štajner (2015) proposed a resource-light, unsupervised lexical simplification system called LIGHT-LS. It relied on large regular text corpus for lexical simplification. A similar web interface to Azab et al. (2015) was introduced by Paetzold and Specia (2016). The tool was called Anita: An Intelligent Text Adaptation Tool and it relied on the LEXenstein framework by Paetzold and Specia (2015). Anita followed four steps in the simplification process where first candidate substitutes were produced based on a word embedding model followed by selection, ranking and replacement of the complex word. Additional information like synonyms and definitions were also provided in the system if a user requested it. Their method created user profiles intending to obtain users' feedback to improve the results. Bingel et al. (2018) introduced a text simplification tool called Lexi which also addressed obtaining users' feedback. The proposed system relied on the pipeline introduced by Shardlow (2014) and included complex word identification, substitution generation, selection, and ranking components. In addition, Lexi used users' feedback to personalise the experience to the target users.

Pioneering frameworks and systems for both lexical and syntactic simplification processes were also introduced over the years. Saggion et al. (2015) presented the Simplext project that effectively managed both lexical and syntactic simplification processes for Spanish. For lexical simplification, Simplext relied on a synonym-based and a rule-based simplification component, while for syntactic simplification handwritten computational grammars were used. Similarly, YATS by Ferrés et al. (2016) consisted of lexical and syntactic components to improve text readability and understandability for English. Its lexical simplification relied on a vector space model and word frequency simplicity measures to rank synonyms while its syntactic simplification used rule-based syntactic analysis and generation techniques based on part-of-speech tags and syntactic dependency information. Following a similar approach to YATS, a lexical simplification architecture for Spanish, Portuguese, Catalan, and Galician was introduced by Ferrés et al. (2017).

Focusing on the improved lexical simplicity of text, Orlando et al. (2021) introduced a word sense disambiguation system called AMuSE-WSD: An All-in-one Multilingual System for Easy Word Sense Disambiguation. The proposed system presented a web interface for word sense disambiguation in multiple languages. Addressing another aspect of lexical simplification, Pouran Ben Veyseh et al. (2021) proposed a web-based acronym identification and disambiguation system called MadDog. Its scope was entirely on the complexity added by acronyms.

Even though there have been several systems targeting lexical simplification in the recent past, most of these systems used the traditional lexical simplification pipeline by Shardlow (2014) for simplification, failing to consider the other essential components for improved understandability. Thus, it is important to explore beyond the traditional simplification steps when translating the research outputs into useful applications. Nevertheless, there has been extensive research in the domain of lexical simplification over the years that predominantly rely on transformer-based language models to improve the understandability of text (Saggion et al., 2022; Štajner et al., 2022).

3 User Study

The development of a functional text simplification system for practical use requires identifying what contributes to the complexity of the text, the aspects that should be considered, and the components that should be included. Thus, we conducted a user study to obtain user input on essential components for text simplification. Ethical approval (Protocol 2021/708) for the user study was obtained from the ANU Human Research Ethics Committee. The user responses were collected in a survey format.

3.1 Survey Process

To identify the essential components in a practical text simplification, we conducted a preliminary user study in the form of an online survey. We co-

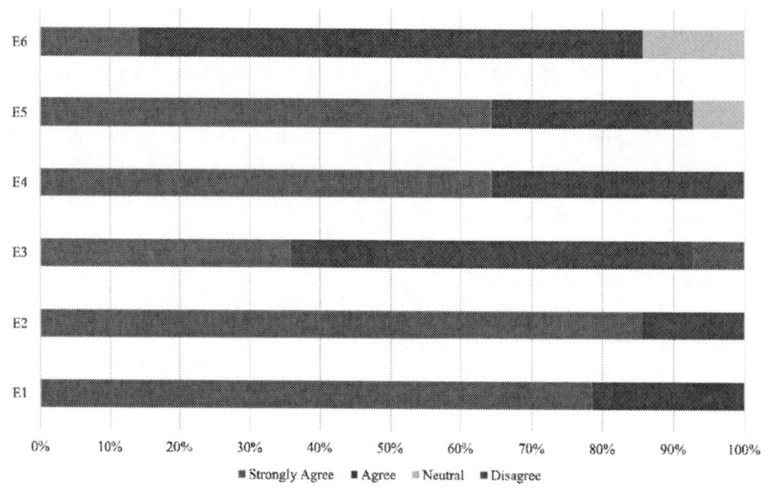

Figure 1: Evaluation results from the user study for all 14 participants. Labels of the $y - axis$ are as follows:
E1: Providing the correct expansion of shortened words is important for better understanding of unfamiliar acronyms.
E2: Inclusion of synonyms/similar substitutes for complex words is important for better understanding of complex text.
E3: Inclusion of additional information about words supplementing with definitions, links to more information can improve understandability of complex text.
E4: Systems that identify complex words and acronyms as well as provide substitutes, correct expansions, and additional information are useful.
E5: Grammatical structures and sentence structures can add complexity to text.
E6: Content simplification is more important than simplifying grammatical structures and sentence structures.

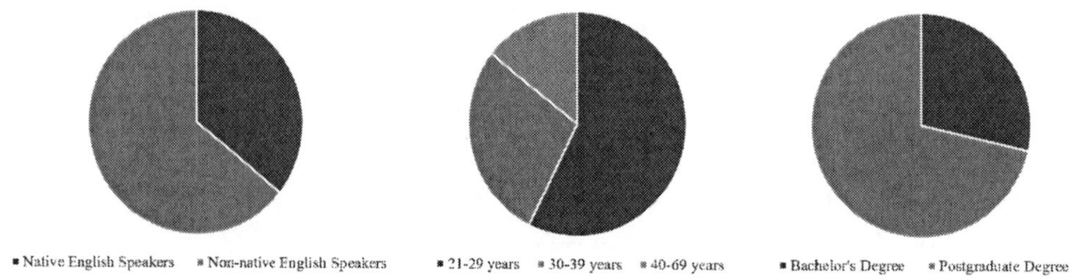

Figure 2: Participants' demographics based on their English-speaking background, age, and highest education.

created the survey questions included in this preliminary user study with user and health experience experts of the Our Health in Our Hands (OHIOH) health experience team (Figure 1). With the survey questions, we mainly targeted the complexities frequently found in complex medical text and the simplification of complex medical text. Each participant was asked to answer the set of survey questions, based on their experience, to identify what contributes to the complexity and components required for simplification. For each question, we provided four answer options (i.e., *strongly agree*, *agree*, *neutral*, and *disagree*).

3.2 Participants

We recruited participants from different English-speaking backgrounds, ages, and educational qualifications for the user study. In total, we recruited 14 participants, of which 9 were non-native English speakers and 5 were native English speakers. Most participants were in the age range of 21–29. In addition, the participants varied in their educational qualifications. For example, there were 4 participants with a bachelor's degree and 10 participants with a postgraduate degree (Figure 2).

3.3 Evaluation Results

Seven out of the nine non-native participants expressed that they frequently or always encountered complex words in the text and found complex text challenging to understand. The native English speakers also indicated that they occasionally struggled to understand certain complex content, suggesting that despite their English-speaking background text can be complex. One reason might be that text from domains like medical or scientific domains we come across daily contains technical terms that are difficult for lay people to understand. Moreover, the exponential growth of information has resulted in a rapid increase of new words and terminologies that can be quite new to lay people.

All 14 participants, that is, both native and non-native English speakers, agreed that the inclusion of synonyms or alternative substitutes for complex words could improve text understandability. Moreover, through the survey, we asked the participants about acronyms and their associated complexities. We focused on the acronyms mainly because most technical domains often use shorthand for ease of use. This can result in complex text due to the availability of multiple possible expansions for one single acronym. All the participants agreed that identifying and disambiguating acronyms could improve text understandability.

Some of the previous systems provided supplementary information for complex text. Thus, in the survey, we asked the participants about their opinion on components to provide additional information. All the non-native participants agreed that including additional information could help the reader.

In addition to content simplification, we asked participants about the complexities of grammatical structures. The majority of the participants ($n = 13$) indicated that grammatical structures and sentence structures could contribute to the complexity of the text. Nevertheless, the results indicated that simplifying complex content is essential for understandability (Figure 1).

In the survey, we asked the participants their most commonly used methods to understand and simplify complex text. The majority of the participants indicated that they use internet searches, google, and dictionaries to find meanings of words. Some participants also indicated that they rely on Wikipedia for information needs relating to complex text. Regarding complex text in technical domains (e.g., medical), the participants stated that they would seek help from an expert in the field for clarification.

4 Proposed Framework

We proposed a modular text simplification framework for improved lexical simplicity based on feedback from the user study. The proposed framework extends beyond the conventional text simplification systems and pipelines and incorporates components targeting a much broader area of aspects related to lexical simplification.

Our work is founded on the pipeline by Shardlow (2014) with components for complex word identification, substitution generation, selection, and ranking. This can be converted into a pipeline with two components at a more abstract level forming it as a pipeline with complex word identification and lexical substitution, with the latter three components of the traditional pipeline falling under lexical substitution. The feedback from the user study indicated that acronyms also contribute to the complexity of text, and hence, we have incorporated an additional component for the acronym identification task. Following the acronym identification module, we have integrated a disambiguation module focusing on identifying the correct expansion of an acronym. Moreover, because the participants of the user study expressed the importance of a module to provide supplementary information for improved understandability, we have incorporated an information module into the pipeline.

Our proposed improved framework targets the understandability of natural language (Figure 3). It consists of 5 main modules: complex word identification, lexical substitution, acronym identification, acronym disambiguation, and information module.

5 System Design

We developed a modular, context-sensitive text simplification system based on the proposed framework focused on improved understandability (Figure 4) that we have made available at `http://130.56.247.69:8501/`. Each major component in the framework is a separate subfield in lexcal simplification. Hence, when translating the framework to the development stage, we have proposed new methods and relied on previous works for each component. The datasets used for experiments come

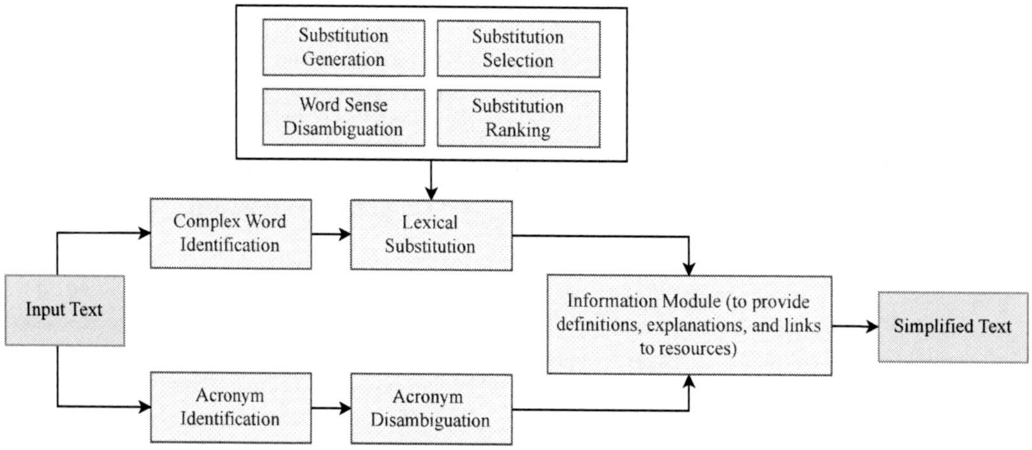

Figure 3: Our modular, extensible, and context-sensitive text simplification pipeline for improved understandability.

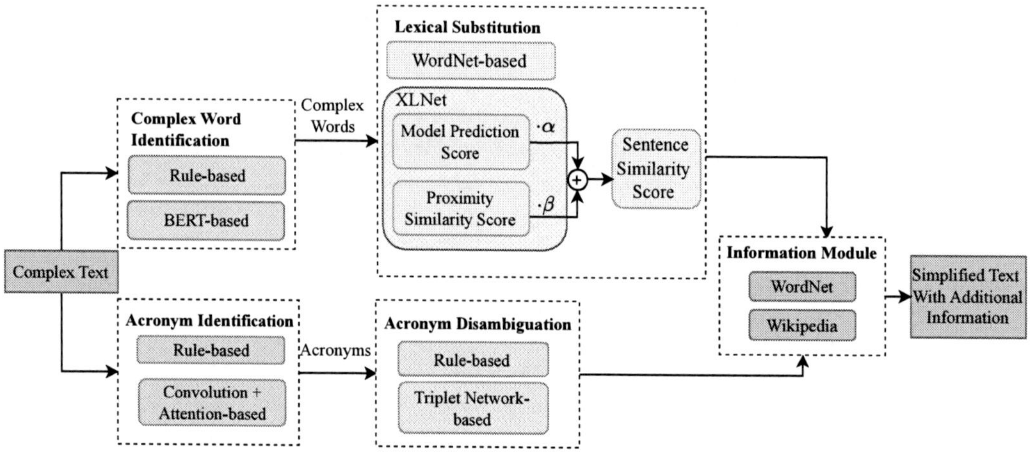

Figure 4: The system development of the proposed framework.

from general and specialised (scientific/medical) text. Its design and development consider dependencies of each of these components.

5.1 Complex Word Identification

In our system, we modeled identifying complex words as a token classification task, where the model predicts if the tokens in the input text are complex or not. We used the pre-trained Bidirectional Encoder Representations from Transformers (BERT) model considering its effectiveness in many natural language processing tasks (Tenney et al., 2019; Qiang et al., 2020). The model was fine-tuned on the complex word identification dataset (Yimam et al., 2017) and achieved an F1 score of 75%. In addition to the BERT-based model, a much simpler frequency-based complex word identification method, which used the frequency of a word per million words of English text based on Google Books Ngrams was included.

5.2 Lexical Substitution

The proposed toolkit has three lexical substitution methods. The first method generates WordNet-based synonyms for complex words while the other two methods are based on pre-trained language models proposed in Arefyev et al. (2020).

The lexical substitution method by Arefyev et al. (2020) relied on XLNet to produce layman-friendly alternatives for complex words by incorporating i) a model prediction score $P(w|c)$ where c is the context and w is any word from the XLNet vocabulary and ii) a proximity similarity score $P(w|x)$ where x is the target complex word as follows:

$$S_{\texttt{XLNet}} = \alpha P(w|c) + \beta P(w|x) \quad (1)$$

Method	P@1	
	LS07	**CoInCo**
BERT-based*	31.7	43.5
XLNet+embs	49.53	51.5
LexSubCon	51.7	50.5
CILex	53.38	55.73

Table 1: Results of substitution generation for LS07 and CoInCo datasets in %. We included reproduced results of the BERT-based substitution method (Zhou et al., 2019) by Michalopoulos et al. (2021) which is shown in *, reproduced the results of both i) XLNet+embs (Arefyev et al., 2020) and ii) LexSubCon (Michalopoulos et al., 2021). Our TextSimplifier uses the method in **bold**.

where α and β weigh the two scores.

Extending the XLNet-based method, we used CILex (Seneviratne et al., 2022a) a lexical substitution method that evaluates the added value of sentence context to ensure that the produced substitutions are semantically consistent and do not change the overall meaning of the sentences.

To evaluate the suitability of the possible candidates and their influence in the global context of the given sentence, we computed an additional score. Given a sentence s with a target word, we obtained an updated sentence (s') by replacing the target word with a possible substitution. For each possible substitution, a sentence similarity score was then calculated using cosine similarity using the sentence embeddings for the original sentence s and the updated sentence s':

$$S_{\texttt{sent}} = \texttt{cos}(s, s'). \quad (2)$$

The model score $S_{\texttt{XLNet}}$ and sentence similarity score $S_{\texttt{sent}}$ were linearly combined to rank and filter the final set of substitutions.

This proposed approach was tested on two publicly available datasets; Semeval 2007 task dataset (LS07) (McCarthy and Navigli, 2009) and the Concepts in Context (CoInCo) (Kremer et al., 2014) dataset. For both datasets, the proposed approach achieved state-of-the-art results in lexical substitution (Table 1).

5.3 Acronym Identification

We saw acronyms, formed from the first letters of words, as a sub-category of complex words in this study because of their contribution to the complexity. Hence, similar to complex word identification, we modeled acronym identification by defining the task as a token classification problem. To facilitate building the acronym identification model, we adopted the publicly available acronym identification dataset from the Scientific Document Understanding task, which consisted of labels for both acronyms and expansions (Pouran Ben Veyseh et al., 2020). For our experiments, we only considered the acronyms in the dataset. The model architecture consisted of convolutional neural networks and attention layers and achieved an `F1` score of 93.94% for the prediction of acronyms. Additionally, we also included a domain-independent rule-based acronym identification method proposed in Schwartz and Hearst (2002) in the toolkit which achieved an `F1` score of 92% .

5.4 Acronym Disambiguation

We modeled acronym disambiguation as a binary classification task to predict if the given expansion is the correct expansion or not for the corresponding acronym. We used a contrastive learning-based method to learn better representations of text and effectively disambiguate acronyms (Seneviratne et al., 2022b).

In the proposed approach, triplet loss

$$||f(x_i^a) - f(x_i^p)||_2^2 + \alpha < ||f(x_i^a) - f(x_i^n)||_2^2 \quad (3)$$

and triplet networks were leveraged to learn semantic differences among the different expansions of the same acronym through sentence triplet creation which included defining an anchor sentence, a positive sentence, and negative sentences. We defined the following process to sentence triplets: i) To obtain the list of anchor sentences, for each expansion of an acronym, we extracted a sentence randomly from the training subset of the data. The resultant set includes sentences with acronyms. ii) To obtain the positive sentences, we replaced the acronyms in the list of given sentences with their correct expansions. iii) To obtain negative sentences, first we obtained all the likely expansions of an acronym in the given sentence except for its correct expansion. Then, we obtained a list of sentences by replacing the given sentences' acronyms with these expansions. The resulting sentences were considered negative sentences. Consequently, we used the obtained anchor, positive, and negative sentences to train the triplet network-based architecture[1].

We validated the proposed approach both in the scientific and medical domains (Seneviratne

[1]More information on how the acronym disambiguation task was performed can be found at Seneviratne et al. (2022b).

Method	F1	
	SDU	MeDAL
Baseline method	59.73	44.39
Span prediction method	84.24	74.91
Triplet Network-based	85.70	75.19

Table 2: Results of acronym disambiguation for the validation data of SDU dataset and test data of MeDAL datasets in %. We included results reproduced using the i) frequency-based baseline method by Veyseh et al. (2020), ii) span prediction method by Singh and Kumar (2021), and iii) triplet network-based method by Seneviratne et al. (2022b). Our TextSimplifier is uses the method in **bold**.

et al., 2022b) using two publicly available datasets; acronym disambiguation dataset from Scientific Document Understanding Task (SDU) (Pouran Ben Veyseh et al., 2020) and a part of Medical Abbreviation Disambiguation Dataset (MeDAL) (Wen et al., 2020). Triplet Network-based method gave comparable performance as the baseline for both the datasets (Table 2). Furthermore, we included the domain-independent frequency-based baseline method by Pouran Ben Veyseh et al. (2020) in TextSimplifier toolkit.

5.5 Information Module

We engineered our Information Module to collect additional information related to predicted complex words and acronym expansions. Each complex word and acronym expansion was linked to its corresponding web page from Wikipedia. Web pages from both English and simple Wikipedia were used for this purpose. We envisioned users clicking on links to obtain further information. For better text understanding, definitions obtained from WordNet and disambiguated using sentence-Transformers (Reimers and Gurevych, 2019) were provided and integrated as a component in the system.

6 Discussion

In this paper, we have proposed a text simplification framework targeting improved lexical simplicity/language understandability using the feedback obtained through a user study on text complexities. Based on the feedback, we have extended the conventional lexical simplification pipeline to incorporate additional components essential for natural language understanding. As a result, we have derived a framework of complex word identification, lexical substitution, acronym identification, and acronym disambiguation components followed by an information module to supplement the simplified output.

Even though the typical lexical simplification systems focus only on the complexities of complex words and phrases, the evaluation results of the user study indicated that the acronyms contribute to the complexity of the text. One reason might be that acronyms are heavily used in technical domains like scientific and medical domains we come across daily. Moreover, the exponential growth in information has increased the use of acronyms. Hence, it is essential to identify and disambiguate them to determine the correct expansion corresponding to the meaning of the context and incorporate the relevant components in simplification pipelines. The results from the user study also indicated the importance of providing additional information related to the complexities in the text to improve understandability, thereby helping the readers grasp the knowledge effectively. Therefore, it is crucial to incorporate components that supplement the simplified versions of complex text.

In our proposed text simplification framework, we have integrated multiple components that all relate to lexical simplification. We have validated and assessed each component separately to ensure their effectiveness. Nevertheless, because each task was trained using datasets from different sources, this could potentially impact the final output. Therefore, exploring the compatibility of these separate models within a unified system is crucial. Moreover, the end-to-end pipeline as a whole was not evaluated. Thus, as future work, we expect to create datasets that provide annotations for each important task in a consistent manner, which could further enhance the effectiveness of text simplification methods. Given these challenges, the output generated by the complete pipeline has not been evaluated using a simplicity metric in this study.

The proposed simplification framework incorporates additional components required for improved language understandability compared to existing simplification systems. It also follows a modular or task-based approach in tackling different aspects related to simplification, which is much more explainable compared to models that rely on one black-box architecture for the simplification task. Moreover, its modular architecture eases the integration of new modules addressing other aspects of simplification and new components for each module in the

Input	The purpose of RL is for the agent to learn an optimal, or nearly-optimal, policy that maximizes the reward function .
TextSimplifier	The purpose of **RL (reinforcement learning)** is for the agent to learn an optimal, or nearly-optimal, policy that maximizes the **reward (payoff, incentive, benefit)** function (reinforcement learning: https://en.wikipedia.org/wiki/Reinforcement_learning reward: https://simple.wikipedia.org/wiki/Reward, reward: act or give recompense in recognition of someone's behavior or actions)
MadDog	The purpose of **RL (Reward Learning)** is for the agent to learn an optimal , or nearly - optimal , policy that maximizes the reward function .
Lexi (Hero)	The purpose of RL is to learn the best policy. The best policy will give the best reward.

Table 3: Comparison with existing toolkits; Lexi (Bingel et al., 2018), MadDog (Pouran Ben Veyseh et al., 2021).

framework. These features of the framework facilitate uncomplicated translation of the framework to the functional systems.

This paper has proposed a text simplification framework targeting the improved understandability of complex text. However, the evaluation results from the user study indicated the complexities of grammatical and sentence structures; hence, incorporating components for syntactic simplification is important. Therefore, future work is welcome to explore the addition of syntactical simplification components along with other modules that can be incorporated into the current framework for improved understandability.

Limitations

The main focus of the proposed user study is limited to the the simplification of complex words and acronyms. This could further be extended to incorporate the role of coherence/cohesion or the impact of syntactic complexity on understanding. Moreover, the participants of the user study are all well-educated even though some have English as their second language. Thus, the feedback could not be representative of the general audience requiring simplification of complex words.

We used the proposed framework for the development of a sample prototype system as a first step towards translating research into the real world. However, developing a text simplification system for practical use requires consideration of many different aspects, thus, is more complex. For example, given that the system aims to assist readers in improving their understandability, the system should have accurate and fast responses. This requires further validation of the outputs from the models to ensure that they do not generate incorrect responses, misinforming the readers. Moreover, the current methods rely heavily on deep learning models; hence, the efficient integration of the models is required. Our current prototype system is in early stages of development and hence it is advisable to be aware of the risks.

Ethics Statement

Ethical approval (Protocol 2021/708) was obtained from the ANU Human Research Ethics Committee for the user study. According to the National Statement on Ethical Conduct in Human Research (2007) — Updated 2018 (National Health and Medical Research Council, 2018), a new ethics approval was not required, and, to the best of our knowledge, all the datasets used were created ethically.

Acknowledgement

This research was funded by and has been delivered in partnership with Our Health in Our Hands (OHIOH), a strategic initiative of the ANU, which aims to transform health care by developing new personalised health technologies and solutions in collaboration with patients, clinicians and healthcare providers. We gratefully acknowledge the funding from the ANU School of Computing and OHIOH for the first author's PhD studies and the related travel. We also thank Dr. Nicola Brew-Sam of OHIOH Health Experience Team for her valuable insights on the user study. This work was supported by computational resources provided by the Australian Government through the National Computational Infrastructure (NCI) under the ANU Merit Allocation Scheme. We wish to thank NCI Australia for providing cloud resources for the project *ny83*, to host the demonstration system.

Lay Summary

Understanding language can be difficult due to complex words, acronyms, and abbreviations. People with limited reading skills, non-native speakers, and those learning a new language find it challenging. To simplify text, at present, automated text simplification methods are used. In this paper, we introduced a text simplification system that uses natural language processing and machine learning techniques. We conducted a user study to figure out different components important in text simplification systems. The proposed text simplification system first identifies complex terms that might confuse readers and then replaces them with simpler words. This TextSimplifier system also identifies acronyms or shortened words in text, provides their long expansion, and gives more information for complex words and acronyms to make things even clearer. This helps make information open to everyone, no matter their language skills.

References

Nikolay Arefyev, Boris Sheludko, Alexander Podolskiy, and Alexander Panchenko. 2020. Always keep your target in mind: Studying semantics and improving performance of neural lexical substitution. In *Proceedings of the 28th International Conference on Computational Linguistics*, pages 1242–1255, Barcelona, Spain (Online). International Committee on Computational Linguistics.

Mahmoud Azab, Chris Hokamp, and Rada Mihalcea. 2015. Using word semantics to assist English as a second language learners. In *Proceedings of the 2015 Conference of the North American Chapter of the Association for Computational Linguistics: Demonstrations*, pages 116–120, Denver, Colorado. Association for Computational Linguistics.

Joachim Bingel, Gustavo Paetzold, and Anders Søgaard. 2018. Lexi: A tool for adaptive, personalized text simplification. In *Proceedings of the 27th International Conference on Computational Linguistics*, pages 245–258, Santa Fe, New Mexico, USA. Association for Computational Linguistics.

Raman Chandrasekar and Bangalore Srinivas. 1997. Automatic induction of rules for text simplification. *Knowledge-Based Systems*, 10(3):183–190.

Siobhan Devlin and Gary Unthank. 2006. Helping aphasic people process online information. In *Proceedings of the 8th International ACM SIGACCESS Conference on Computers and Accessibility*, pages 225–226.

Daniel Ferrés, Montserrat Marimon, Horacio Saggion, and Ahmed AbuRa'ed. 2016. Yats: yet another text simplifier. In *Natural Language Processing and Information Systems: 21st International Conference on Applications of Natural Language to Information Systems, NLDB 2016, Salford, UK, June 22-24, 2016, Proceedings 21*, pages 335–342. Springer.

Daniel Ferrés, Horacio Saggion, and Xavier Gómez Guinovart. 2017. An adaptable lexical simplification architecture for major Ibero-Romance languages. In *Proceedings of the First Workshop on Building Linguistically Generalizable NLP Systems*, pages 40–47, Copenhagen, Denmark. Association for Computational Linguistics.

Goran Glavaš and Sanja Štajner. 2015. Simplifying lexical simplification: Do we need simplified corpora? In *Proceedings of the 53rd Annual Meeting of the Association for Computational Linguistics and the 7th International Joint Conference on Natural Language Processing (Volume 2: Short Papers)*, pages 63–68, Beijing, China. Association for Computational Linguistics.

Tomoyuki Kajiwara, Hiroshi Matsumoto, and Kazuhide Yamamoto. 2013. Selecting proper lexical paraphrase for children. In *Proceedings of the 25th Conference on Computational Linguistics and Speech Processing (ROCLING 2013)*, pages 59–73, Kaohsiung, Taiwan. The Association for Computational Linguistics and Chinese Language Processing (ACLCLP).

Gerhard Kremer, Katrin Erk, Sebastian Padó, and Stefan Thater. 2014. What substitutes tell us - analysis of an "all-words" lexical substitution corpus. In *Proceedings of the 14th Conference of the European Chapter of the Association for Computational Linguistics*, pages 540–549, Gothenburg, Sweden. Association for Computational Linguistics.

Mounica Maddela, Fernando Alva-Manchego, and Wei Xu. 2021. Controllable text simplification with explicit paraphrasing. In *Proceedings of the 2021 Conference of the North American Chapter of the Association for Computational Linguistics: Human Language Technologies*, pages 3536–3553, Online. Association for Computational Linguistics.

Diana McCarthy and Roberto Navigli. 2009. The english lexical substitution task. *Language resources and evaluation*, 43(2):139–159.

George Michalopoulos, Ian McKillop, Alexander Wong, and Helen Chen. 2021. Lexsubcon: Integrating knowledge from lexical resources into contextual embeddings for lexical substitution. *arXiv preprint arXiv:2107.05132*.

National Health and Medical Research Council. 2018. National Statement on Ethical Conduct in Human Research (2007). `https://www.nhmrc.gov.au/about-us/publications/national-statement-ethical-conduct-human-research-2007-updated-2018`. [Online; accessed 06-January-2022].

Sergiu Nisioi, Sanja Štajner, Simone Paolo Ponzetto, and Liviu P. Dinu. 2017. Exploring neural text simplification models. In *Proceedings of the 55th Annual Meeting of the Association for Computational Linguistics (Volume 2: Short Papers)*, pages 85–91, Vancouver, Canada. Association for Computational Linguistics.

Riccardo Orlando, Simone Conia, Fabrizio Brignone, Francesco Cecconi, and Roberto Navigli. 2021. AMuSE-WSD: An all-in-one multilingual system for easy Word Sense Disambiguation. In *Proceedings of the 2021 Conference on Empirical Methods in Natural Language Processing: System Demonstrations*, pages 298–307, Online and Punta Cana, Dominican Republic. Association for Computational Linguistics.

Gustavo Paetzold and Lucia Specia. 2015. LEXenstein: A framework for lexical simplification. In *Proceedings of ACL-IJCNLP 2015 System Demonstrations*, pages 85–90, Beijing, China. Association for Computational Linguistics and The Asian Federation of Natural Language Processing.

Gustavo Paetzold and Lucia Specia. 2016. Anita: An intelligent text adaptation tool. In *Proceedings of COLING 2016, the 26th International Conference on Computational Linguistics: System Demonstrations*, pages 79–83, Osaka, Japan. The COLING 2016 Organizing Committee.

Amir Pouran Ben Veyseh, Franck Dernoncourt, Walter Chang, and Thien Huu Nguyen. 2021. MadDog: A web-based system for acronym identification and disambiguation. In *Proceedings of the 16th Conference of the European Chapter of the Association for Computational Linguistics: System Demonstrations*, pages 160–167, Online. Association for Computational Linguistics.

Amir Pouran Ben Veyseh, Franck Dernoncourt, Quan Hung Tran, and Thien Huu Nguyen. 2020. What does this acronym mean? introducing a new dataset for acronym identification and disambiguation. In *Proceedings of the 28th International Conference on Computational Linguistics*, pages 3285–3301, Barcelona, Spain (Online). International Committee on Computational Linguistics.

Jipeng Qiang, Yun Li, Zhu Yi, Yunhao Yuan, and Xindong Wu. 2020. Lexical simplification with pretrained encoders. *Thirty-Fourth AAAI Conference on Artificial Intelligence*, page 8649–8656.

Nils Reimers and Iryna Gurevych. 2019. Sentence-BERT: Sentence embeddings using Siamese BERT-networks. In *Proceedings of the 2019 Conference on Empirical Methods in Natural Language Processing and the 9th International Joint Conference on Natural Language Processing (EMNLP-IJCNLP)*, pages 3982–3992, Hong Kong, China. Association for Computational Linguistics.

Horacio Saggion, Sanja Štajner, Stefan Bott, Simon Mille, Luz Rello, and Biljana Drndarevic. 2015. Making it simplext: Implementation and evaluation of a text simplification system for spanish. *ACM Transactions on Accessible Computing (TACCESS)*, 6(4):1–36.

Horacio Saggion, Sanja Štajner, Daniel Ferrés, Kim Cheng Sheang, Matthew Shardlow, Kai North, and Marcos Zampieri. 2022. Findings of the TSAR-2022 shared task on multilingual lexical simplification. In *Proceedings of the Workshop on Text Simplification, Accessibility, and Readability (TSAR-2022)*, pages 271–283, Abu Dhabi, United Arab Emirates (Virtual). Association for Computational Linguistics.

Ariel S Schwartz and Marti A Hearst. 2002. A simple algorithm for identifying abbreviation definitions in biomedical text. In *Biocomputing 2003*, pages 451–462. World Scientific.

Sandaru Seneviratne, Elena Daskalaki, Artem Lenskiy, and Hanna Suominen. 2022a. CILex: An investigation of context information for lexical substitution methods. In *Proceedings of the 29th International Conference on Computational Linguistics*, pages 4124–4135, Gyeongju, Republic of Korea. International Committee on Computational Linguistics.

Sandaru Seneviratne, Elena Daskalaki, Artem Lenskiy, and Hanna Suominen. 2022b. m-networks: Adapting the triplet networks for acronym disambiguation. In *Proceedings of the 4th Clinical Natural Language Processing Workshop*, pages 21–29, Seattle, WA. Association for Computational Linguistics.

Sandaru Seneviratne, Elena Daskalaki, and Hanna Suominen. 2022c. CILS at TSAR-2022 shared task: Investigating the applicability of lexical substitution methods for lexical simplification. In *Proceedings of the Workshop on Text Simplification, Accessibility, and Readability (TSAR-2022)*, pages 207–212, Abu Dhabi, United Arab Emirates (Virtual). Association for Computational Linguistics.

Matthew Shardlow. 2014. A survey of automated text simplification. *International Journal of Advanced Computer Science and Applications*, 4(1):58–70.

Advaith Siddharthan. 2006. Syntactic simplification and text cohesion. *Research on Language and Computation*, 4:77–109.

Aadarsh Singh and Priyanshu Kumar. 2021. Scidr at sdu-2020: Ideas-identifying and disambiguating everyday acronyms for scientific domain. In *In SDU@AAAI-21*.

Sanja Štajner, Daniel Ferrés, Matthew Shardlow, Kai North, Marcos Zampieri, and Horacio Saggion. 2022. Lexical simplification benchmarks for english, portuguese, and spanish. *Frontiers in Artificial Intelligence*, 5:991242.

Hanna Suominen, Liadh Kelly, Lorraine Goeuriot, et al. 2018. Scholarly influence of the conference and labs of the evaluation forum ehealth initiative: review and bibliometric study of the 2012 to 2017 outcomes. *JMIR research protocols*, 7(7):e10961.

Ian Tenney, Dipanjan Das, and Ellie Pavlick. 2019. BERT rediscovers the classical NLP pipeline. In *Proceedings of the 57th Annual Meeting of the Association for Computational Linguistics*, pages 4593–4601, Florence, Italy. Association for Computational Linguistics.

Amir Pouran Ben Veyseh, Franck Dernoncourt, Thien Huu Nguyen, Walter Chang, and Leo Anthony Celi. 2020. Acronym identification and disambiguation shared tasks for scientific document understanding. *arXiv preprint arXiv:2012.11760*.

Zhi Wen, Xing Han Lu, and Siva Reddy. 2020. MeDAL: Medical abbreviation disambiguation dataset for natural language understanding pretraining. In *Proceedings of the 3rd Clinical Natural Language Processing Workshop*, pages 130–135, Online. Association for Computational Linguistics.

Seid Muhie Yimam, Sanja Štajner, Martin Riedl, and Chris Biemann. 2017. CWIG3G2 - complex word identification task across three text genres and two user groups. In *Proceedings of the Eighth International Joint Conference on Natural Language Processing (Volume 2: Short Papers)*, pages 401–407, Taipei, Taiwan. Asian Federation of Natural Language Processing.

Xingxing Zhang and Mirella Lapata. 2017. Sentence simplification with deep reinforcement learning. In *Proceedings of the 2017 Conference on Empirical Methods in Natural Language Processing*, pages 584–594, Copenhagen, Denmark. Association for Computational Linguistics.

Sanqiang Zhao, Rui Meng, Daqing He, Andi Saptono, and Bambang Parmanto. 2018. Integrating transformer and paraphrase rules for sentence simplification. In *Proceedings of the 2018 Conference on Empirical Methods in Natural Language Processing*, pages 3164–3173, Brussels, Belgium. Association for Computational Linguistics.

Wangchunshu Zhou, Tao Ge, Ke Xu, Furu Wei, and Ming Zhou. 2019. BERT-based lexical substitution. In *Proceedings of the 57th Annual Meeting of the Association for Computational Linguistics*, pages 3368–3373, Florence, Italy. Association for Computational Linguistics.

Cross-lingual Mediation: Readability Effects

Maria Kunilovskaya
Saarland University
maria.kunilovskaya@uni-saarland.de

Ruslan Mitkov
University of Lancaster
r.mitkov@lancaster.ac.uk

Eveline Wandl-Vogt
Ludwig Boltzmann Gesellschaft / Austrian Academy of Sciences
eveline.wandl-vogt@oeaw.ac.at

Abstract

This paper explores the readability of translated and interpreted texts compared to the original source texts and target language texts in the same domain. It was shown in the literature that translated and interpreted texts could exhibit lexical and syntactic properties that make them simpler, and hence, easier to process than their sources or comparable non-translations. In translation, this effect is attributed to the tendency to simplify and disambiguate the message. In interpreting, it can be enhanced by the temporal and cognitive constraints. We use readability annotations from the Newsela corpus to formulate a number of classification and regression tasks and fine-tune a multilingual pre-trained model on these tasks, obtaining models that can differentiate between complex and simple sentences. Then, the models are applied to predict the readability of sources, targets, and comparable target language originals in a zero-shot manner. Our test data – parallel and comparable – come from English-German bidirectional interpreting and translation subsets from the Europarl corpus. The results confirm the difference in readability between translated/interpreted targets against sentences in standard originally-authored source and target languages. Besides, we find consistent differences between the translation directions in the English-German language pair.

1 Introduction

Cross-lingual mediation is known to be a specific type of communication, where a message in one language is rendered into the other language either in spoken or written mode. The documents produced as a result of interpreting and translation were shown to have specific linguistic patterns, which makes them distinct from comparable originally-authored (non-mediated) documents. Distinctive features of translated language, usually captured by statistical analyses, are traditionally referred to as *translationese*. Recent studies based on interpreting data demonstrated that the outcomes of cross-lingual mediation in the written and spoken modes are very dissimilar in their linguistic properties. The term *interpretese* was introduced to refer to the specificity of linguistic choices in interpreting.

In the literature, some trends in translational behaviour (in particular, *simplification, explicitation and normalisation*) are in part explained by a conscious strategy or subconscious tendencyto clarify the communicative intent of the source text for the target audience (Olohan, 2001), and to improve document readability (Puurtinen, 2003). In simultaneous interpreting studies, simplification is viewed as a part of the coping strategy to mitigate the temporal and cognitive constraints imposed by the process. Shlesinger and Ordan (2012) found that simultaneous interpreting emphasises the spoken features of the language, which can contribute to simplification.

Theoretically, in terms of the readability outcomes of the mediation process, the effects of simplification, normalisation and explicitation together can be overcome by *interference*, a tendency which was more recently shown to have the stronger influence on the properties of translation (Evert and Neumann, 2017; Kunilovskaya and Lapshinova-Koltunski, 2020; Chowdhury et al., 2021).

This study aims to estimate the integral impact of cross-lingual mediation on the readability of translated and interpreted texts. For the purposes of this study, we do not make a distinction between readability and complexity/simplicity, assuming that the texts that are easier to read are also less complex, and vice versa, the texts that are simpler on any linguistic level are also easier to read. This assumption is often made in the related literature.

Unlike a lot of previous work, this study relies

Proceedings of the Second Workshop on Text Simplification, Accessibility and Readability associated with RANLP-2023, pages 33–43,
held in Varna Bulgaria, Sept 7, 2023.
https://doi.org/10.26615/978-954-452-086-1_004

on a computational, modelling-driven approach instead of corpus-based and statistical methods. The readability of translated and interpreted segments is captured as dependent on their respective sources and is contrasted with originally-authored data in the target language. The paper presents the results of two experiments comparing mediated segments (a) to their aligned sources and (b) to comparable originals (non-mediated segments) in the target language. Depending on the experimental setup, we train neural models that can distinguish original and simplified versions of the same segment or predict the readability level/score of unaligned segments with unrelated content, and apply these models to translated/interpreted segments aligned with their sources or to target language segments annotated as originals or mediated, respectively. If mediated language is simpler than sources, we expect the model to recognise the target segments in an aligned segment pair as simpler/more readable than the respective source. If mediated language is simpler than comparable non-mediated language in the target language, we expect mediated segments to get lower readability scores, signalling lower complexity.

The results are reported with regard to the mediation mode (written or spoken) and translation direction (German-English and English-German).

The rest of the paper is structured as follows. Section 2 provides a more in-depth analysis of the relations between readability and translational tendencies, especially simplification. In Section 3, we explain the rationale behind the proposed methodology and describe the setup of the two experiments. Subsection 3.1 contains the details on the textual data used to train and evaluate the models, and the testing data to for zero-shot transfer to translations and simultaneous interpreting. Subsection 3.2 offers a description of the modelling process and the measure used to estimate the readability of mediated segments. The results of the experiments are detailed and interpreted in Section 4. We conclude with Section 5, which summarises the study and highlights the findings.

2 Cross-lingual Mediation and Readability

In the context of this research, the specificity of cross-lingual mediation as a type of communicative activity can be viewed as dominated by two opposite trends. On the one hand, mediated language is expected to feature increased readability as an integral effect of simplification, explicitation and standardisation. On the other hand, translated and interpreted segments are likely to exhibit traits of interference from the source language, which might make them more difficult to read. Below, we give a brief overview of tendencies in translational behaviour that can be linked to readability.

One of the most discussed trends in both translators' and interpreters' behaviour is *simplification*. It can be described as "a subconscious tendency to simplify the language or message or both of the source" (Baker, 1996, p. 176). Evidence for various types of simplification in translation was reported in a number of corpus-based and computational studies, especially earlier ones (Puurtinen, 2003; Corpas Pastor et al., 2008, to name just a few). Readability scores are used as an indicator of simplification on the assumption that easier-to-read texts must be less complex (Williams, 2005; Corpas Pastor et al., 2008; Redelinghuys, 2016). Importantly, most simplification-supporting evidence comes from lexical features, such as those used by (Volansky et al., 2015): TTR, mean word length, syllable ratio, lexical density, mean word rank, and mean sentence length. For example, Redelinghuys and Kruger (2015) reported some evidence in favour of a number of translationese trends, especially simplification, in translated English. However, if simplification is operationalised at the syntactic level, as in (Hu and Kübler, 2021), who looked at news articles in seven languages translated into Chinese, simplification hypothesis does not hold. Kunilovskaya (2023, p. 163, 222) also disproved simplification: sentences in English-to-Russian translations of mass-media texts had a strong tendency to be longer and more complex than in comparable non-translations.

Other tendencies that can be viewed as contributing to increased readability of mediated output are *normalisation* and *levelling-out*. They describe the trend in translation to prefer linguistic expressions that constitute prototypical features of the target language, which might lead to exaggerating these features (over-normalisation) and make translations more similar to each other than originals in either source or target language (Baker, 1996). The empirical support for this claim also varies depending on the language pair. For example, Hu and Kübler (2021) did not find evidence for normalisation in translated Chinese, while the research on translated

Russian suggests ample evidence that translators actually over-emphasise some of the features of the target language (Kunilovskaya, 2023). (Nikolaev et al., 2020) demonstrated that the relative contribution of normalisation depended on the distance between the source and target languages. Translations from structurally-similar languages were found to demonstrate greater conformity to the TL norms and were more predictable, while translations from structurally-divergent source languages contained more non-idiomatic features making them more entropic and unusual in terms of lexical density, mean sentence length, frequencies of conjunctions and passives, etc.

Finally, the tendency to make translations more explicit is usually linked to the potential readability gains. *Explicitation* is described as a trend of the target texts to spell out components that are implicit on the linguistic surface of the source text. The most studied explicitation phenomenon is the increased explicitness of cohesion in translations manifested by a greater number of connectives. Other explicitation phenomena include additional explanatory phrases and deciphered implicatures. Although the findings from the translationese studies are mixed, it is not uncommon to conclude that "compared to original texts, translations tend to be simpler, more standardised, and more explicit" (Toral, 2019).

From the readability perspective, a translationese trend that might work against increasing fluency of the text, is *shining-through* (Teich, 2003) or interference. This term is used to refer to a tendency in translation to follow the source language patterns where possible. Interference drives up the frequencies of the linguistic features shared by the source and target languages and results in unusual awkward wordings. Similarly, the potential effects of mediation (at least in the written mode) sometimes include *sentence lengthening* (Chesterman, 2010). Volansky et al. (2015) found that the mean sentence length in English translated from a number of languages (based on Europarl data) is higher than in comparable English originals, which contradicts the simplification hypothesis.

Investigations into simultaneous interpreting often compare the results to written translation. The findings usually align with (Shlesinger and Ordan, 2012), who concluded that interpreting is associated with a strong simplification effect. For example, (Kajzer-Wietrzny and Grabowski, 2021) established reduced lexical variation in English-Polish interpreting based on Europarl speeches. (Dayter, 2018), using transcripts of speeches in the United Nations confirmed simplification (measured by lexical variety and density) for interpreting into English, but not into Russian. (Gast and Borges, 2023) found that there were fewer nouns and more pronouns in interpreted German than in comparable originals and translations, which was explained by the similarity of interpreting and unplanned spoken conversation.

To sum up, previous feature-based research on the properties of mediated language makes it difficult to judge about its comparative complexity/readability, mostly because of the atomistic nature of the features, pointing in opposite directions. Besides, the translational tendencies described above may overlap in terms of their operationalisation and interpretation with regard to readability. On the one hand, explicitation aims to make the text more accessible to the target audience and on the other hand, it increases the sentence length, and well-established readability formulae such as Flesh-Kincaid Reading Ease treat longer sentences as more difficult to read. Nonetheless, the previous research indicated that there might be good reasons to expect professional cross-lingual mediation, especially in interpreting, to increase text readability.

The motivation behind this study is to leverage the power of modern language models and estimate the readability of translated and interpreted texts in a holistic manner, refraining from designing features and detecting specific trends. Translation scholars convincingly hypothesise that clarification of the original communicative intent and disambiguation of the original message are integral parts of cross-lingual mediation, which should improve the comprehensibility of mediated texts for the target audience. If the effects of simplification, explicitation and normalisation were not counteracted by shining-through, it is not unreasonable to suggest that mediated subcorpora should have higher readability scores than non-mediated subcorpora in the source or target language. This claim is stronger for high-quality professional translation/interpreting (used in this study) because professional translators and interpreters (unlike amateurs or students) can be expected to effectively counteract interference and follow the best practices disseminated and established through professional training (Redelinghuys, 2016).

3 Methodology

Our methodology is based on fine-tuning a multilingual neural model on English readability-annotated data and applying the resulting models to English-German translational data in a zero-shot transfer scenario. This approach is inspired by (Artetxe and Schwenk, 2019) who reported remarkably strong zero-short performance for large multilingual models, fine-tuned on English and evaluated on cross-lingual inference and classification tasks. The assumed reliability of zero-shot transfer helps us circumvent the lack of readability data in German.

3.1 Data

This subsection gives a general description of the readability corpus used to train models and translation/interpreting subcorpora used to obtain readability estimates and address our research question of the impact of cross-lingual mediation on the readability/complexity of language.

The parameters of the datasets in Tables 1 and 2 are reported after filtering and preprocessing, including sentence and word tokenisation. Segments shorter than 5 words were filtered out from all datasets.

Readability corpus The fine-tuning tasks are formulated based on the annotated data from the Newsela corpus[1] which was officially obtained for this study under an academic licensing agreement. The corpus contains 1130 news articles simplified by professional editors several times to fit the reading proficiency of children at different grade levels. Each text comes with extensive metadata, including annotations for grade level and Lexile level[2]. This corpus is distributed with a segment-aligned Newsela-based dataset created by (Xu et al., 2015) to facilitate research on text simplification. The dataset maps grade and readability levels of Newsela to 5 versions of the same text (or simplification levels, ranging from the original V0 version to the most simple V4 version). The sentences from all versions of the same text were automatically aligned pairwise (using Jaccard similarity on overlapping word lemmas) resulting in pairs of sentences like V0-V1, V3-V4, V0-V3, etc, where the first member of the segment pair is from the more complex document.

For our purposes, we filtered out all segment pairs that did not contain V0 as the more complex version.

A closer inspection of the filtered dataset revealed that the aligned version of the Newsela corpus does not respect sentence splitting and explicitation as simplification strategies. The same original sentence (V0) can be multiply aligned with various parts of the simplified version at the same level. For example, according to the full-text V4 Newsela version (see corporal-punishment.en.4.txt) ORIGINAL (V0) in (1) was rendered as two sentences (given in SIMPLIFIED (V4)). Each of these sentences is paired to the original sentence in the aligned dataset.

(1) ORIGINAL (V0): *"All studies point to the fact that corporal punishment does not make for a more peaceful, happier child," she said at the Capitol on Wednesday.*
SIMPLIFIED (V4): *Corporal punishment does not work, she said. It "does not make for a more peaceful, happier child."*

Non_unique originals within the same simplification level were grouped together, and split bits of their simplified versions were concatenated. The number of segment pairs that were affected by multiple alignments varied across levels from 1370 (V1) to 2930 (V3) (1-2% of the input number of segment pairs for each readability level). This preprocessing step reduced the repetitiveness of V0 and de-noised the association between V0 and the simplified versions.

Table 1 displays the quantitative parameters of the resulting dataset for each type of alignment. It can be seen that the number of V0 segments aligned to VN versions varies across simplified versions. It means that in many cases V0 segments do not have corresponding versions at all simplification levels. In fact, we detected only 290 V0 segments that were aligned to all four VN.

The average segment length for V0 (original document) is about 28 words. The segment length for the simplified versions ranges between 25.1 (V1) and 16.8 (V4).

Importantly, this dataset ignores text-level simplification strategies such as reordering or deleting entire sentences containing unimportant de-

[1] https://newsela.com/

[2] a quantitative readability metric based on individual words and sentence lengths (see https://en.wikipedia.org/wiki/Lexile)

aligned	docs	segs	wc V0	wc VN
V0-V1	1,130	15,1K	440 K	382 K
V0-V2	1,130	17,4K	497 K	389 K
V0-V3	1,129	16,6K	466 K	322 K
V0-V4	1,125	13,2K	365 K	221 K

Table 1: Description of the aligned Newsela for English

		docs	segs	src_wc	tgt_wc
DE-EN	sp	165	2,748	56,720	57,880
	wr	170	2,896	68,358	77,721
EN-DE	sp	137	2,965	66,146	57,020
	wr	170	2,930	72,296	70,327

Table 2: Balanced subsets of bidirectional English(EN)-German(DE) corpus representing spoken (sp) and written (wr) mediation modes by translation direction

tails. It only reflects sentence-level simplification transformations and seems to omit sentence pairs where sentences from two simplification versions coincide. Only 37% of the original V0 sentences present in the full-text documents are found in the aligned version of Newsela (20621 out of 55946 V0 segments). The aligned version is thus a focused sentence-level simplification dataset, which is not diluted by sentence pairs without simplification transformations. It is particularly suited for training models that can distinguish complex and simple sentences.

The aligned dataset was used to construct training data in Experiments 1 and 2, as detailed in Section 3.2.

Translation/interpreting data The results from the translation data in all settings are reported for each translation direction in the English-German language pair and for each mode (written and spoken). EPIC-UdS (Przybyl et al., 2022) and Europarl-UdS (Karakanta et al., 2018) were used as the sources of document- and segment-aligned parallel data, representing *spoken* and *written* mode of cross-lingual mediation, respectively. EPIC-UdS was built from transcribed speeches by MEPs and their transcribed simultaneous interpretation, whereas Europarl-UdS includes officially published speeches and their written translations. Throughout this paper, we will refer to interpreted or translated text as *targets* (tgt) or *mediated*, to the source language segments aligned with mediated text as *sources* (src), and to comparable material in the target language as *originals* (org).

3.2 Experimental setup

We are interested in comparing targets to their sources in the other language (cross-lingual comparison) as well as to domain-comparable originals in the same target language (monolingual comparison). To account for the specificity of each task, we designed two experiments. In Experiment 1 *paired* Newsela segments were used to obtain fine-tuned models that could be applied to aligned sources and targets and establish which of the two was estimated as more complex. Experiment 2 had a different type of training data, namely single segments that did not share semantic content. The models obtained in this setup were applied to compare targets to the originals in the target language. The paragraphs below provide more details on how we approached each task.

The models in both experiments were trained in the same neural networks framework, simple transformers library (Rajapakse, 2019) build on top of Hugging Face's Transformers (Wolf et al., 2020). As a starting point in all experiments, we used pre-trained *xlm-roberta-base* model (Conneau et al., 2019) available from the Hugging Face repository. The initial training hyper-parameters were set to the following values: batch 32, epochs 10, learning rate 2e-6, warmup_ratio 0.05. We trained models with an adaptive learning rate, using the AdamW optimizer with the weight_decay 1e-6 to improve regularization and to avoid overfitting. The training process is also equipped with the early_stopping rule (delta: 1e-5, patience: 3). Thirty percent (30%) of the data available for each training process was reserved for validation during training (10%) and for measuring the models' skill on Newsela-based readability tasks (20%).

Experiment 1: Paired segments The comparison of aligned segments was cast as a binary classification task, based on paired segments as input. We trained four models: one for each set of V0 segments aligned with V1, V2, V3, V4 versions. Fifty percent (50%) of paired instances in each set had V0-VN order and were assigned label 0, while the other 50% had the order of segments swapped (VN-V0) and were labelled 1. We expect that the accuracy of these classifiers would increase for subsets using simpler versions. Additionally, we experimented with a model trained on all V0 paired with a simpler version regardless of the level of simplification (see 'V0-any' in Tables 4 and 5). Arguably, it is a more challenging task, with more heterogeneous and noisy instances, where the same V0 can be aligned to several dissimilar versions. These binary classifiers were perfectly balanced across 0 and 1 classes, and we evaluate them on accuracy only, reporting the size of support for each classifier.

These models are applied to predict source-target pairs in a zero-shot manner. Unlike the training data, translations are full-text documents aligned at the segment level. The explored readability relation between sources and targets in the individual segment pairs can vary. To obtain an overall estimate of targets' simplicity in comparison to their sources, we calculate the ratio of 0 returned for source-target pairs in each mode subcorpus and translation direction. Recall that 0 is used to label pairs where the first member is more complex than the second one (e.g. V0-V4). The higher the ratio of 0, the more target sentences in a document were predicted as simpler by our simplification-aware models.

Experiment 2: Content-unique segments This experimental setup aims to facilitate the comparison between targets and similar originals in the target language. Unlike the source-target case, segments do not share semantic content and cannot be reasonably paired. For this experiment, we constructed balanced subsets of content-unique Newsela segments annotated with V0, V1, V2, V3, V4 simplification version labels. To obtain these subsets, each original segment was aligned with all simplification versions available for it. Each set of aligned versions was represented in the new dataset only once: one item from a set of versions for each original segment was selected in accordance with its version. This ensured that there were no segments with very similar content across the simplification levels. Besides, each segment was matched in the alternative Newsela format to access grade and Lexile readability scores, available for it. The segments that did not match were skipped. The number of skipped segments varied from 2% in V3 to 29% in V1. Table 3 presents a quantitative description of the resulting dataset.

As can be seen from Table 3, the five version-based categories in the unique-content segments datasets are reasonably balanced in size. The dataset spans 11 grade values and 125 Lexile level

	docs	segs	wc	grade	lexile
V0	1,066	3,948	121 K	12	1288
V1	1,061	4,182	101 K	8	1112
V2	1,101	4,369	94 K	6	972
V3	1,095	4,462	83 K	5	834
V4	1,025	3,630	60 K	4	710

Table 3: Parameters of the dataset based on unique-content segments annotated for various complexity levels, including mean scores for grade and lexile level

values, with their averages consistent with the expected decrease in text complexity from V0 to V4.

This dataset was used to train five classifiers, similar to Experiment 1, except the input was single segments annotated for complexity level: four classifiers use [V0, V1], [V0, V2] etc. as categories plus a multiclass classifier on the five labels [V0, V1, V2, V3, V4]. Additionally, the entire dataset was used to train two regressors using grade level and Lexile level as training targets.

4 Results and Discussion

The results are reported by experiment, starting with the evaluation study on Newsela and then, focusing on the outcomes of the zero-shot transfer to translated/interpreted data.

4.1 Experiment 1: Are Targets Simpler than their Sources?

In this experiment, we fine-tuned *xlmr-roberta-base* to recognise the order of more complex and less complex versions of the same segment in a pair with a view to apply trained models to predict source-target pairs. Five models were produced: four models based on the alignment of the original V0 segments with each of the four simplified versions plus a model on the entire dataset, where the simplified member of the pair was not differentiated by simplification level. The evaluation results for the five models on Newsela are listed in Table 4.

model	acc	train	test
V0-V1	0.79	12 K	3,040
V0-V2	0.88	14 K	3,479
V0-V3	0.92	13 K	3,325
V0-V4	0.95	11 K	2,633
V0-any	0.91	50 K	12,477

Table 4: Binary classifiers results on aligned Newsela

The results are intuitively expected: the greater the difference in complexity between the aligned segments, the higher the performance of the classifier. The lowest accuracy of 79% was seen for V0-V1 pairs, which was still higher than the random baseline of 50%. The best results of 95% accuracy were seen on V0-V4, where the original was aligned to its simplest version. A generic model, which was supposed to capture the different complexity of the segments regardless the annotated readability level, returned a high score of 91%.

The preliminary fine-tuning experiments with other values for batch and starting learning rate returned some fluctuation but the overall ranking of models' performance on Newsela and the relation between mediation modes and translation directions predicted by the models were the same.

The results of the zero-shot transfer of the English Newsela models to the Europarl spoken and written mediation data for German-English and English-German are displayed in Table 5.

direction	model	spoken	written
DE-EN	V0-V1	0.96	0.93
	V0-V2	0.87	0.78
	V0-V3	0.80	0.71
	V0-V4	0.89	0.86
	V0-any	0.61	0.49
EN-DE	V0-V1	0.81	0.59
	V0-V2	0.64	0.45
	V0-V3	0.56	0.34
	V0-V4	0.65	0.50
	V0-any	0.42	0.28

Table 5: Ratio of segment pairs where the target was estimated as more readable than its source by model, translation direction and mediation mode

Table 5 invites a few observations. First, most models predicted targets as easier to read than their sources. The ratio of source-target segment pairs predicted as 0 was over 50%. This ratio was higher for the V0-V1 model, which was fine-tuned on pairs with small complexity contrast between the aligned segments. Interestingly, the V0-V4 model, which was trained on the segment pairs with the greatest complexity contrast, also had a tendency to predict targets as easier than their sources in both modes and translation directions. This might mean that the nature of transformations performed in translation/interpreting is more similar to simplification transformations typical for V1 and V4. Also, recall that the V0-V1 model had a relatively low accuracy on Newsela (79% vs 95% for the V0-V4 model). Therefore, the predictions by this model might be less reliable.

Second, the ratios of segment pairs where targets were predicted as simpler than their sources were consistently higher for interpreting (spoken) than for translation (written). For spoken production, the ratios of cross-lingual pairs with the simpler target were over 50% for all testing conditions, except the V0-any model. For written production, these ratios were not only consistently lower, but in English-to-German direction some models predicted the prevalence of segment pairs where targets were more complex than their sources.

Finally, as prompted above, the results from this experiment are suggestive of some asymmetry between translation directions. Any mediation into English leads to a greater simplification effect (against the aligned sources) than mediation into German. The asymmetry in translational properties of translation into English and into other languages, including German, attracted some attention from the research community before. In particular, results reported by Kunilovskaya et al. (2023) obtained using other methods, confirm our current observation that written translation into German seems to increase text complexity (unlike all other mediation settings). However, this can also be an effect of a zero-shot setup: the models were fine-tuned on the English data only.

4.2 Experiment 2: Are Targets Simpler than Comparable Originals?

The models trained in this experiment were designed to compare the complexity of mediated text vs. originals in the target language. Table 6 reports the performance of the four binary classifiers and a multiclass classifier, described in Section 3.2, on the Newsela corpus.

As was the case with the classification of the paired segments, the performance of the classifier followed the increase in the contrast between the classes, achieving the best accuracy score of 0.88 for V0-vs-V4 classifier. The confusion matrix for the multiclass indicates that the classifier struggles most with V2 and returns the highest accuracy for the extreme classes: V0 and V4.

A regressor fine-tuned on grade level values re-

model classes	acc	train	test
V0-vs-V1	0.66	6,504	1,626
V0-vs-V2	0.74	6,652	1,665
V0-vs-V3	0.84	6,728	1,682
V0-vs-V4	0.88	6,061	1,517
V0,V1,V2,V3,V4	0.41	16,472	4,119

Table 6: Newsela evaluation results for classifiers on content-unique segments

turned a Pearson correlation of 0.664 and root mean square error (RMSE) of 2.12 (grades spanned 11 values from 2 to 12). The results on 125 types of Lexile scores were very similar: Pearson 0.669 and RMSE 165.59 (Lexile score range from 320 to 1640).

Models' transfer to the translation/interpreting data yielded the following results. In this classification setup, targets and target language originals were predicted independently of each other. Table 7 reports the aggregated predictions on the translational data from the binary classifiers. For considerations of space, it omits the outcomes for the intermediate simplification levels (V0 vs V2 and V0 vs V3).

	type	spoken	written
V0 vs V1			
DE	org	0.27	0.35
	tgt	0.15	0.44
EN	org	0.28	0.39
	tgt	0.17	0.41
V0 vs V4			
DE	org	0.4	0.51
	tgt	0.24	0.62
EN	org	0.46	0.65
	tgt	0.34	0.67

Table 7: Ratios of instances predicted as the more complex class (V0) by the classifiers fine-tuned on the least and most contrasting classes for originals and targets in each language by mode

The results from the omitted models were consistent with the trend established by the reported simplification models: in spoken production, targets had a twice lower ratio of complex sentences than comparable target language originals, while in written mode, targets were a bit more difficult than the originals. Unlike the cross-lingual experiments, this observation holds for both translation directions. For example, in German, the V0-vs-V4 model predicted 40% of spoken originals and 24% of spoken targets as complex, while in written production 51% of originals and 62% of targets were complex. This finding is corroborated by the results from the multiclass model given in Table 8. The ratios of segments predicted as the complex V0 class were twice lower for spoken targets than for spoken originals in both languages and were higher for written targets than for written originals. While in the multiclass model, the V0 option was one of the five categories, the absolute values were lower compared to predictions of binary classifiers, as expected.

	type	spoken	written
DE	org	0.15	0.20
	tgt	0.06	0.30
EN	org	0.19	0.30
	tgt	0.09	0.33

Table 8: Ratios of instances predicted as the more complex class (V0) by the multiclass classifier for originals and targets in each language by mode

The predictions from zero-shot transferred regressors were well-aligned with the observation from classifiers in this experiment. They confirmed that cross-lingual mediation in spoken mode comes with a considerable simplification effect against similar target language originals. Tables 9 and 10 present average predicted grade and Lexile levels, respectively, for originals and targets in each language. For both metrics the lower the score, the lower the text complexity.

	type	spoken	written
DE	org	6.7 (+/-1.7)	7.2 (+/-1.6)
	tgt	6.0 (+/-1.4)	7.5 (+/-1.6)
EN	org	7.0 (+/-1.7)	7.9 (+/-1.6)
	tgt	6.6 (+/-1.5)	7.9 (+/-1.6)

Table 9: Mean predicted *grade levels* for originals and targets in each language by mode

It can be seen that the scores predicted for the targets tend to be lower than for the originals in the spoken mode, but higher in the written mode,

	type	spoken	written
DE	org	914.0 (+/-136)	951.8 (+/-133)
	tgt	844.9 (+/-121)	978.3 (+/-132)
EN	org	972.6 (+/-160)	1047.1 (+/-156)
	tgt	927.6 (+/-138)	1056.4 (+/-156)

Table 10: Mean predicted *Lexile levels* for originals and targets in each language by mode

except for written English where the difference was small and outside of the number of decimal places reported in Table 9.

5 Conclusion

This project adopts a modelling-driven approach to the study of readability/complexity of translated and interpreted texts against their sources and comparable originals in the target language. It is designed to test a theoretical claim, often made in translation studies and supported by some empirical evidence, that professional translation, and especially interpreting, entails a considerable simplification effect. In this study, the properties of translations and interpreting are contrasted with the sources (based on parallel segment-aligned data) and with comparable originals in the target language. Our method consists in fine-tuning a pre-trained multilingual model in a number of settings (required to respect the specificity of the two types of comparisons – targets to sources and targets to originals) and applying the fine-tuned models to texts produced in various cross-lingual mediation conditions in a zero-shot transfer scenario. We use the annotations in the Newsela readability corpus to create computational models of linguistic complexity and then transfer them to the bidirectional English-German translational data from Europarl reporting the results for spoken and written mediation mode in each translation direction separately.

Our findings from several experimental setups reveal a certain pattern of readability/simplification effects in cross-lingual mediation. When compared to their sources, targets tend to be easier to read, especially in interpreting and in German-to-English direction. Written translation into German might be an exception to this trend: German written targets were more often predicted as more complex than their sources. When compared to the originals in the target language, targets are simpler in interpreting, but not in translation. Written translations were found more difficult to read than originally-authored tests in the same language, possibly with some exceptions for English, where the difference between the categories was small.

It is important to bare in mind that the nature and strength of any translationese effects are register- and language-pair-dependent. The claims made in this study are only applicable to the specific register and domain of the underlying translational data. We plan to extend this study to Spanish Newsela data and Spanish segment of Europarl to explore the properties of zero-shot predictions. Also, we leave the qualitative analysis of simplification transformations in the Newsela simplification versions and in translation data as well as the analysis of the models' training process for future work.

Acknowledgments

This research was funded within the CHIST-ERA programme under the following national grant agreement: FWF-I 3441 (FWF Austrian Science Fund, Austria)

Lay Summary

This paper explores the impact of translation and interpreting on the readability of texts comparing the outcomes to originally-authored texts in the source and target languages. Previous studies of translated language demonstrate that translators have a tendency to make texts simpler, more readable and less ambiguous than originals in either source or target language. We expect that this general trend is stronger in simultaneous interpreting. Interpreters experience additional difficulties because they have to deliver their interpretations in the other language as they process the incoming original speech in the source language. This general expected trend towards simpler output in translation/interpreting can be counteracted by the tendency to render the original word-for-word, where possible. This tendency is known as shining-through and leads to a familiar Master Yoda talk in translations. So, we are interested in whether overall translated/interpreted messages are more readable than their sources and comparable texts in the target language. Our translated/interpreted materials come from a collection of speeches delivered in the European Parliament. The written edited versions of the original speeches and their written translations are available on their website, while the spoken versions and their simultaneous interpretations were transcribed from the video recordings. Our approach is based on training computational models that can distinguish between sentences with higher and lower readability scores. The sentences for training were obtained from the Newsela corpus, which contains news articles in English manually simplified by experts in creating reading materials for schoolchildren of various ages. The trained models demonstrated a good ability to tell apart (1) more readable and less readable versions of the same sentence and (2) more readable and less readable sentences of unrelated content. These models were applied to translational data in two conditions corresponding to the two training setups: classification of sentence pairs into those where the source is more complex than the target or where it is not, and classification of sentences into marked as translated/interpreted or originally-authored in the target language. Our experiments yielded evidence that simultaneous interpreting comes with a strong simplification effect for both translation directions and both types of comparison (vs sources in the other language and vs non-translations in the same language). However, in written translation, the results are more varied. The simplification effect was only seen for the comparison against sources in the German-to-English direction.

References

Mikel Artetxe and Holger Schwenk. 2019. Massively Multilingual Sentence Embeddings for Zero-Shot Cross-Lingual Transfer and Beyond. *Transactions of the Association for Computational Linguistics*, 7:597–610.

Mona Baker. 1996. Corpus-based translation studies: the challenges that lie ahead. *Terminology, LSP and translation: Studies in language engineering, in honour of Juan C. Sager.*, pages 175–186.

Andrew Chesterman. 2010. Why study translation universals? *Kiasm. Acta Translatologica Helsingiensia*, 1:38–48.

Koel Dutta Chowdhury, Cristina España i Bonet, and Josef van Genabith. 2021. Tracing source language interference in translation with graph-isomorphism measures. In *Proceedings of the International Conference on Recent Advances in Natural Language Processing (RANLP 2021)*, pages 380–390. INCOMA Ltd.

Alexis Conneau, Kartikay Khandelwal, Naman Goyal, Vishrav Chaudhary, Guillaume Wenzek, Francisco Guzmán, Edouard Grave, Myle Ott, Luke Zettlemoyer, and Veselin Stoyanov. 2019. Unsupervised cross-lingual representation learning at scale. *CoRR*, abs/1911.02116.

Gloria Corpas Pastor, Ruslan Mitkov, Naveed Afzal, and Viktor Pekar. 2008. A corpus-based NLP study of convergence and simplification. In *Proceedings of the 8th Conference of the Association for Machine Translation in the Americas (AMTA'08)*, pages 75–81. Association for Computational Linguistics.

Daria Dayter. 2018. Describing lexical patterns in simultaneously interpreted discourse in a parallel aligned corpus of russian-english interpreting (siren). *FORUM: International Journal of Interpretation and Translation*, 16.

Stefan Evert and Stella Neumann. 2017. The impact of translation direction on characteristics of translated texts: A multivariate analysis for English and German. *Empirical Translation Studies: New Methodological and Theoretical Traditions*, 300:47–80.

Volker Gast and Robert Borges. 2023. Nouns, verbs and other parts of speech in translation and interpreting: Evidence from english speeches made in the european parliament and their german translations and interpretations. *Languages*, 8(1):39.

Hai Hu and Sandra Kübler. 2021. Investigating Translated Chinese and Its Variants Using Machine Learning. *Natural Language Engineering*, 27(3):339–372.

Marta Kajzer-Wietrzny and Lukasz Grabowski. 2021. Formulaicity in constrained communication: An intermodal approach. *MonTi Monografías de Traducción e Interpretación*, 13:148–183.

Alina Karakanta, Mihaela Vela, and Elke Teich. 2018. Europarl-UdS: Preserving metadata from parliamentary debates. In *Proceedings of the 11th International Conference on Language Resources and Evaluation (LREC 2018)*. European Language Resources Association (ELRA).

Maria Kunilovskaya. 2023. *Translationese indicators for human translation quality estimation (based on English-to-Russian translation of mass-media texts)*. Ph.D. thesis, University of Wolverhampton.

Maria Kunilovskaya and Ekaterina Lapshinova-Koltunski. 2020. Lexicogrammatic translationese across two targets and competence levels. In *Proceedings of the 12th Conference on Language Resources and Evaluation (LREC 2020)*, pages 4102–4112. The European Language Resources Association (ELRA).

Maria Kunilovskaya, Heike Przybyl, Elke Teich, and Ekaterina Lapshinova-Koltunski. 2023. Simultaneous Interpreting as a Noisy Channel: How Much Information Gets Through. In *Proceedings of the International Conference on Recent Advances in Natural Language Processing (RANLP 2023)*, page in print. INCOMA Ltd.

Dmitry Nikolaev, Taelin Karidi, Neta Kenneth, Veronika Mitnik, Lilja Saeboe, and Omri Abend. 2020. Morphosyntactic predictability of translationese. *Linguistics Vanguard*, 6(1):1–12.

Maeve Olohan. 2001. Spelling out the optionals in translation: a corpus study. In Paul Rayson, Andrew Wilson, Tony McEnery, Andrew Hardie, and Shereen Khoja, editors, *Proceedings of the Corpus Linguistics*, pages 423–432. Lancaster University.

Heike Przybyl, Ekaterina Lapshinova-Koltunski, Katrin Menzel, Stefan Fischer, and Elke Teich. 2022. Epic uds - creation and applications of a simultaneous interpreting corpus. In *Proceedings of the 13th Conference on Language Resources and Evaluation (LREC 2022)*, pages 1193–1200, Marseille, France. ELDA.

Tiina Puurtinen. 2003. Genre-specific features of translationese? Linguistic differences between translated and non-translated Finnish children's literature. *Literary and Linguistic Computing*, 18(4):389–406.

Thilina Rajapakse. 2019. Simple transformers. `https://www.simpletransformers.ai/`. [Online; accessed Feb. 12, 2021].

Karien Redelinghuys. 2016. Levelling-out and register variation in the translations of experienced and inexperienced translators: A corpus-based study. *Stellenbosch Papers in Linguistics*, 45(1):189–220.

Karien Redelinghuys and Haidee Kruger. 2015. Using the features of translated language to investigate translation expertise: A corpus-based study. *International Journal of Corpus Linguistics*, 20(3):293–325.

Miriam Shlesinger and Noam Ordan. 2012. More spoken or more translated?: Exploring a known unknown of simultaneous interpreting. *Target. International Journal of Translation Studies*, 24(1):43–60.

Elke Teich. 2003. *Cross-Linguistic Variation in System und Text. A Methodology for the Investigation of Translations and Comparable Texts.* Mouton de Gruyter, Berlin.

Antonio Toral. 2019. Post-editese: an Exacerbated Translationese. In *Proceedings of MT Summit XVII*, pages 273–281, Dublin.

Vered Volansky, Noam Ordan, and Shuly Wintner. 2015. On the features of translationese. *Digital Scholarship in the Humanities*, 30(1):98–118.

Donna A Williams. 2005. *Recurrent features of translation in Canada: A corpus-based study.* Ph.D. thesis, University of Ottawa (Canada).

Thomas Wolf, Lysandre Debut, Victor Sanh, Julien Chaumond, Clement Delangue, Anthony Moi, Pierric Cistac, Tim Rault, Rémi Louf, Morgan Funtowicz, et al. 2020. Transformers: State-of-the-art natural language processing. In *Proceedings of the 2020 conference on empirical methods in natural language processing: system demonstrations*, pages 38–45.

Wei Xu, Chris Callison-Burch, and Courtney Napoles. 2015. Problems in Current Text Simplification Research: New Data Can Help. *Transactions of the Association for Computational Linguistics*, 3:283–297.

Simplification by Lexical Deletion

Matthew Shardlow
Manchester Metropolitan University,
Manchester, United Kingdom
m.shardlow@mmu.ac.uk

Piotr Przybyła
Universitat Pompeu Fabra, Barcelona, Spain
and Institute of Computer Science,
Polish Academy of Sciences, Warsaw, Poland
piotr.przybyla@upf.edu

Abstract

Lexical simplification traditionally focuses on the replacement of tokens with simpler alternatives. However, in some cases the goal of this task (simplifying the form while preserving the meaning) may be better served by removing a word rather than replacing it. In fact, we show that existing datasets rely heavily on the deletion operation. We propose supervised and unsupervised solutions for lexical deletion based on classification, end-to-end simplification systems and custom language models. We contribute a new silver-standard corpus of lexical deletions (called SimpleDelete), which we mine from simple English Wikipedia edit histories and use to evaluate approaches to detecting superfluous words. The results show that even unsupervised approaches (TerseBERT) can achieve good performance in this new task. Deletion is one part of the wider lexical simplification puzzle, which we show can be isolated and investigated.

1 Introduction

Lexical simplification aims to identify words that are too difficult for readers and apply an intervention that will enable them to better understand the term. In almost all lexical simplification studies, the primary intervention is the **replacement** operation, in which the target word is substituted for a simpler alternative (Carroll et al., 1998; Shardlow, 2014). Some studies have also considered applying an **addition** operation by adding a definition or explanation of the difficult term (Srikanth and Li, 2020; Kloehn et al., 2018). We propose that a new operation should be considered for lexical simplification, which is that of **deletion**.

Lexical deletion is a vital element in making texts easier to understand. A prior analysis of simple English Wikipedia showed that 47% of sentence simplifications involved deleting words (Coster and Kauchak, 2011b). To better understand the role of deletions in modern TS datasets, we performed an analysis of reference datasets in the EASSE package for text simplification evaluation (Alva-Manchego et al., 2019). The results in Table 1 show that deletions are important, making up 26.82% of the operations for the turkcorpus and 37.42% of operations for PWKP. Whilst other operations are still essential for full sentence simplification, deletion is a vital yet understudied edit operation, on which we choose to focus this study.

Reference	Delete	Add	Keep
Turk Corpus	26.82	20.19	53.00
PWKP	37.42	23.17	39.41

Table 1: The proportion of operation types between two common text simplification evaluation reference sets.

Consider the following sentence, in which the word 'erudite' has been highlighted as a candidate for simplification:

"Aristotle was an ***erudite*** *scholar."*

We could choose to substitute the difficult term by searching for a simpler alternative (learned, knowledgeable, intelligent, etc.). However, we could also simply omit the term, leading to the sentence[1]:

"Aristotle was a scholar."

The new sentence loses some details from the original meaning (was Aristotle a particularly well read scholar or just a mediocre one?), yet is undoubtedly simpler for a reader to understand. The overall meaning of the sentence is preserved and a reader is less likely to stumble over the difficult term. This goes beyond traditional lexical simplification, where only complex words are considered, as it may be beneficial to delete simple words from a sentence without losing any meaning (e.g. dropping 'located' in: 'Times Square is **located** in New York'). We present further examples of deletions taken directly from our corpus in Table 2.

[1]We make the article agree manually, which is not strictly part of the task but can be done with a simple algorithm.

Proceedings of the Second Workshop on Text Simplification, Accessibility and Readability associated with RANLP-2023, pages 44–50,
held in Varna Bulgaria, Sept 7, 2023.
https://doi.org/10.26615/978-954-452-086-1_005

2 Related Work

Simplification by deletion has been studied as an emergent property of systems which perform simplification through sentence to sentence translation (Coster and Kauchak, 2011a; Nisioi et al., 2017; Kumar et al., 2020). These systems are trained on parallel datasets that contain a variety of operations including deletion (Alva-Manchego et al., 2017). It is also possible to force these systems to provide certain types of operations through the use of control tokens (Martin et al., 2020).

Sentence deletion has also been studied as a means of discourse simplification, where the aim is to drop redundant sentences in a passage (Štajner and Glavaš, 2017; Stajner et al., 2013). This is similar to the task of extractive summarisation (Knight and Marcu, 2002; Nenkova and McKeown, 2012) where the task is to only retain the relevant sentences. Conversely, lexical deletion is similar to sentence compression (Filippova and Altun, 2013), where the goal is to remove all redundant information from a sentence.

Typical evaluation of simplification has focussed on either matching n-grams (Štajner et al., 2014; Wubben et al., 2012) (e.g., BLEU-score (Papineni et al., 2002)) or analysing the lexical simplification pipeline (Paetzold and Specia, 2016). SARI score (Xu et al., 2016) has become dominant in the evaluation of text simplification, however it is designed for full sentence simplification, and does not explicitly measure text coherence. Nonetheless, SARI score has been used to measure the ability of a system to perform deletions (Kumar et al., 2020). The recent Shared Task on Multilingual Lexical Simplification at the TSAR workshop (Saggion et al., 2022) popularised several metrics for the evaluation of lexical simplification, including Accuracy@k@top1 and Mean Average Precision (MAP@k). These evaluation methods are appropriate when a ranked list of candidates is produced.

Our work leverages simple English Wikipedia edit histories, drawing on a long line of prior simplification studies to generate corpora using this resource. Simple English Wikipedia has been shown to contain the type of language that is useful for simplification models (Kauchak, 2013). The edit histories have been used previously to mine examples (Yatskar et al., 2010) and corpora (Shardlow, 2013) of complex words. English Wikipedia has also previously been used to generate candidate sentences for the complex word identification task (Yimam et al., 2017). Parallel articles from simple and regular English Wikipedia have also been aligned to generate examples of parallel sentences for training text simplification models (Zhu et al., 2010; Jiang et al., 2020).

3 Corpus Development

We take an approach similar to our prior work (Shardlow, 2013), by mining simple English Wikipedia edit histories. We hypothesise that editors are typically trying to simplify the texts when editing them and so any cases we find of a single word being dropped (with some caveats listed below) are likely to be examples of simplification by deletion.

We download the most recent version of the Simple Wikipedia edit histories as an XML file[2] and compare successive revisions of each page using the following pipeline of operations:

1. Converting the WikiText to plain text using *Sweble* (Dohrn and Riehle, 2011).

2. Parsing the document for sentences and tokens using *Stanford CoreNLP* (Manning et al., 2014).

3. Identifying candidate sentences that contained all but one of the tokens, preserving order, from a sentence in the prior revision.

4. Checking if the deleted word was a dictionary word (defined as any token with frequency above 10,000 in the Google Web1T (Brants and Franz, 2006)).

5. Ignoring sentences longer than 30 tokens, as such lines often tended to be spam or vandalism (unfortunately, Wikipedia edit histories exhibit wilful acts of destruction or overwriting to the contents therein, usually quickly reverted by an editor — yet recorded in the edit history).

6. Removing contexts containing very long tokens (20+ characters), usually resulting from errors in parsing malformed wikitext.

7. Ensuring that each deleted word was a single token in lowercase and contained no punctuation.

[2] `https://dumps.wikimedia.org/simplewiki/latest/`, our version was dated 2021-04-01

ID	Example
1	Naturalization makes them **naturalized** citizens of their new country.
2	Plants include **familiar** types such as tree, herb, bushes, grass, vine, fern, moss, and green algae.
3	There were many brooks providing **fresh** water.
4	Bullock is the **usual** word for beef cattle.
5	He was best known for his **trenchant** secularism.

Table 2: Examples from the SimpleDelete Corpus. The dropped token is in boldface type.

8. Excluding cases where the dropped word was the first token in the sentence, as these were often superfluous headings that were being removed.

9. Removing cases, where the deleted word is included in a list of offensive terms[3], extended with several malicious terms (vandalism, etc.) that occurred frequently in the corpus.

10. Ensuring that all examples were a minimum of 2 characters long.

This procedure yields 18,082 cases of lexical deletions. We split these data into train, validation and test subsets according to the deleted token (to prevent the same token occurring in test and train sets). We select one non-deleted token per context to create a negative class (preserving the original token-based stratification) to give a final corpus size of 36,164 instances (train: 28,836, validation: 3,678, test: 3,650). We release the data, the partitions and the code used to generate the corpus via GitHub[4].

Examples of the types of deletions in our corpus are provided in Table 2. Whereas examples 1 and 5 are potentially difficult words, 2–4 are undoubtedly simple. Yet, removing these makes each sentence more intelligible, whilst preserving the meaning.

To validate our silver standard corpus, the first author examined 600 examples from the validation set (300 from each class), deciding on the correctness of each instance. The result of this showed that 92.33% of the positive class (true deletions) in this sample of our corpus were valid, as were 96.00% of the negative class. Rejected examples in the positive class included cases of vandalism that were not picked up by our token blacklist or simply words that had been removed in error by the editor, whereas cases in the negative class represented cases where the randomly selected word was also a good candidate for removal. We did not perform a full validation of our entire corpus due to the high number of instances contained therein. In total, 94.17% of examples in our silver standard corpus were acceptable based on the entire 600 instance sample.

[3]taken from: `https://www.cs.cmu.edu/~biglou/resources/bad-words.txt`

[4]`https://github.com/MMU-TDMLab/SimpleDelete`

4 Prediction of Lexical Deletions

We test the following four methods for predicting lexical deletion, covering unsupervised and supervised techniques, as well as a sentence simplification system capable of deletions.

4.1 TerseBERT (Unsupervised)

The core question any solution for this problem must address can be stated as: *Is the given word necessary in this context?*. We can easily see how similar this is to the main question of language modelling, namely *What word is likely in this context?*. Therefore, in our first approach, we build on a pretrained language model, namely BERT (Devlin et al., 2018).

As the regular version of BERT can only predict the most probable replacements for a given word in context but not estimate the probability of no word being required, it is not suitable for the purpose of this study. Therefore, we use *TerseBERT* (Przybyła and Shardlow, 2020), which is a custom version of the BERT model, originally developed for multi-word lexical simplification. TerseBERT includes a special token, `[NONE]`, which reflects the probability that the left and right context of the given mask position occur directly after each other, with no words between them. Here we use the model by obtaining its predictions for each token, masked separately, and treating the probability of `[NONE]` as a deletion score.

4.2 SVM with fastText Embeddings (Supervised)

We use the Scikit-Learn (Pedregosa et al., 2011) implementation of the linear kernel SVM (Fan et al., 2008). The features include: *fastText* embeddings (Joulin et al., 2016) for the candidate token, whole context, context preceding the candidate token (left-context) and context following the candidate token (right-context). To calculate the embedding for the multi-word context(s) we collect the embeddings for each token in the fragment and select the maximum value across each dimension to give a single embedding vector. Whilst we did check for the relevance of each feature set using the validation data, we found that the best policy was to use all feature sets during training. The SVM is trained using the training portion of our data which contains true deletions (class label = 1) and randomly selected examples (class label = 0).

4.3 Fine-tuned BERT-large (Supervised)

We use the HuggingFace implementation of the PyTorch BERT-Large-uncased model[5]. We fine-tune for 5 epochs on our data using the given parameters (Adam optimiser, warmup steps = 500, weight decay = 0.01, learning rate = 0.001). All experiments are evaluated using the validation data to check configurations of our task. The final results are given by applying the fine-tuned model to the test data. To encode our problem we provide the following sequence: `Context [SEP] Token`. Where the context and token are provided by our corpus and the class variable is assigned as previously.

4.4 ACCESS (Baseline)

We select a state-of-the-art simplification model, ACCESS (Martin et al., 2020), which is capable of lexical or clausal deletion and ran it over the contexts in our test dataset using the default configuration. We check for each context whether a word was still present or not in the simplified outputs of these models. We did not constrain ACCESS to only perform deletes, however this is to the system's benefit as other operations, such as replacements, will be considered deletes.

5 Results

We evaluate our task and methods in a variety of settings as described below in order to better understand the nature of the lexical deletion problem.

5.1 Candidate Rank According to Deletion Score

We calculate the deletion score using TerseBERT for every word in each context in our validation set and check the rank of the candidate token, normalising by sentence length. Figure 1 shows that

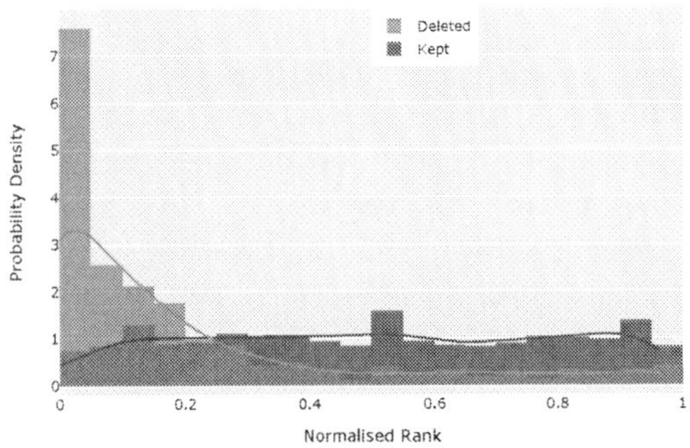

Figure 1: The normalised rank of deleted tokens vs. kept tokens on the validation set.

Type	System	P	R	F1
U	TerseBert$_{0.03}$	0.677	0.942	0.788
U	TerseBert$_{0.27}$	0.746	0.850	0.795
U	ACCESS	0.719	0.472	0.570
S	SVM	0.766	0.666	0.712
S	BERT-large	0.870	0.830	0.850

Table 3: Deletion prediction (as binary classification) performance of different approaches on our dataset. TerseBert$_X$ refers to the deletion score being thresholded at X to give a binary classification. U and S refer to unsupervised and supervised systems with respect to our corpus.

whereas the positive class (truly deleted tokens) follows an exponential decrease, the negative class (tokens not deleted by the editors) follows a flat distribution, which is expected as these were randomly selected.

5.2 Binary Classification

We evaluate in a binary classification setting using the positive and negative classes in our corpus. We find thresholds for converting the deletion score of TerseBERT to a binary decision by selecting the value that gave the highest F1 score (0.02) or the best balance of precision and recall (0.27) on our training and validation data combined. We then perform a further analysis on our test set, which is reported in Table 3. We compare these results on our test set to ACCESS, the SVM and fine-tuned BERT-Large as described previously.

6 Discussion

We introduced the task of lexical deletion in the new context of lexical simplification. This is the first work of which we are aware to explicitly investigate lexical deletion as a simplification operation.

[5]https://huggingface.co/transformers/

We also developed a new silver-standard corpus, SimpleDelete, mined from simple English Wikipedia edit histories and tested our results on it. Future work could move our corpus from silver to gold standard by verifying all 18,082 instances either manually or semi-automatically.

In our binary classification setting, we demonstrated supervised methods trained on our corpus (SVM, BERT-large) and unsupervised methods (TerseBERT, ACCESS) for the task of lexical deletion. ACCESS gives a low recall, but competitive precision, indicating it is capable of the type of deletions we have identified but does not perform these consistently. TerseBERT with a thresholded deletion score of 0.27 gave an F1 score of 0.795, which was higher than the SVM, but lower than BERT-large. As our corpus is silver standard, it is possible that the supervised methods may have also learnt corpus specific factors.

Our simplifications come directly from simple Wikipedia edit histories and we assume that editors remove words to improve the simplicity of the language. The examples in Table 2 and our manual validation indicate that this assumption is correct and that we have collected true examples of simplification by deletion.

In conclusion, we have introduced and evaluated the capacity of lexical deletion for simplification. As a result, we hope that future works in lexical simplification will also take the deletion operation into account as an alternative to lexical replacement.

Acknowledgements

The work of Piotr Przybyła was supported by the *Polish National Agency for Academic Exchange* through a *Polish Returns* grant number PPN/PPO/2018/1/00006.

Lay Summary

Text Simplification is the task of making written language easier to understand. It is a very natural task for a person, such as when explaining an idea or talking to a child. Research has shown that computer algorithms can be used to automatically make language easier to understand. Some simplification algorithms first identify the difficult words or phrases in a sentence and replace these with easier alternatives. This is usually called 'lexical simplification' (lexical here is a term from linguistics that refers to words). A typical lexical simplification system is composed of several operations:

- First, the system identifies any words that might be difficult for the reader.
- Second, the system proposes candidates that may be useful replacements for the difficult word.
- Next, the possible candidates are ranked according to factors such as their simplicity and contextual fit.
- Finally, the highest ranking candidate is inserted into the sentence in place of the original term.

We wanted to know whether difficult words can be deleted, instead of replaced as in previous research. In many sentences, the difficult words are not necessary to the overall meaning. Take the following example:

> He was best known for his **trenchant** secularism.

We could find a simpler word for 'trenchant', but we could also remove it and the sentence would mean the same. In particular we wanted to find out whether an algorithm could be used to predict when to delete words.

Our research looked at articles from Simple Wikipedia. Specifically, we examined how editors had changed these articles over time. We used a set of rules to find examples of words that had been deleted to make a sentence easier to read. We kept a record of the original sentence and the word that had been deleted from it. This allowed us to find over 36,000 examples. We noticed that many examples were 'easy' words that had been deleted. This was surprising as we did not know that you could make a sentence easier to read by removing simple words. Finally, we compared several algorithms for predicting deletions. We showed that it is possible to automatically find words to delete.

Our work could be used to help make language easier to read. One possible area that it could be used in is education. For example, a student could use a simplification tool to make difficult texts on the web easier to read.

References

Fernando Alva-Manchego, Joachim Bingel, Gustavo Paetzold, Carolina Scarton, and Lucia Specia. 2017. Learning how to simplify from explicit labeling of complex-simplified text pairs. In *Proceedings of the Eighth International Joint Conference on Natural Language Processing (Volume 1: Long Papers)*, pages 295–305, Taipei, Taiwan. Asian Federation of Natural Language Processing.

Fernando Alva-Manchego, Louis Martin, Carolina Scarton, and Lucia Specia. 2019. Easse: Easier automatic sentence simplification evaluation. In *Proceedings of the 2019 Conference on Empirical Methods in Natural Language Processing and the 9th International Joint Conference on Natural Language Processing (EMNLP-IJCNLP): System Demonstrations*, pages 49–54.

Thorsten Brants and Alex Franz. 2006. Web 1T 5-gram version 1. LDC2006T13.

John Carroll, Guido Minnen, Yvonne Canning, Siobhan Devlin, and John Tait. 1998. Practical simplification of english newspaper text to assist aphasic readers. In *Proceedings of the AAAI-98 Workshop on Integrating Artificial Intelligence and Assistive Technology*, pages 7–10.

Will Coster and David Kauchak. 2011a. Learning to simplify sentences using Wikipedia. In *Proceedings of the Workshop on Monolingual Text-To-Text Generation*, pages 1–9, Portland, Oregon. Association for Computational Linguistics.

William Coster and David Kauchak. 2011b. Simple English Wikipedia: A new text simplification task. In *Proceedings of the 49th Annual Meeting of the Association for Computational Linguistics: Human Language Technologies*, pages 665–669, Portland, Oregon, USA. Association for Computational Linguistics.

Jacob Devlin, Ming-Wei Chang, Kenton Lee, and Kristina Toutanova. 2018. BERT: Pre-training of Deep Bidirectional Transformers for Language Understanding. In *Proceedings of the 2019 Conference of the North American Chapter of the Association for Computational Linguistics: Human Language Technologies*, pages 4171–4186. Association for Computational Linguistics.

Hannes Dohrn and Dirk Riehle. 2011. Design and implementation of the Sweble wikitext parser: unlocking the structured data of Wikipedia. In *Proceedings of the 7th International Symposium on Wikis and Open Collaboration*, pages 72–81.

Rong-En Fan, Kai-Wei Chang, Cho-Jui Hsieh, Xiang-Rui Wang, and Chih-Jen Lin. 2008. Liblinear: A library for large linear classification. *the Journal of machine Learning research*, 9:1871–1874.

Katja Filippova and Yasemin Altun. 2013. Overcoming the lack of parallel data in sentence compression. In *Proceedings of the 2013 Conference on Empirical Methods in Natural Language Processing*, pages 1481–1491, Seattle, Washington, USA. Association for Computational Linguistics.

Chao Jiang, Mounica Maddela, Wuwei Lan, Yang Zhong, and Wei Xu. 2020. Neural CRF model for sentence alignment in text simplification. In *Proceedings of the 58th Annual Meeting of the Association for Computational Linguistics*, pages 7943–7960, Online. Association for Computational Linguistics.

Armand Joulin, Edouard Grave, Piotr Bojanowski, Matthijs Douze, Hérve Jégou, and Tomas Mikolov. 2016. Fasttext.zip: Compressing text classification models. *arXiv preprint arXiv:1612.03651*.

David Kauchak. 2013. Improving text simplification language modeling using unsimplified text data. In *Proceedings of the 51st Annual Meeting of the Association for Computational Linguistics (Volume 1: Long Papers)*, pages 1537–1546, Sofia, Bulgaria. Association for Computational Linguistics.

Nicholas Kloehn, Gondy Leroy, David Kauchak, Yang Gu, Sonia Colina, Nicole P Yuan, and Debra Revere. 2018. Improving consumer understanding of medical text: Development and validation of a new subsimplify algorithm to automatically generate term explanations in english and spanish. *Journal of medical Internet research*, 20(8):e10779.

Kevin Knight and Daniel Marcu. 2002. Summarization beyond sentence extraction: A probabilistic approach to sentence compression. *Artificial Intelligence*, 139(1):91–107.

Dhruv Kumar, Lili Mou, Lukasz Golab, and Olga Vechtomova. 2020. Iterative edit-based unsupervised sentence simplification. In *Proceedings of the 58th Annual Meeting of the Association for Computational Linguistics*, pages 7918–7928, Online. Association for Computational Linguistics.

Christopher D. Manning, Mihai Surdeanu, John Bauer, Jenny Finkel, Steven J. Bethard, and David McClosky. 2014. The Stanford CoreNLP natural language processing toolkit. In *Association for Computational Linguistics (ACL) System Demonstrations*, pages 55–60.

Louis Martin, Éric de la Clergerie, Benoît Sagot, and Antoine Bordes. 2020. Controllable sentence simplification. In *Proceedings of the 12th Language Resources and Evaluation Conference*, pages 4689–4698, Marseille, France. European Language Resources Association.

Ani Nenkova and Kathleen McKeown. 2012. A survey of text summarization techniques. In *Mining text data*, pages 43–76. Springer.

Sergiu Nisioi, Sanja Štajner, Simone Paolo Ponzetto, and Liviu P. Dinu. 2017. Exploring neural text simplification models. In *Proceedings of the 55th Annual Meeting of the Association for Computational*

Linguistics (Volume 2: Short Papers), pages 85–91, Vancouver, Canada. Association for Computational Linguistics.

Gustavo Paetzold and Lucia Specia. 2016. Benchmarking lexical simplification systems. In *Proceedings of the Tenth International Conference on Language Resources and Evaluation (LREC'16)*, pages 3074–3080, Portorož, Slovenia. European Language Resources Association (ELRA).

Kishore Papineni, Salim Roukos, Todd Ward, and Wei-Jing Zhu. 2002. Bleu: a method for automatic evaluation of machine translation. In *Proceedings of the 40th Annual Meeting of the Association for Computational Linguistics*, pages 311–318, Philadelphia, Pennsylvania, USA. Association for Computational Linguistics.

F. Pedregosa, G. Varoquaux, A. Gramfort, V. Michel, B. Thirion, O. Grisel, M. Blondel, P. Prettenhofer, R. Weiss, V. Dubourg, J. Vanderplas, A. Passos, D. Cournapeau, M. Brucher, M. Perrot, and E. Duchesnay. 2011. Scikit-learn: Machine learning in Python. *Journal of Machine Learning Research*, 12:2825–2830.

Piotr Przybyła and Matthew Shardlow. 2020. Multi-Word Lexical Simplification. In *Proceedings of the 28th International Conference on Computational Linguistics (COLING 2020)*, pages 1435–1446, Barcelona, Spain. International Committee on Computational Linguistics.

Horacio Saggion, Sanja Štajner, Daniel Ferrés, Kim Cheng Sheang, Matthew Shardlow, Kai North, and Marcos Zampieri. 2022. Findings of the TSAR-2022 shared task on multilingual lexical simplification. In *Proceedings of the Workshop on Text Simplification, Accessibility, and Readability (TSAR-2022)*, pages 271–283, Abu Dhabi, United Arab Emirates (Virtual). Association for Computational Linguistics.

Matthew Shardlow. 2013. The CW corpus: A new resource for evaluating the identification of complex words. In *Proceedings of the Second Workshop on Predicting and Improving Text Readability for Target Reader Populations*, pages 69–77, Sofia, Bulgaria. Association for Computational Linguistics.

Matthew Shardlow. 2014. Out in the open: Finding and categorising errors in the lexical simplification pipeline. In *Proceedings of the Ninth International Conference on Language Resources and Evaluation (LREC'14)*, pages 1583–1590.

Neha Srikanth and Junyi Jessy Li. 2020. Elaborative simplification: Content addition and explanation generation in text simplification.

Sanja Stajner, Biljana Drndarevic, and Horacio Saggion. 2013. Corpus-based sentence deletion and split decisions for spanish text simplification. *Computacion y Sistemas. 2013; 17 (2): 251-62.*

Sanja Štajner, Ruslan Mitkov, and Horacio Saggion. 2014. One step closer to automatic evaluation of text simplification systems. In *Proceedings of the 3rd Workshop on Predicting and Improving Text Readability for Target Reader Populations (PITR)*, pages 1–10, Gothenburg, Sweden. Association for Computational Linguistics.

Sander Wubben, Antal van den Bosch, and Emiel Krahmer. 2012. Sentence simplification by monolingual machine translation. In *Proceedings of the 50th Annual Meeting of the Association for Computational Linguistics (Volume 1: Long Papers)*, pages 1015–1024, Jeju Island, Korea. Association for Computational Linguistics.

Wei Xu, Courtney Napoles, Ellie Pavlick, Quanze Chen, and Chris Callison-Burch. 2016. Optimizing statistical machine translation for text simplification. *Transactions of the Association for Computational Linguistics*, 4:401–415.

Mark Yatskar, Bo Pang, Cristian Danescu-Niculescu-Mizil, and Lillian Lee. 2010. For the sake of simplicity: Unsupervised extraction of lexical simplifications from Wikipedia. In *Human Language Technologies: The 2010 Annual Conference of the North American Chapter of the Association for Computational Linguistics*, pages 365–368, Los Angeles, California. Association for Computational Linguistics.

Seid Muhie Yimam, Sanja Štajner, Martin Riedl, and Chris Biemann. 2017. CWIG3G2 - complex word identification task across three text genres and two user groups. In *Proceedings of the Eighth International Joint Conference on Natural Language Processing (Volume 2: Short Papers)*, pages 401–407, Taipei, Taiwan. Asian Federation of Natural Language Processing.

Zhemin Zhu, Delphine Bernhard, and Iryna Gurevych. 2010. A monolingual tree-based translation model for sentence simplification. In *Proceedings of the 23rd International Conference on Computational Linguistics (Coling 2010)*, pages 1353–1361, Beijing, China. Coling 2010 Organizing Committee.

Sanja Štajner and Goran Glavaš. 2017. Leveraging event-based semantics for automated text simplification. *Expert Systems with Applications*, 82:383–395.

Comparing Generic and Expert Models for Genre-Specific Text Simplification

Zihao LI[1] and **Matthew Shardlow**[1] and **Fernando Alva-Manchego**[2]
[1] Manchester Metropolitan University
[2] School of Computer Science and Informatics, Cardiff University, UK
21443696@stu.mmu.ac.uk, m.shardlow@mmu.ac.uk,
alvamanchegof@cardiff.ac.uk

Abstract

We investigate how text genre influences the performance of models for controlled text simplification. Regarding datasets from Wikipedia and PubMed as two different genres, we compare the performance of genre-specific models trained by transfer learning and prompt-only GPT-like large language models. Our experiments showed that: (1) the performance loss of genre-specific models on general tasks can be limited to 2%, (2) transfer learning can improve performance on genre-specific datasets up to 10% in SARI score from the base model without transfer learning, (3) simplifications generated by the smaller but more customized models show similar performance in simplicity and a better meaning preservation capability to the larger generic models in both automatic and human evaluations.

1 Introduction

Controllable text simplification is a technique whereby the features of a generated simplification (e.g. its length) can be determined at inference time. Control tokens prepended to the input with specific features' values can be regarded as a way of prompting text simplification systems to generate outputs with certain desired characteristics. This gives rise to flexible and controllable simplification systems that satisfy various demands from different user groups or scenarios with regulated output (Kikuchi et al., 2016; Scarton and Specia, 2018; Nishihara et al., 2019; Martin et al., 2019; Maddela et al., 2021). A use case for such types of models is making specialised information (e.g. related to medicine) more accessible to lay users.

We present genre-specific text simplification research alongside a study on the effects of different genres. We followed the idea of Multilingual Unsupervised Sentence Simplification (MUSS) (Martin et al., 2020), which is the State-of-the-art (SOTA) of controlled text simplification, to build the base model and expert models. Different from MUSS, in which the authors combined the explicit control tokens with the mined paraphrase corpus, we combined the control tokens with two small expert-level genre-specific training subsets derived from Simple TICO-19 corpus (Shardlow and Alva-Manchego, 2022). The base model reimplements the MUSS without the fine-tuning on the paraphrase corpus, while the expert models are further fined-tuned on the genre-specific training subsets.

We choose the newly published Simple TICO-19 dataset (Shardlow and Alva-Manchego, 2022) as our training and test bench of genre-specific tasks for the expert models, because of the manual simplification from experienced annotators and expert-level information in COVID-19. Based on Simple TICO-19, we created the two subsets with unified data source labels as two different genre-specific corpora and designed the genre-specific tasks with different permutations of each kind of subset.

To verify the improvement before and after transfer learning, we tested the performance of the expert models over the base model in the above-mentioned genre-specific scenarios. In addition, considering the strong competitiveness of more updated and larger language models than the base model (Radford et al., 2018; Devlin et al., 2019; Liu et al., 2019; Raffel et al., 2019; Brown et al., 2020), it is worth finding whether the large language models targeting generic content can outperform lightweight custom models that have been specialized for specific tasks. Thus, we also compared the expert models with the leading generic models for generative NLP, covering GPT-3 (Brown et al., 2020) and ChatGPT.

In this paper, we leveraged a newly published text simplification dataset, designed a test scenario for controlled text simplification with different genres, proved the effects of transfer learning on the genre-specific datasets, compared the performance of generic and expert models in SARI score and

Proceedings of the Second Workshop on Text Simplification, Accessibility and Readability associated with RANLP-2023, pages 51–67,
held in Varna Bulgaria, Sept 7, 2023.
https://doi.org/10.26615/978-954-452-086-1_006

BERTScore, and discussed the cost-effectiveness between expert models and generic models.

2 Related Work

Text simplification consists of reducing linguistic complexity at both syntactic and lexical levels without significant loss in the main content (Alva-Manchego et al., 2020b). In practice, this task can be treated as monolingual machine translation (Zhu et al., 2010; Wubben et al., 2012). Research in English highly relies on Wikipedia and Simple Wikipedia (Zhu et al., 2010; Coster and Kauchak, 2011; Woodsend and Lapata, 2011; Kauchak, 2013; Zhang and Lapata, 2017). High-quality manually-made corpora are rare and some may come with restrictions (Xu et al., 2015; Alva-Manchego et al., 2020a; Shardlow and Alva-Manchego, 2022). To alleviate this problem, we combined the large automated corpus with the small manual-made corpus.

Text simplification researchers have recently turned to larger pre-trained language models (Peters et al., 2018; Martin et al., 2020; Omelianchuk et al., 2021; Lu et al., 2021; Sheang and Saggion, 2021; Štajner et al., 2022). From Long-short term memory (LSTM) to transformer-based pre-trained models (Hochreiter and Schmidhuber, 1997; Raffel et al., 2019; Lewis et al., 2020), the order of magnitude of parameters used in models for text simplification has increased dramatically, The parameter count in Bidirectional Auto-Regressive Transformers (BART) is 140 million (Lewis et al., 2020), the value in Text-to-Text Transfer Transformer (T5) reaches 220 million (Raffel et al., 2019), the value in GPT-3 increases to 170 billion (Brown et al., 2020), and the value in Switch Transformer even reaches an astonishing 1.6 trillion (Fedus et al., 2021). With the advent of pre-trained language models in NLP, the SOTA of many common tasks and leaderboard is refreshed (Schwartz et al., 2014; Rajpurkar et al., 2016; Wang et al., 2018). Models with more parameters tend to perform better on downstream tasks (Kaplan et al., 2020). However, larger models require more energy to run (Puvis de Chavannes et al., 2021) and are inaccessible to a typical researcher, hampering reproducibility. Besides, the correlation between large models and high performance is still worth exploring and the necessity of extremely huge models is questionable. To find out the exact situation in text simplification, we leveraged the latest pre-trained large language model ChatGPT.

In addition to the general models, there are also researches focusing on controlled text simplification (Martin et al., 2019, 2020; Sheang and Saggion, 2021). Due to the various demands of lay users in text simplification, the generic output can hardly satisfy the main user group (Xu et al., 2015). Controlled text simplification is introduced to satisfy the various demands of different user groups or in different scenarios with explicit or implicit restraints on the output. In AudienCe-CEntric Sentence Simplification (ACCESS), Martin et al. (Martin et al. (2019)) present the 4 control tokens used in this paper, Sheang and Saggion (Sheang and Saggion (2021) replace the BART model (Lewis et al., 2020) with T5 model(Raffel et al., 2019), further extend the control tokens to 5 and refresh the SOTA. The performance and flexibility of controlled text simplification make it possible to compete with the large pre-trained language models, and they will be tested in this paper.

3 Methodology

In this section we describe the experiments that were undertaken. A visual representation of our methodology is provided in Figure 1, which is explained in further detail throughout the following subsections.

3.1 Datasets

Wikilarge. The Wikilarge dataset (Zhang and Lapata, 2017) is one of the biggest parallel complex-simple sentence datasets based on various existing corpora and contains 296,402 sentence pairs in the training set. We use this training set to fine-tune the base models in this paper.

Simple TICO-19. We leveraged a newly published dataset, simple TICO-19 (Shardlow and Alva-Manchego, 2022) as the test bench for genre-specific simplification, which is based on the dataset: Translation Initiative for COVID-19 (TICO-19) (Anastasopoulos et al., 2020). This dataset contains translations and simplifications related to COVID-19 from multiple resources. Simple TICO-19 contains 3,173 parallel sentences in both English and Spanish. Only the English section is applied in this paper. We split this dataset based on the data source and regard the subsets from different sources as different genres. The subsets are further divided into training, validation and test sets for the expert models.

ASSET. The Abstractive Sentence Simplification Evaluation and Tuning dataset (ASSET) (Alva-Manchego et al., 2020a) is widely used to evaluate the performance of text simplification models. The dataset contains validation and test sets, both are equipped with 10 reference sets. Only the test sets are used as a general test benchmark for both generic and expert models.

3.2 Metrics and Evaluation

We use **SARI score** (Xu et al., 2016) as the main metric for evaluating the simplicity of our systems outputs. It compares the output with reference sentences and calculates the F1-score of *add*, *keep* and *delete* operations from system output compared to the reference sentences. Although there have been criticisms of the metric (Alva-Manchego et al., 2021) recently, it is still the most widely used automatic metric in the evaluation of text simplification (Alva-Manchego et al., 2020b). To increase the reliability of our results, we also include other automatic metrics and human evaluation.

It is worth noting that there is only one reference sentence per instance in Simple TICO-19 and its subsets for genre-specific tasks. This differs from other datasets with multiple references such as ASSET. Thus, the SARI score of uncomparable among different test sets, and the reliability of SARI for Simple TICO-19 may be lower compared with ASSET.

BERTScore (Zhang et al., 2019) is a metric that measures the likelihood between the output and reference sentences. It is calculated by maximizing the cosine distance in vector spaces in the most possible likelihood matrix. According to Scialom et al. (2021), BERTScore has a higher correlation to human evaluation than SARI and shows how similar the output and references are in the aspect of meaning instead of words. We apply BERTScore as a co-reference in both general and genre-specific tasks.

Human evaluation. We also conduct a human evaluation for the results of the genre-specific experiments as the gold reference, compared to the automatic evaluation metrics. We recruited 17 human annotators via Amazon Mechanical Turk. The annotators were selected to have the 'Masters' qualification, indicating that they are trusted workers on the platform. All annotators reported an educational level of undergraduate or above. Twelve annotators are non-native English speakers, whereas five are native speakers of English. Each annotator was presented with 20 instances. Each instance contained an original sentence and a pair of corresponding simplifications from either the generic or expert models, whose order is random to avoid bias. Annotators were asked to evaluate the following two questions on a 5-point Likert scale:

> 1) *Simplicity*: To what extent do you agree the simplified sentence is easy to understand?
>
> 2) *Meaning preservation*: To what extent do you agree the simplified sentence keeps the important information?

There is a total of 340 instances with 50% overlap in the adjacent forms to ensure a more comprehensive score from two annotators. For disagreement, we use the average value as the final score. The results are shown in Table 6 and the sample form is shown in Appendix A.

3.3 Preprocessing

Following the MUSS implementation (Martin et al., 2020), the four control tokens are introduced as follow:

- ⟨DEPENDENCYTREEDEPTH_x⟩ **(DTD)** representing syntactic complexity
- ⟨WORDRANK_x⟩ **(WR)** representing lexical complexity
- ⟨REPLACEONLYLEVENSHTEIN_x⟩ **(LV)** representing the token difference ratio
- ⟨LENGTHRATIO_x⟩ **(LR)** representing the difference in length

Each control token is calculated by comparing the above ratios in complex-simple sentence pairs. After the calculation of the control tokens for the training set, the calculated value of complex sentences is added as a prompt to the beginning of the corresponding complex sentences. The value of these control tokens is rounded to 0.05 and limited in the range of 0.2 to 1.5, except for the LV, which is limited from 0.2 to 1.

In Simple Tico-19 (Shardlow and Alva-Manchego, 2022), due to the manual translation, there are some sentences marked as sentences that require no more simplification. These were removed in the following experiments. The number

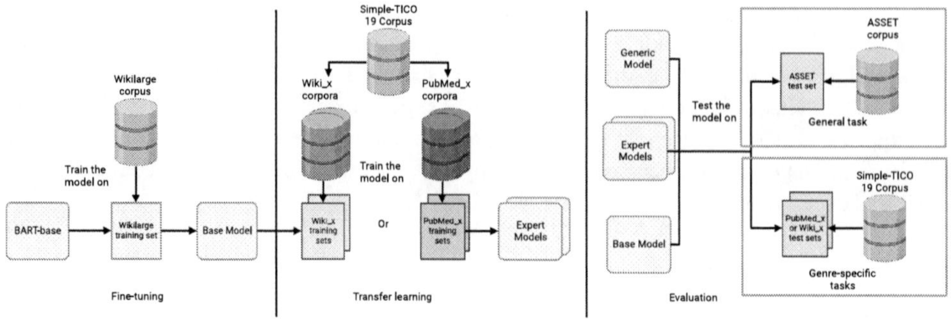

Figure 1: The methodology is represented in three sections. In the left section, we fine-tune BART-base on the WikiLarge training set to give the **base model**. In the middle section, we regard the task as transfer learning and further fine-tune the base model on our Wikipedia_x and PubMed_x training sets to generate the **expert model(s)**. In the right section, we add 2 zero-shot **generic models** through publicly available APIs. We then evaluate our base model, expert models and generic models in the generic simplification task (The Asset test set) and the genre-specific tasks (the Wikipedia_x and Pubmed_x test sets) and compare the results for the models.

Data source	Number of instances
CMU	122
PubMed	809
Wikinews	76
Wikivoyage	206
Wikipedia	1224
Wikisource	101

Table 1: Number of instances in each data source

of instances after the filtering of each data source is shown in Table 1.

Considering the target audience and sentence count, we choose the **PubMed** and **Wikipedia** subsets as representative of two different genres, namely public literature and academic literature, to be applied in the genre-specific tasks. To create training, validation and test sets, we further randomly split the **PubMed** and **Wikipedia** subsets into 3 sections in a ratio of 8:1:1 with a random seed. The generated permutations of the two subsets with a certain random seed $\boldsymbol{x}$ is then marked as **PubMed$\boldsymbol{x}$** and **Wikipedia$\boldsymbol{x}$**, such as **PubMed0** and **Wikipedia0**. As a result, there are 978, 122 and 124 sentence pairs in each **Wikipedia$\boldsymbol{x}$** permutation and 647, 81 and 81 sentence pairs in each **PubMed$\boldsymbol{x}$** permutation as train, validation and test set respectively.

3.4 Models for Text Simplification

In this paper, we propose to compare the performance among three versions of a text simplification model: the base model, the generic model and the expert model.

The **base model** is based on BART-base (Lewis et al., 2020) with 6 layers in both encoder and decoder and 140 million parameters. The base model is fine-tuned on the training set of Wikilarge (Zhang and Lapata, 2017) only with the above-mentioned 4 control tokens. The following hyper-parameters were applied: Learning rate: 2e-5, Weight Decay: 0.01, Training epochs: 10. After fine-tuning, the training loss reaches 0.85 without overfitting. By comparing the SARI score of our model on the ASSET test set (Alva-Manchego et al., 2020a) with the original results in MUSS (Martin et al., 2020), it is reasonable to claim that it has reached to the designed performance level.

For **generic models**, we apply the GPT-3 (Brown et al., 2020) and ChatGPT via the API and online platform by OpenAI. Instead of training or fine-tuning, we leverage the 2 models as zero-shot models by promoting. The prompt is set to "Please simplify this sentence for me: " and will be added to the beginning of each complex sentence, then the model will try to generate a simplified version of the input text after the colon. The exact model prompted in the GPT-3 is called "text-davinci-003", which is the latest version, the parameters are set as follows: temperature: 1, frequency_penalty: 0, presence_penalty: 0.

As for ChatGPT, due to the fast iteration speed, the only information available is "ChatGPT Jan 9

Version". During our experiment, since there is no official API released, we accessed the ChatGPT via a fake web browser with session IDs to request responses in batches. The ChatGPT is then accessed on the online platform in the conversations automatically. There is no guarantee of performance compared to the results of API access and different versions of ChatGPT.

The **expert model(s)** are composed of base models after transfer learning on corresponding permutations of subsets. By fine-tuning the pre-trained model on the preprocessed Wikilarge training set (Zhang and Lapata, 2017), the base model learns how to generate simplifications based on the value of control tokens. To leverage the base model as an expert text simplification model, we further fine-tune the model on the preprocessed training set of **Wikipedia$x$** and **PubMed$x$** and then have the corresponding expert models for each permutation of **Wikipedia$x$** and **PubMed$x$**. The setting of fine-tuning hyper-parameters is the same as fine-tuning the base model. In the experiment, we build 30 expert models from different permutations of **Wikipedia$x$** and 30 from **PubMed$x$**. Due to time constraints, we only evaluate the performance of expert models over 20 permutations of subsets for each genre. In total, we have 40 permutations of subsets with 31 expert models evaluated on each dataset permutation.

3.5 Optimization

Since the values of control tokens influence the quality of the generated output and overall model performance, it is necessary to find an optimal value of the control tokens for the model on the test sets. This is in line with the previous state of the art, but does mean that the results reported are specific to the given test set and alternative parameters may be optimal for another dataset. The value options of most control tokens fall between 0.2 to 1.5 (or 0 to 1 for Levenshtein), so there is only finite options are provided during optimization, and the optimization problem is reduced to finding the best value combination of control tokens within the optimization budget. The optimization budget limits the total number of attempts to find the set of values of control tokens to maximize the metric, which is set to the SARI score. The optimization budget for the general tasks on the ASSET valid set (Alva-Manchego et al., 2020a) is 128, while the value for genre-specific tasks on the valid sets of permutations of **Wikipedia$x$** and **PubMed$x$** is reduced to 64 for time-saving. We used Nevergrad (Rapin and Teytaud, 2018) to find out the local optimal value within the budgets.

3.6 Genre-specific Experiments

To verify the effect of transfer learning, we computed the SARI score on the test set of **PubMed$x$**s and **Wikipedia$x$**s. Since there is only one reference sentence in the Simple TICO-19, the SARI score on these test sets is only applicable and comparable within the experiment. We tested the base model, generic model and expert models on the test sets from 20 permutations of **PubMed$x$**s and **Wikipedia$x$**s. For expert models from the same genre of the test set, we only evaluate the expert model trained on the corresponding training set of the test set to avoid data leakage. The average of these models is reported as 'Average corresponding ⟨genre⟩ models' in Tables 3 and 4. As for the expert models from the other genre, we tested 30 expert models from different permutations. The overall results are shown in Table 3 and 4, and the details are shown in Figures 2 and 3. The full results are available in Appendix B.

4 Results

4.1 General task

	Model	SARI	BERTScore
Base	BART-base	44.05	0.777
Generic	GPT-3	41.73	0.703
	ChatGPT	**46.42**	0.731
Expert	**Wikipedia0**	43.24	**0.835**
	PubMed0	43.67	0.812

Table 2: SARI and BERTScore on ASSET test

Table 2 shows the SARI scores and BERTScores on the ASSET test set. ChatGPT reaches the highest SARI score known so far on the ASSET test set, while the expert model **Wikipedia0** obtains the highest BERTScore. Compared to the base model, GPT-3 attains a lower SARI score, whereas ChatGPT attains an improved SARI score. However, the BERTScore is lower for both generic models compared to the base model. Within the 2 general models, the ChatGPT outperforms the GPT-3 in both metrics, which aligns with the model structure and scale. As for the expert models, we find that the SARI scores on the general task drop marginally,

	Model	SARI	BERTScore
Base	BART-base	40.78	0.741
Generic	GPT-3	29.03	0.530
	ChatGPT	31.12	0.542
Expert	Average corresponding expert **Wikipedia** models	**44.30**	**0.756**
	Average **PubMed** models	42.75	0.741

Table 3: Average SARI and BERTScore on all **Wikipedia*x***

	Model	SARI	BERTScore
Base	BART-base	40.56	0.723
Generic	GPT-3	30.72	0.547
	ChatGPT	31.55	0.515
Expert	Average Corresponding expert **PubMed** models	**45.05**	**0.741**
	Average **Wikipedia** models	43.38	0.726

Table 4: Average SARI and BERTScore on all **PubMed*x***

while **Wikipedia0** shows the highest BERTScore among all models.

4.2 Genre-specific task

Table 3 shows the average SARI and BERTScores over all 20 test sets of different permutations from different models. The first row shows the average SARI and BERTScore of the base model, which is only fine-tuned on the WikiLarge training set. The following two rows show the SARI and BERTScore of two generic models on the test sets. The last two rows show the SARI and BERTScore of all expert models. The corresponding **Wikipedia** or **Pubmed** models refer to the corresponding expert models after transfer learning on the training sets (e.g., model **Wikipedia0** to test set **Wikipedia0** and model **Pubmed19** to test set **Pubmed19**). The last row shows a combined average SARI and BERTScore of expert models trained in the other genre. The detailed SARI and BERTScore can be found in Appendix B. The same rules also apply to Table 4.

In both Table 3 and 4, the corresponding expert models, which is the expert model transfer learned on the corresponding training set, have the highest SARI and BERTScore. Although the generic models show very competitive performance in the general task, the lack of fine-tuning led to lower performance in terms of SARI score in the genre-specific scenarios. The fine-tuned models also take advantage of learning the text style in the training set. The overall performance gap between the two generic models is aligned to the gap in Table 2. As for the expert models, they have a much higher SARI score and appear to have a much higher performance, but the actual performance gap between the generic models and expert models needs further exploration. What the SARI score can tell is how they benefit from the transfer learning compared to the base model. It is surprising to see the improvement for both kinds of expert models, which is presumably caused by the sharing characteristics in the two subsets (both are related to Covid-19 information). As a result, the improvement of the overall SARI score for expert models shows the effectiveness of transfer learning for genre-adaptive text simplification.

We also evaluated BERT-score for our generic and expert models on the expert datasets. The BERTScore similarly shows that the simplifications produced by generic models in the expert setting are of worse quality than those produced by the expert models. In Table 3, we notice that there is an improvement in BERTScore on the corresponding expert models over the base model, while no improvement on the average **PubMedx** models in the other genre. The base model was also fine-tuned on the Wikilarge, which belongs to the same genre of the **Wikipediax** models. This may explain why there was no performance gain for the **PubMedx** models. In Table 4, both kinds of expert models gain improvement when measured against the Base model. The genre-specific PubMed expert models attain a higher BERTScore than those fine-tuned on the Wikipedia subsets.

4.3 Detailed SARI score in genre-specific task

Generally, the detailed SARI score is aligned with the overall performance. The corresponding expert model outperforms the other four models in the SARI score across all permutations and the generic models have a much lower SARI score than the base model. The SARI score also shows some similarities among models. We listed the detailed SARI score in Figures 2 and 3 and the remaining tables.

Figure 2 shows the SARI score of 20 **Wikipediax** test sets. Most models follow the order of average score, except for text sets **Wikipedia0**,

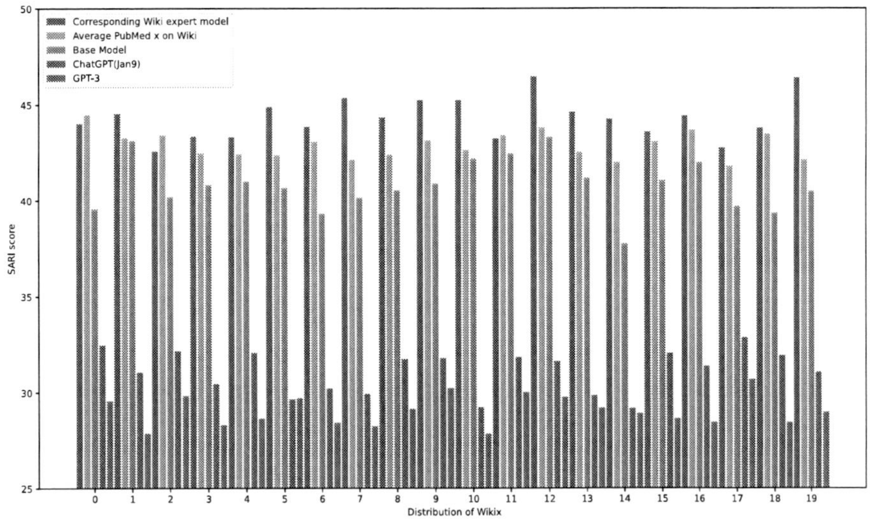

Figure 2: SARI score on **Wikipedia$x$** for expert models

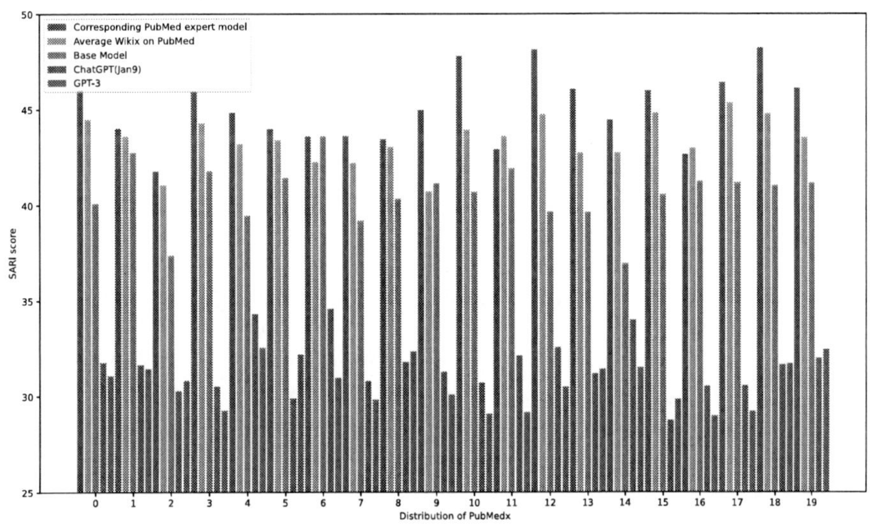

Figure 3: The SARI score on **PubMed$x$** for expert models

Wikipedia2 and **Wikipedia11**. In the above-mentioned test sets, the average SARI score of the other genre outperforms the corresponding expert model. This may be caused by the similarity between the training sets in the other genre and test sets. The fluctuation of the SARI score demonstrates the effect of permutation in the genre-specific experiments and also shows that some of the permutations are not ideal distribution of training and test sets.

In Figure 3, similar to the detailed SARI score for **Wikipediax**, there are several divergences on certain permutations of **PubMedx**. In **PubMed11** and **PubMed16**, the average performance of expert models from **Wikipedia** outperforms the corresponding expert model. While in **PubMed6** and **PubMed9**, the average **Wikipedia** expert models show worse SARI scores than the base model. A similar inconsistency of the SARI score with the expected performance happens between the two generic models too. Considering the big performance gap between the GPT-3 and ChatGPT, the lack of more reference sentences may be one reason. The inconsistency of the detailed SARI score also shows the necessity of repeated experiments.

Comparing the base models with the generic

models, it is unclear why the generic models perform so poorly on the test sets in terms of the SARI score. One possible reason is that both base models and expert models are fitted with the optimal value of control tokens to maximize the SARI score while the prompted generic models are not. The calculation method of the SARI score prefers the sentence that keeps the most of original content under the condition of lack of reference sentences.

4.4 Case study

Table 5 shows the picked examples from the system. In the first example, ChatGPT demonstrates the ability of abbreviation explanation for the PoCT, while the other only follows the original text. In the second example, ChatGPT generates an inaccurate text that simplify the domestic animals as pets, which raises some concerns about the factuality of the simplification. In the third example, the generic models even removed the explanation of the abbreviation, which potentially decreased the readability of the sentence. The inconsistency of the performance of generic models can be an obstacle to applying such models to downstream tasks. In addition to that, the definition of simplicity for the generic models is also vague. We found that some of the outputs of ChatGPT are much shorter than the outputs of expert models. However, the short sentences don't always align with the simplicity and better readability.

4.5 Human evaluation

Table 6 shows the results of human evaluation. The scores range from 1 to 5, from strongly disagree to strongly agree. For the simplicity question, the generic model (ChatGPT) obtains a similar, but marginally higher score than the expert models under evaluation (**Wiki0** and **PubMed0**). However, for the meaning preservation question, ChatGPT was evaluated to have worse performance than the expert model. This implies that ChatGPT may have omitted some important details that the expert models were able to retain correctly. It also implies that the expert models retained much of the original text, making more conservative edits than the paraphrasing that was performed by GPT-3 and ChatGPT. Similar situations can also be found in Table 5 that the expert models tend to maintain the source content. Unlike the SARI score shown in Table 3 and 4, the performance gap between generic models and expert models is not as high as expected.

5 Discussion and Future Work

The performance of generic models is impressive in the general task. The generic model can become the new SOTA in many natural language processing tasks with proper prompts. However, the scale of the parameters in LLM like ChatGPT makes it almost impossible to be deployed locally. In addition, it can hardly be fine-tuned by an individual or a small group of researchers due to the high requirement for computation power. Even though it can be leveraged by prompts, when it comes to the specialised domain or private information, data privacy prevents it from becoming a universal solution for all people, which limits the applications in real-life scenarios. Another issue is low BERTScore in both general and genre-specific tasks, which indicates deviation in meaning preservation.

When it comes to genre-specific tasks, the generic model is less competitive than it is in general tasks. Based on the human evaluation (Table 6), the expert model shows similar or higher performance than the generic model. Although the generic model trained with a much larger corpus contains more internal knowledge, it is hard to determine where to stop the simplification without quantitive prompts. Considering the lower BERTScore from the generic models, it seems that the ChatGPT over-paraphrased the input, compared to the expert models. Results from human evaluation also agree that the expert models appear to preserve the meaning better than the generic model. However, the expert models are equipped with control tokens and inevitably will delete some content or information based on the control token they are given as well. This result shows that human annotators may prefer the more conservative settings of the expert models as opposed to the paraphrasing of the generic models in terms of meaning preservation.

The results in Table 3 and 4 prove the effectiveness of transfer learning after fine-tuning. As mentioned in the results, both expert models benefit from transfer learning in the genre-specific task. One possible reason for the improvement of the other kind of expert models may be the common ground between the two subsets of different genres, the topic and context for example. Yet the performance gap between the two types of expert models shows that genre or text style still matters and causes performance differences. The genre-adapted model can be a potential solution to better

Source:	For PoCT a single specimen of blood is usually obtained by skin puncture.
Reference:	For PoCT, a single specimen of blood is usually obtained by skin puncture.
GPT-3:	A skin puncture usually gets one sample of blood for PoCT.
ChatGPT:	For Point of Care Testing (PoCT), a small sample of blood is usually taken by pricking the skin.
Expert:	For PoCT, a single specimen of blood is usually obtained through skin puncture.
Source:	It is possible that many mammals including domestic animals are susceptible to SARS-CoV-2.
Reference:	It is possible that many mammals, including domestic animals, are susceptible to SARS-CoV-2.
GPT-3:	Mammals, including domestic animals, may be vulnerable to SARS-CoV-2.
ChatGPT:	Many types of animals, including pets, may be able to get infected with SARS-CoV-2.
Expert:	Many mammals including domestic animals may be susceptible to SARS-CoV-2.
Source:	Personal protective equipment (PPE) is considered less effective than engineering and administrative controls, but can help prevent some exposures.
Reference:	Personal protective equipment (PPE) is considered less effective than engineering and administrative controls. However, it can help prevent some exposures.
GPT-3:	PPE is not as good as engineering and admin controls but can prevent some exposures.
ChatGPT:	PPE is not as good as other ways to prevent exposure, but it can help some.
Expert:	Personal protective equipment (PPE) is considered less effective than engineering and administrative controls, but can help prevent some exposures.

Table 5: Examples of simplifications from different models

Model	Simplicity	Meaning Preservation
Generic	3.55	3.86
Expert	3.46	4.17

Table 6: Human evaluation score on test set of **Wiki0** and **PubMed0** (out of 5)

fit the requirements of different groups of lay users.

Even with highly capable generic or expert models, there is still the possibility for the introduction of factual errors in the output. With the convincing performance of generic models like ChatGPT, the hallucination problem become more serious than ever before. When the task is related to a crucial area such as medicine or legal help, the introduction of misleading information may cause severe problems. To improve the robustness of the simplification system, it is necessary to build a factual evaluation system in the future (Devaraj et al., 2022; Ma et al., 2022). Unlike other text generation tasks, simplification maintains the essential information in the input, thus it is easier to judge whether there is misleading content or hallucinations. BERTScore, which measures the meaning preservation for the implications, could be extended into a tool to measure the deviation of original meanings in future work.

Another problem is the explanation of abbreviations. For lay users unfamiliar with the abbreviations and technical terms, it is important to explain the meaning of these unique words or phases. ChatGPT has a huge knowledge base to understand common abbreviations. However, technical terms in certain domains may be unknown for the generic model and the abbreviations may refer to different phrases in different contexts. To avoid the above problem, the model needs to have a genre-specific knowledge base in future work, which allows the model to identify and explain the abbreviations and terms. To achieve this goal, a model competitive with an external source of knowledge base is required. In addition, the knowledge base should be combined with lexical complexity evaluation to decide which term needs explanation.

6 Conclusion

In this paper, we compared the performance differences between generic models and expert models on general and genre-specific simplification datasets. We showed the effect and practicality of transfer learning in genre-specific datasets with less amount of samples. The performance drop on general tasks after transfer learning is acceptable and may be further reduced in future studies. The performance, cost-effectiveness and portability of expert models prove themselves as one of the practical solutions for domains-specific or genres-specific tasks.

7 Lay Summary

Text simplification is a technique for making written language easier to read. This is helpful for people with reading difficulties such as dyslexia, or people who are learning a language. In this paper, we investigated how well tools built to simplify one type of text can be used to simplify another type of text. The two types of text we looked at were academic articles and Wikipedia articles. To make these types of articles easier to read, we used large language models (such as ChatGPT), which were not designed for the task. Large Language Models are a new type of technology that are trained to complete a sentence, or write an appropriate response to a question. Language models are usually trained on general purpose data, so might not be useful for specialist areas such as academic articles and Wikipedia articles. We also designed our own customised models which were smaller, but trained on data that helped them to learn the task. As a result, we found that:

- the type of text (known as its genre) **does affect the performance** of text simplification models targeting general corpus;
- the **zero-shot large language models are competitive** but require tweaks to reach the same level of performance as the customized models;
- the smaller customized models may **still hold their position as the best model**.

References

Fernando Alva-Manchego, Louis Martin, Antoine Bordes, Carolina Scarton, Benoît Sagot, and Lucia Specia. 2020a. ASSET: A dataset for tuning and evaluation of sentence simplification models with multiple rewriting transformations. In *Proceedings of the 58th Annual Meeting of the Association for Computational Linguistics*, pages 4668–4679, Online. Association for Computational Linguistics.

Fernando Alva-Manchego, Carolina Scarton, and Lucia Specia. 2020b. Data-driven sentence simplification:: Survey and benchmark. *Computational Linguistics*, 46(1):135–187.

Fernando Alva-Manchego, Carolina Scarton, and Lucia Specia. 2021. The (Un)Suitability of Automatic Evaluation Metrics for Text Simplification. *Computational Linguistics*, 47(4):861–889.

Antonios Anastasopoulos, Alessandro Cattelan, Zi-Yi Dou, Marcello Federico, Christian Federmann, Dmitriy Genzel, Franscisco Guzmán, Junjie Hu, Macduff Hughes, Philipp Koehn, Rosie Lazar, Will Lewis, Graham Neubig, Mengmeng Niu, Alp Öktem, Eric Paquin, Grace Tang, and Sylwia Tur. 2020. TICO-19: the translation initiative for COvid-19. In *Proceedings of the 1st Workshop on NLP for COVID-19 (Part 2) at EMNLP 2020*, Online. Association for Computational Linguistics.

Tom Brown, Benjamin Mann, Nick Ryder, Melanie Subbiah, Jared D Kaplan, Prafulla Dhariwal, Arvind Neelakantan, Pranav Shyam, Girish Sastry, Amanda Askell, Sandhini Agarwal, Ariel Herbert-Voss, Gretchen Krueger, Tom Henighan, Rewon Child, Aditya Ramesh, Daniel Ziegler, Jeffrey Wu, Clemens Winter, Chris Hesse, Mark Chen, Eric Sigler, Mateusz Litwin, Scott Gray, Benjamin Chess, Jack Clark, Christopher Berner, Sam McCandlish, Alec Radford, Ilya Sutskever, and Dario Amodei. 2020. Language models are few-shot learners. In *Advances in Neural Information Processing Systems*, volume 33, pages 1877–1901. Curran Associates, Inc.

Lucas Høyberg Puvis de Chavannes, Mads Guldborg Kjeldgaard Kongsbak, Timmie Rantzau, and Leon Derczynski. 2021. Hyperparameter power impact in transformer language model training. In *Proceedings of the Second Workshop on Simple and Efficient Natural Language Processing*, pages 96–118, Virtual. Association for Computational Linguistics.

Will Coster and David Kauchak. 2011. Learning to simplify sentences using Wikipedia. In *Proceedings of the Workshop on Monolingual Text-To-Text Generation*, pages 1–9, Portland, Oregon. Association for Computational Linguistics.

Ashwin Devaraj, William Sheffield, Byron Wallace, and Junyi Jessy Li. 2022. Evaluating factuality in text simplification. In *Proceedings of the 60th Annual Meeting of the Association for Computational Linguistics (Volume 1: Long Papers)*, pages 7331–7345, Dublin, Ireland. Association for Computational Linguistics.

Jacob Devlin, Ming-Wei Chang, Kenton Lee, and Kristina Toutanova. 2019. BERT: Pre-training of deep bidirectional transformers for language understanding. In *Proceedings of the 2019 Conference of the North American Chapter of the Association for Computational Linguistics: Human Language Technologies, Volume 1 (Long and Short Papers)*, pages 4171–4186, Minneapolis, Minnesota. Association for Computational Linguistics.

William Fedus, Barret Zoph, and Noam Shazeer. 2021. Switch transformers: Scaling to trillion parameter models with simple and efficient sparsity. *CoRR*, abs/2101.03961.

Sepp Hochreiter and Jürgen Schmidhuber. 1997. Long short-term memory. *Neural computation*, 9(8):1735–1780.

Jared Kaplan, Sam McCandlish, Tom Henighan, Tom B. Brown, Benjamin Chess, Rewon Child, Scott Gray, Alec Radford, Jeffrey Wu, and Dario Amodei. 2020. Scaling laws for neural language models. *CoRR*, abs/2001.08361.

David Kauchak. 2013. Improving text simplification language modeling using unsimplified text data. In *Proceedings of the 51st Annual Meeting of the Association for Computational Linguistics (Volume 1:*

Long Papers), pages 1537–1546, Sofia, Bulgaria. Association for Computational Linguistics.

Yuta Kikuchi, Graham Neubig, Ryohei Sasano, Hiroya Takamura, and Manabu Okumura. 2016. Controlling output length in neural encoder-decoders. In *Proceedings of the 2016 Conference on Empirical Methods in Natural Language Processing*, pages 1328–1338, Austin, Texas. Association for Computational Linguistics.

Mike Lewis, Yinhan Liu, Naman Goyal, Marjan Ghazvininejad, Abdelrahman Mohamed, Omer Levy, Veselin Stoyanov, and Luke Zettlemoyer. 2020. BART: Denoising sequence-to-sequence pre-training for natural language generation, translation, and comprehension. In *Proceedings of the 58th Annual Meeting of the Association for Computational Linguistics*, pages 7871–7880, Online. Association for Computational Linguistics.

Yinhan Liu, Myle Ott, Naman Goyal, Jingfei Du, Mandar Joshi, Danqi Chen, Omer Levy, Mike Lewis, Luke Zettlemoyer, and Veselin Stoyanov. 2019. Roberta: A robustly optimized BERT pretraining approach. *CoRR*, abs/1907.11692.

Xinyu Lu, Jipeng Qiang, Yun Li, Yunhao Yuan, and Yi Zhu. 2021. An unsupervised method for building sentence simplification corpora in multiple languages. In *Findings of the Association for Computational Linguistics: EMNLP 2021*, pages 227–237, Punta Cana, Dominican Republic. Association for Computational Linguistics.

Yuan Ma, Sandaru Seneviratne, and Elena Daskalaki. 2022. Improving text simplification with factuality error detection. In *Proceedings of the Workshop on Text Simplification, Accessibility, and Readability (TSAR-2022)*, pages 173–178, Abu Dhabi, United Arab Emirates (Virtual). Association for Computational Linguistics.

Mounica Maddela, Fernando Alva-Manchego, and Wei Xu. 2021. Controllable text simplification with explicit paraphrasing. In *Proceedings of the 2021 Conference of the North American Chapter of the Association for Computational Linguistics: Human Language Technologies*, pages 3536–3553, Online. Association for Computational Linguistics.

Louis Martin, Angela Fan, Éric de la Clergerie, Antoine Bordes, and Benoît Sagot. 2020. Multilingual unsupervised sentence simplification. *CoRR*, abs/2005.00352.

Louis Martin, Benoît Sagot, Éric de la Clergerie, and Antoine Bordes. 2019. Controllable sentence simplification. *CoRR*, abs/1910.02677.

Daiki Nishihara, Tomoyuki Kajiwara, and Yuki Arase. 2019. Controllable text simplification with lexical constraint loss. In *Proceedings of the 57th Annual Meeting of the Association for Computational Linguistics: Student Research Workshop*, pages 260–266, Florence, Italy. Association for Computational Linguistics.

Kostiantyn Omelianchuk, Vipul Raheja, and Oleksandr Skurzhanskyi. 2021. Text simplification by tagging. *CoRR*, abs/2103.05070.

Matthew E. Peters, Mark Neumann, Mohit Iyyer, Matt Gardner, Christopher Clark, Kenton Lee, and Luke Zettlemoyer. 2018. Deep contextualized word representations. In *Proceedings of the 2018 Conference of the North American Chapter of the Association for Computational Linguistics: Human Language Technologies, Volume 1 (Long Papers)*, pages 2227–2237, New Orleans, Louisiana. Association for Computational Linguistics.

Alec Radford, Karthik Narasimhan, Tim Salimans, Ilya Sutskever, et al. 2018. Improving language understanding by generative pre-training.

Colin Raffel, Noam Shazeer, Adam Roberts, Katherine Lee, Sharan Narang, Michael Matena, Yanqi Zhou, Wei Li, and Peter J. Liu. 2019. Exploring the limits of transfer learning with a unified text-to-text transformer. *CoRR*, abs/1910.10683.

Pranav Rajpurkar, Jian Zhang, Konstantin Lopyrev, and Percy Liang. 2016. SQuAD: 100,000+ questions for machine comprehension of text. In *Proceedings of the 2016 Conference on Empirical Methods in Natural Language Processing*, pages 2383–2392, Austin, Texas. Association for Computational Linguistics.

J. Rapin and O. Teytaud. 2018. Nevergrad - A gradient-free optimization platform. `https://GitHub.com/FacebookResearch/Nevergrad`.

Carolina Scarton and Lucia Specia. 2018. Learning simplifications for specific target audiences. In *Proceedings of the 56th Annual Meeting of the Association for Computational Linguistics (Volume 2: Short Papers)*, pages 712–718, Melbourne, Australia. Association for Computational Linguistics.

Lane Schwartz, Timothy Anderson, Jeremy Gwinnup, and Katherine Young. 2014. Machine translation and monolingual postediting: The AFRL WMT-14 system. In *Proceedings of the Ninth Workshop on Statistical Machine Translation*, pages 186–194, Baltimore, Maryland, USA. Association for Computational Linguistics.

Thomas Scialom, Louis Martin, Jacopo Staiano, Éric Villemonte de la Clergerie, and Benoît Sagot. 2021. Rethinking automatic evaluation in sentence simplification. *CoRR*, abs/2104.07560.

Matthew Shardlow and Fernando Alva-Manchego. 2022. Simple TICO-19: A dataset for joint translation and simplification of COVID-19 texts. In *Proceedings of the Thirteenth Language Resources and Evaluation Conference*, pages 3093–3102, Marseille, France. European Language Resources Association.

Kim Cheng Sheang and Horacio Saggion. 2021. Controllable sentence simplification with a unified text-to-text transfer transformer. In *Proceedings of the*

14th International Conference on Natural Language Generation, pages 341–352, Aberdeen, Scotland, UK. Association for Computational Linguistics.

Sanja Štajner, Kim Cheng Sheang, and Horacio Saggion. 2022. Sentence simplification capabilities of transfer-based models. *Proceedings of the AAAI Conference on Artificial Intelligence*, 36(11):12172–12180.

Alex Wang, Amanpreet Singh, Julian Michael, Felix Hill, Omer Levy, and Samuel Bowman. 2018. GLUE: A multi-task benchmark and analysis platform for natural language understanding. In *Proceedings of the 2018 EMNLP Workshop BlackboxNLP: Analyzing and Interpreting Neural Networks for NLP*, pages 353–355, Brussels, Belgium. Association for Computational Linguistics.

Kristian Woodsend and Mirella Lapata. 2011. Learning to simplify sentences with quasi-synchronous grammar and integer programming. In *Proceedings of the 2011 Conference on Empirical Methods in Natural Language Processing*, pages 409–420, Edinburgh, Scotland, UK. Association for Computational Linguistics.

Sander Wubben, Antal van den Bosch, and Emiel Krahmer. 2012. Sentence simplification by monolingual machine translation. In *Proceedings of the 50th Annual Meeting of the Association for Computational Linguistics (Volume 1: Long Papers)*, pages 1015–1024, Jeju Island, Korea. Association for Computational Linguistics.

Wei Xu, Chris Callison-Burch, and Courtney Napoles. 2015. Problems in current text simplification research: New data can help. *Transactions of the Association for Computational Linguistics*, 3:283–297.

Wei Xu, Courtney Napoles, Ellie Pavlick, Quanze Chen, and Chris Callison-Burch. 2016. Optimizing statistical machine translation for text simplification. *Transactions of the Association for Computational Linguistics*, 4:401–415.

Tianyi Zhang, Varsha Kishore, Felix Wu, Kilian Q. Weinberger, and Yoav Artzi. 2019. Bertscore: Evaluating text generation with BERT. *CoRR*, abs/1904.09675.

Xingxing Zhang and Mirella Lapata. 2017. Sentence simplification with deep reinforcement learning. In *Proceedings of the 2017 Conference on Empirical Methods in Natural Language Processing*, pages 584–594, Copenhagen, Denmark. Association for Computational Linguistics.

Zhemin Zhu, Delphine Bernhard, and Iryna Gurevych. 2010. A monolingual tree-based translation model for sentence simplification. In *Proceedings of the 23rd International Conference on Computational Linguistics (Coling 2010)*, pages 1353–1361.

A Template of human evaluation form

Please mark the score of simplicity and meaning preservation on a 5-point Likert scale. There are 2 sets of simplified sentences, please compare and mark the score. Meaning preservation: To what extent do you agree the simplified sentence keeps the important information? Simplisity: To what extent do you agree the simplified sentence is easy to understand?			
Original Text	Simplified sentences	Meaning Preservation	Simplicity
It is possible that many mammals including domestic animals are susceptible to SARS-CoV-2.	Many types of animals, including pets, may be able to get infected with SARS-CoV-2.	Disagree	Agree
	Many mammals including domestic animals may be susceptible to SARS-CoV-2.	Agree	Agree

Table 7: Sample of the human evaluation form

B Detailed Scores

	SARI score / Test set / Model	Wiki0	Wiki1	Wiki2	Wiki3	Wiki4	Wiki5	Wiki6	Wiki7	Wiki8	Wiki9	Wiki10	Wiki11	Wiki12	Wiki13	Wiki14	Wiki15	Wiki16	Wiki17	Wiki18	Wiki19	**Overall**
Base	BART-base	39.58	43.13	40.20	40.82	40.99	40.67	39.33	40.14	40.53	40.88	42.18	42.43	43.30	41.17	37.74	41.03	41.99	39.70	39.34	40.48	40.78
Generic	GPT-3	29.54	27.85	29.82	28.29	28.62	29.70	28.41	28.22	29.12	30.22	27.83	30.01	29.76	29.18	28.88	28.62	28.44	30.68	28.42	28.95	29.03
	ChatGpt	32.46	31.05	32.16	30.45	32.07	29.63	30.21	29.93	31.73	31.79	29.21	31.83	31.62	29.85	29.16	32.04	31.37	32.86	31.92	31.07	31.12
Expert	Corresponding **Wiki** model	43.99	44.53	42.56	43.33	43.30	44.88	43.83	45.36	44.33	45.23	45.24	43.22	46.46	44.62	44.25	43.56	44.41	42.74	43.76	46.39	**44.30**
	PubMed0	43.52	43.36	42.62	44.94	44.33	41.31	41.79	42.81	42.02	43.25	41.68	41.51	44.38	43.41	42.90	43.36	43.03	41.57	45.32	44.14	43.06
	PubMed1	41.28	42.73	42.70	41.37	44.00	42.15	43.62	40.72	42.36	43.18	44.35	43.65	43.34	43.23	41.94	42.69	42.15	42.33	41.42	40.74	42.50
	PubMed2	42.72	43.78	43.01	43.16	41.49	44.52	40.69	41.39	42.03	42.19	40.90	43.48	45.08	42.52	41.60	43.95	44.92	40.46	43.88	41.42	42.66
	PubMed3	40.90	43.55	43.09	42.51	44.50	42.13	43.98	41.93	41.92	41.23	42.43	43.70	43.71	42.74	41.82	42.96	45.02	39.59	42.79	43.29	42.69
	PubMed4	40.04	43.34	44.72	43.26	43.14	43.85	43.09	40.27	41.62	44.31	41.43	42.11	42.56	42.43	42.25	41.42	43.33	41.50	41.79	42.54	42.45
	PubMed5	40.53	43.62	44.39	40.24	41.17	43.00	41.95	43.09	42.73	43.81	41.05	44.11	42.80	43.42	42.48	43.08	44.77	41.62	40.68	42.69	42.56
	PubMed6	43.11	42.98	43.84	42.94	40.59	42.03	43.91	40.63	40.95	42.81	44.03	43.80	43.05	42.59	41.02	43.49	44.00	42.00	42.28	42.95	42.65
	PubMed7	41.15	42.38	42.30	43.87	43.19	40.27	42.03	43.76	40.98	43.93	44.08	42.72	44.52	41.97	42.32	42.48	43.38	42.22	45.01	40.97	42.68
	PubMed8	43.59	43.58	41.92	43.81	42.54	42.74	44.77	41.77	42.25	43.69	40.03	43.96	44.83	42.11	41.88	44.40	44.89	41.48	42.48	43.39	43.01
	PubMed9	42.51	41.79	45.22	42.24	41.55	41.35	42.12	42.41	42.72	41.80	43.03	43.69	44.03	43.58	40.82	41.90	42.43	41.87	41.66	42.18	42.45
	PubMed10	42.11	44.12	45.41	42.17	42.80	41.11	42.83	43.29	42.80	41.20	43.50	43.33	42.80	43.29	42.55	42.22	43.43	41.15	42.33	42.58	42.75
	PubMed11	43.47	44.30	44.72	43.85	43.13	42.05	43.93	43.40	40.71	42.67	44.10	43.44	43.38	39.46	42.08	42.87	42.54	42.17	44.31	43.42	43.00
	PubMed12	42.17	44.73	43.65	43.23	42.29	40.96	41.82	41.15	43.31	44.12	42.38	44.00	42.25	40.82	41.67	43.07	43.19	40.36	42.72	40.23	42.41
	PubMed13	40.95	41.53	42.46	41.70	42.44	43.36	41.62	43.52	41.59	43.72	43.18	44.42	45.20	41.20	42.96	42.90	43.84	42.39	42.88	45.04	42.84
	PubMed14	41.49	43.38	44.17	42.49	42.83	42.85	44.60	42.53	41.09	44.83	43.16	42.87	44.32	42.02	43.41	43.98	44.91	43.21	44.16	41.56	43.19
	PubMed15	42.00	43.81	43.83	42.49	41.53	42.69	41.97	41.16	44.18	40.93	41.33	44.95	43.23	42.90	41.28	41.99	44.42	41.84	44.49	42.35	42.67
	PubMed16	43.38	41.63	42.97	42.11	41.39	42.59	42.32	43.22	42.85	45.12	41.27	42.06	44.34	43.17	41.33	42.46	44.40	42.24	44.35	39.71	42.65
	PubMed17	40.74	43.04	41.75	41.40	41.53	44.47	42.83	38.51	43.79	43.70	41.13	43.03	42.70	43.21	43.61	43.85	41.05	41.35	45.01	41.20	42.40
	PubMed18	42.27	43.16	45.59	41.33	44.20	41.83	43.75	42.24	41.86	43.91	41.39	43.87	44.77	44.06	41.01	43.57	43.79	41.16	44.14	43.23	43.06
	PubMed19	43.03	43.61	42.38	40.75	44.17	42.53	43.99	42.73	42.33	43.94	42.24	43.39	43.03	42.67	42.67	43.00	43.83	42.96	45.40	41.66	43.02
	PubMed20	42.67	42.60	42.72	42.02	42.76	42.95	43.42	42.08	43.34	39.79	43.97	42.78	44.28	42.11	41.81	42.49	43.82	42.77	42.26	41.22	42.59
	PubMed21	39.71	42.36	43.71	40.99	41.71	41.45	43.12	42.68	42.69	43.52	44.16	44.25	44.72	42.29	39.49	45.07	42.72	42.25	44.75	40.79	42.62
	PubMed22	42.09	41.96	42.83	41.27	41.09	43.91	42.91	41.61	42.06	42.85	42.64	42.87	44.37	43.12	42.54	43.15	42.30	42.59	43.21	41.46	42.54
	PubMed23	42.96	45.08	44.38	44.48	40.52	40.83	44.83	42.74	43.85	44.42	43.57	42.65	44.62	43.88	41.23	42.52	42.42	42.45	42.81	41.99	43.11
	PubMed24	43.37	43.43	43.09	40.50	40.55	42.57	43.25	41.98	43.70	43.95	43.88	43.19	45.14	42.82	42.61	43.41	44.45	42.12	44.37	41.20	42.98
	PubMed25	42.62	42.82	43.36	41.35	42.47	44.20	44.17	42.58	42.96	44.46	44.03	43.38	42.76	42.41	40.80	41.88	44.23	42.25	44.01	43.94	43.03
	PubMed26	42.76	44.63	42.64	43.09	42.91	42.57	43.57	42.71	41.95	42.63	44.82	42.51	42.08	41.11	40.34	43.53	44.59	41.85	44.50	41.92	42.84
	PubMed27	41.20	45.43	41.81	42.15	41.46	41.58	43.78	39.74	43.47	41.50	42.22	43.24	43.07	42.06	43.63	43.27	43.10	41.66	43.36	41.43	42.46
	PubMed28	39.86	41.25	43.70	44.96	42.41	41.11	42.69	43.74	40.87	42.40	41.69	44.37	44.64	41.88	43.59	42.84	44.57	41.20	44.66	41.58	42.70
	PubMed29	41.65	44.38	42.92	42.73	43.82	41.81	42.48	42.51	42.31	44.10	41.01	44.26	43.33	43.17	42.54	43.37	44.67	40.71	42.29	42.17	42.81
Average of **PubMed**		44.48	43.28	43.40	42.45	42.42	42.36	43.06	42.10	42.38	43.13	42.62	43.39	43.78	42.52	42.01	43.04	43.67	41.78	43.44	42.10	42.75

Table 8: Detailed SARI score on **Wikipedia*x*** (We use **Wiki** to refer the **Wikipedia** in the columns)

	BERTScore / Test set / Model	Wiki0	Wiki1	Wiki2	Wiki3	Wiki4	Wiki5	Wiki6	Wiki7	Wiki8	Wiki9	Wiki10	Wiki11	Wiki12	Wiki13	Wiki14	Wiki15	Wiki16	Wiki17	Wiki18	Wiki19	**Overall**
Base	BART-base	0.743	0.797	0.723	0.722	0.755	0.804	0.721	0.766	0.747	0.781	0.737	0.735	0.753	0.698	0.733	0.760	0.736	0.768	0.602	0.733	0.741
Generic	GPT-3	0.524	0.533	0.541	0.532	0.515	0.557	0.545	0.524	0.523	0.508	0.525	0.518	0.514	0.506	0.536	0.546	0.533	0.548	0.535	0.533	0.530
	ChatGpt	0.559	0.568	0.551	0.547	0.549	0.546	0.555	0.549	0.542	0.521	0.521	0.531	0.552	0.495	0.539	0.552	0.534	0.538	0.548	0.538	0.542
Expert	Corresponding **Wiki** model	0.763	0.756	0.805	0.736	0.745	0.772	0.764	0.771	0.738	0.796	0.749	0.748	0.774	0.727	0.770	0.726	0.711	0.755	0.749	0.763	**0.756**
	PubMed0	0.759	0.742	0.786	0.755	0.746	0.735	0.710	0.741	0.774	0.754	0.700	0.792	0.769	0.717	0.748	0.731	0.742	0.755	0.761	0.741	0.748
	PubMed1	0.669	0.771	0.776	0.731	0.746	0.724	0.781	0.736	0.745	0.784	0.794	0.733	0.772	0.713	0.785	0.744	0.764	0.715	0.786	0.708	0.749
	PubMed2	0.740	0.780	0.760	0.706	0.763	0.754	0.687	0.788	0.744	0.765	0.749	0.751	0.745	0.722	0.673	0.773	0.763	0.767	0.783	0.685	0.745
	PubMed3	0.670	0.781	0.750	0.680	0.747	0.758	0.810	0.769	0.753	0.730	0.756	0.769	0.715	0.710	0.646	0.703	0.759	0.673	0.675	0.729	0.729
	PubMed4	0.647	0.797	0.756	0.776	0.766	0.790	0.779	0.788	0.735	0.759	0.752	0.661	0.727	0.736	0.743	0.727	0.742	0.729	0.732	0.725	0.743
	PubMed5	0.649	0.799	0.736	0.676	0.704	0.763	0.763	0.753	0.762	0.756	0.737	0.737	0.720	0.726	0.743	0.660	0.750	0.735	0.745	0.705	0.731
	PubMed6	0.736	0.748	0.740	0.736	0.688	0.756	0.781	0.696	0.679	0.740	0.764	0.738	0.692	0.728	0.685	0.725	0.752	0.759	0.768	0.757	0.733
	PubMed7	0.734	0.769	0.740	0.788	0.751	0.745	0.756	0.764	0.730	0.761	0.786	0.718	0.745	0.720	0.759	0.691	0.759	0.727	0.771	0.705	0.746
	PubMed8	0.758	0.761	0.795	0.745	0.745	0.757	0.775	0.775	0.701	0.770	0.721	0.768	0.769	0.741	0.723	0.731	0.747	0.740	0.748	0.739	0.750
	PubMed9	0.752	0.811	0.758	0.723	0.778	0.719	0.780	0.758	0.766	0.683	0.751	0.742	0.730	0.736	0.707	0.707	0.747	0.754	0.787	0.709	0.745
	PubMed10	0.735	0.770	0.756	0.730	0.741	0.615	0.810	0.751	0.769	0.682	0.763	0.758	0.711	0.715	0.712	0.732	0.769	0.702	0.754	0.726	0.735
	PubMed11	0.738	0.766	0.773	0.786	0.750	0.762	0.782	0.769	0.660	0.714	0.781	0.759	0.767	0.574	0.761	0.729	0.724	0.762	0.763	0.739	0.743
	PubMed12	0.733	0.770	0.758	0.750	0.729	0.719	0.773	0.760	0.753	0.752	0.746	0.758	0.699	0.615	0.688	0.742	0.755	0.696	0.771	0.692	0.733
	PubMed13	0.726	0.673	0.748	0.713	0.732	0.773	0.726	0.759	0.755	0.756	0.770	0.705	0.764	0.685	0.762	0.713	0.746	0.735	0.754	0.739	0.737
	PubMed14	0.735	0.757	0.747	0.707	0.752	0.773	0.798	0.793	0.711	0.771	0.791	0.783	0.774	0.711	0.753	0.738	0.751	0.726	0.760	0.691	0.751
	PubMed15	0.695	0.784	0.765	0.735	0.703	0.746	0.741	0.726	0.771	0.782	0.715	0.743	0.728	0.737	0.762	0.705	0.783	0.761	0.782	0.727	0.745
	PubMed16	0.756	0.723	0.791	0.732	0.683	0.762	0.702	0.763	0.757	0.758	0.700	0.779	0.750	0.746	0.680	0.683	0.786	0.747	0.771	0.686	0.738
	PubMed17	0.654	0.771	0.701	0.640	0.753	0.750	0.785	0.625	0.758	0.774	0.714	0.743	0.740	0.720	0.752	0.728	0.685	0.725	0.749	0.701	0.723
	PubMed18	0.709	0.757	0.763	0.706	0.757	0.794	0.795	0.758	0.684	0.772	0.752	0.745	0.732	0.748	0.734	0.759	0.742	0.742	0.790	0.726	0.748
	PubMed19	0.750	0.776	0.791	0.692	0.762	0.773	0.793	0.748	0.723	0.755	0.777	0.770	0.698	0.728	0.768	0.720	0.727	0.748	0.768	0.688	0.748
	PubMed20	0.745	0.753	0.789	0.733	0.769	0.779	0.784	0.723	0.740	0.693	0.797	0.775	0.752	0.710	0.668	0.724	0.769	0.730	0.767	0.637	0.742
	PubMed21	0.723	0.812	0.743	0.693	0.761	0.707	0.798	0.748	0.724	0.735	0.800	0.748	0.753	0.713	0.701	0.740	0.711	0.729	0.765	0.681	0.739
	PubMed22	0.753	0.780	0.802	0.726	0.678	0.791	0.773	0.671	0.718	0.756	0.791	0.745	0.711	0.714	0.738	0.729	0.734	0.687	0.782	0.725	0.740
	PubMed23	0.734	0.796	0.774	0.770	0.676	0.698	0.780	0.776	0.766	0.735	0.788	0.739	0.757	0.751	0.707	0.743	0.774	0.759	0.768	0.720	0.750
	PubMed24	0.745	0.789	0.718	0.678	0.683	0.719	0.778	0.779	0.734	0.781	0.784	0.726	0.771	0.715	0.734	0.710	0.743	0.732	0.739	0.696	0.738
	PubMed25	0.768	0.780	0.749	0.753	0.740	0.787	0.784	0.766	0.709	0.759	0.806	0.744	0.757	0.756	0.731	0.714	0.772	0.739	0.765	0.749	0.756
	PubMed26	0.770	0.782	0.758	0.716	0.756	0.720	0.769	0.764	0.745	0.775	0.743	0.753	0.734	0.713	0.701	0.740	0.759	0.748	0.769	0.705	0.746
	PubMed27	0.626	0.790	0.697	0.705	0.762	0.723	0.779	0.632	0.770	0.774	0.756	0.749	0.695	0.744	0.744	0.729	0.744	0.753	0.761	0.691	0.731
	PubMed28	0.602	0.810	0.753	0.744	0.724	0.771	0.783	0.746	0.648	0.760	0.772	0.744	0.772	0.711	0.751	0.712	0.756	0.760	0.782	0.680	0.739
	PubMed29	0.630	0.779	0.749	0.734	0.742	0.772	0.762	0.774	0.751	0.783	0.683	0.733	0.715	0.744	0.742	0.727	0.748	0.745	0.646	0.719	0.734
Average of **PubMed**		0.715	0.773	0.757	0.725	0.736	0.748	0.771	0.747	0.735	0.752	0.758	0.747	0.739	0.717	0.727	0.724	0.750	0.736	0.759	0.711	0.741

Table 9: Detailed BERTScore on **Wikipedia*x*** (We use **Wiki** to refer the **Wikipedia** in the columns)

	SARI score / Test set / Model	Pub0	Pub1	Pub2	Pub3	Pub4	Pub5	Pub6	Pub7	Pub8	Pub9	Pub10	Pub11	Pub12	Pub13	Pub14	Pub15	Pub16	Pub17	Pub18	Pub19	**Overall**
Base	BART-base	40.10	42.76	37.38	41.81	39.44	41.44	43.60	39.19	40.35	41.15	40.70	41.93	39.67	39.64	36.94	40.57	41.26	41.18	41.03	41.17	40.56
Generic	GPT-3	31.06	31.43	30.82	29.25	32.56	32.19	30.96	29.82	32.36	30.09	29.09	29.18	30.50	31.42	31.50	29.84	28.99	29.23	31.70	32.45	30.72
	ChatGpt	31.75	31.63	30.28	30.52	34.32	29.89	34.59	30.80	31.79	31.28	30.71	32.12	32.57	31.18	33.99	28.75	30.53	30.57	31.65	31.99	31.55
Expert	Corresponding **PubMed** model	46.04	44.02	41.77	45.95	44.83	43.98	43.60	43.61	43.45	44.97	47.79	42.92	48.14	46.05	44.45	45.97	42.66	46.41	48.24	46.11	**45.05**
	Wikipedia0	46.06	43.34	40.63	43.85	43.65	42.51	41.89	41.80	43.76	41.32	43.87	42.84	46.94	44.14	44.05	43.79	42.93	45.37	45.34	43.25	43.57
	Wikipedia1	43.39	42.57	40.29	45.24	44.20	45.11	43.38	41.63	41.96	40.52	45.66	42.03	45.38	44.98	43.79	43.27	44.64	45.83	46.75	42.95	43.68
	Wikipedia2	45.31	43.26	40.92	45.10	42.84	44.82	42.80	40.55	43.14	42.57	44.47	43.55	42.91	43.91	42.59	44.53	42.33	44.46	43.98	43.53	43.38
	Wikipedia3	44.41	42.11	40.26	43.42	43.47	44.51	42.58	42.72	42.73	39.74	43.53	43.33	46.24	42.25	43.68	43.69	41.94	46.19	41.94	44.19	43.15
	Wikipedia4	44.70	40.70	41.02	43.48	42.02	43.26	42.17	41.30	43.34	39.49	43.39	44.76	46.35	42.92	41.51	46.17	40.74	46.15	46.13	42.63	43.11
	Wikipedia5	46.16	41.24	40.83	44.85	41.77	42.62	41.47	41.97	42.22	41.37	44.00	43.46	44.24	41.83	41.15	45.41	42.23	47.27	44.74	44.21	43.15
	Wikipedia6	42.23	44.98	40.99	44.10	41.80	42.62	43.02	41.68	42.84	40.82	45.20	44.38	45.67	41.93	42.06	45.43	43.81	45.50	46.08	44.49	43.48
	Wikipedia7	44.93	44.30	40.96	43.90	44.42	44.90	40.82	43.56	42.10	40.39	42.95	43.19	43.69	43.02	41.53	44.58	42.79	43.82	45.91	43.77	43.28
	Wikipedia8	43.85	42.81	41.95	43.02	42.90	41.77	39.76	42.84	41.78	40.11	45.05	44.83	45.78	43.62	42.97	45.73	43.42	44.07	46.07	44.24	43.33
	Wikipedia9	45.88	42.68	41.28	44.54	45.69	43.88	43.34	42.39	42.65	41.62	44.99	45.20	44.93	42.61	42.95	43.88	42.75	43.72	44.58	42.70	43.61
	Wikipedia10	45.14	42.52	40.63	45.48	43.21	45.29	43.57	43.63	43.68	42.19	44.79	44.51	42.59	41.15	40.73	44.78	45.95	44.84	45.45	43.80	43.70
	Wikipedia11	43.05	44.73	42.57	44.13	42.20	42.16	43.28	42.06	43.18	39.55	45.14	44.82	47.42	41.86	44.28	45.07	42.27	44.12	44.45	44.25	43.53
	Wikipedia12	43.74	42.67	41.42	45.30	41.43	41.50	41.39	41.15	43.90	40.54	42.88	44.52	46.35	41.43	42.16	44.76	44.87	46.92	43.65	43.51	43.20
	Wikipedia13	42.95	42.03	41.47	43.44	45.47	42.90	41.41	41.84	42.90	39.49	40.63	42.90	43.59	42.72	41.57	43.80	43.22	46.46	45.58	43.94	42.92
	Wikipedia14	41.49	44.27	42.48	44.06	42.46	43.58	42.98	43.13	42.39	40.88	44.66	42.15	42.47	42.40	44.49	44.27	42.60	45.02	41.65	44.04	43.07
	Wikipedia15	44.64	44.71	40.12	44.81	43.36	42.47	42.25	43.47	42.77	39.17	42.31	44.99	45.34	40.44	43.39	44.06	42.94	45.17	44.63	43.21	43.21
	Wikipedia16	43.01	45.84	41.05	44.86	42.96	44.49	43.00	41.09	43.01	39.56	44.48	43.54	44.58	44.12	42.18	45.60	39.94	45.22	44.71	43.64	43.34
	Wikipedia17	43.33	42.32	40.62	44.18	44.55	43.13	42.40	41.62	43.21	39.36	44.05	41.84	43.14	43.73	44.08	44.30	40.57	44.06	47.49	43.21	43.06
	Wikipedia18	44.74	44.14	40.04	45.04	42.26	41.52	44.70	42.95	43.10	39.69	44.52	42.64	42.61	41.88	41.25	46.20	45.05	45.41	44.07	41.83	43.18
	Wikipedia19	44.72	44.90	40.79	43.83	43.62	44.99	41.02	42.08	43.39	41.20	41.86	43.90	46.57	43.21	44.47	46.07	43.44	46.22	45.68	43.80	43.79
	Wikipedia20	45.78	45.79	39.14	44.39	41.65	44.54	40.85	43.16	42.07	40.49	43.16	43.40	45.53	42.08	42.91	44.46	42.23	43.54	46.00	44.26	43.27
	Wikipedia21	42.83	45.37	42.21	43.96	41.52	44.55	42.12	42.13	43.92	41.05	43.88	42.76	46.10	42.38	40.89	44.05	42.10	46.18	42.55	43.93	43.22
	Wikipedia22	43.98	43.17	41.61	43.62	43.51	43.34	41.60	42.12	42.86	39.97	44.90	43.50	44.82	44.72	43.07	44.65	42.30	44.55	43.78	42.76	43.24
	Wikipedia23	45.41	42.82	40.86	43.01	42.46	42.87	42.14	41.89	45.22	40.58	41.75	43.27	43.70	42.96	43.21	45.18	45.62	47.94	44.51	42.69	43.40
	Wikipedia24	45.29	43.69	41.22	45.13	45.94	45.19	43.28	42.91	44.35	42.44	43.45	43.45	44.02	42.62	44.39	44.78	43.45	47.87	44.89	43.92	44.11
	Wikipedia25	45.31	44.64	43.61	46.07	40.68	42.70	42.50	42.01	44.01	41.90	46.28	45.02	43.01	41.03	43.60	44.47	43.90	42.92	45.81	43.83	43.66
	Wikipedia26	45.61	42.98	39.72	44.76	43.94	42.53	40.98	42.57	43.08	41.54	42.74	41.86	44.59	41.40	43.18	45.23	44.35	43.14	41.99	42.43	42.93
	Wikipedia27	45.89	44.58	41.34	44.53	44.02	41.21	41.74	41.48	42.74	41.51	45.32	43.03	47.85	43.81	41.63	45.04	43.74	48.39	45.90	43.68	43.87
	Wikipedia28	45.80	42.73	40.32	43.46	44.22	41.83	41.92	42.16	41.86	41.03	43.89	43.94	43.00	44.00	41.16	45.65	40.53	46.38	43.78	42.17	42.99
	Wikipedia29	44.68	46.07	40.86	43.56	43.52	45.32	43.29	42.78	42.91	41.47	44.80	44.57	43.20	43.57	43.92	45.95	42.82	43.40	45.21	45.02	43.85
Average of **Wikipedia**		44.48	43.60	41.04	44.30	43.19	43.40	42.26	42.22	43.04	40.72	43.95	43.61	44.75	42.76	42.76	44.83	42.98	45.34	44.78	43.53	43.38

Table 10: Detailed SARI score on **PubMed*x***(We use **Pub** to refer the **PubMed** in the columns)

	BERTScore / Test set / Model	Pub0	Pub1	Pub2	Pub3	Pub4	Pub5	Pub6	Pub7	Pub8	Pub9	Pub10	Pub11	Pub12	Pub13	Pub14	Pub15	Pub16	Pub17	Pub18	Pub19	**Overall**
Base	BART-base	0.739	0.773	0.691	0.725	0.680	0.702	0.735	0.732	0.681	0.756	0.720	0.778	0.646	0.728	0.710	0.741	0.725	0.730	0.731	0.743	0.723
Generic	GPT-3	0.542	0.557	0.549	0.536	0.546	0.565	0.538	0.509	0.550	0.525	0.545	0.549	0.568	0.543	0.519	0.573	0.561	0.572	0.540	0.556	0.547
	ChatGpt	0.517	0.537	0.505	0.511	0.535	0.497	0.527	0.507	0.513	0.509	0.510	0.511	0.508	0.501	0.521	0.512	0.533	0.527	0.491	0.521	0.515
Expert	Corresponding **PubMed** model	0.767	0.774	0.675	0.749	0.725	0.705	0.751	0.748	0.724	0.739	0.758	0.711	0.782	0.768	0.737	0.782	0.701	0.770	0.776	0.688	**0.741**
	Wikipedia0	0.742	0.743	0.723	0.737	0.714	0.658	0.702	0.724	0.709	0.712	0.702	0.723	0.742	0.764	0.686	0.760	0.731	0.722	0.714	0.722	0.721
	Wikipedia1	0.683	0.761	0.713	0.746	0.742	0.755	0.704	0.650	0.720	0.772	0.745	0.681	0.711	0.748	0.670	0.781	0.726	0.750	0.721	0.659	0.722
	Wikipedia2	0.743	0.754	0.711	0.748	0.656	0.756	0.730	0.664	0.758	0.758	0.756	0.754	0.654	0.743	0.668	0.774	0.718	0.748	0.709	0.731	0.727
	Wikipedia3	0.748	0.729	0.720	0.709	0.723	0.750	0.743	0.724	0.712	0.757	0.698	0.710	0.778	0.718	0.647	0.741	0.710	0.745	0.689	0.739	0.725
	Wikipedia4	0.731	0.732	0.688	0.711	0.704	0.716	0.718	0.700	0.740	0.748	0.728	0.773	0.738	0.687	0.689	0.774	0.667	0.757	0.738	0.719	0.723
	Wikipedia5	0.769	0.745	0.704	0.729	0.700	0.696	0.732	0.676	0.732	0.744	0.749	0.771	0.754	0.730	0.684	0.800	0.741	0.762	0.762	0.744	0.736
	Wikipedia6	0.777	0.751	0.725	0.712	0.689	0.674	0.699	0.681	0.747	0.733	0.726	0.741	0.756	0.717	0.707	0.762	0.759	0.761	0.729	0.735	0.729
	Wikipedia7	0.744	0.746	0.650	0.712	0.760	0.761	0.719	0.704	0.697	0.743	0.687	0.707	0.713	0.757	0.672	0.778	0.732	0.758	0.728	0.723	0.725
	Wikipedia8	0.715	0.744	0.730	0.743	0.749	0.701	0.727	0.714	0.695	0.737	0.737	0.765	0.758	0.757	0.698	0.765	0.724	0.731	0.720	0.751	0.733
	Wikipedia9	0.760	0.731	0.688	0.712	0.754	0.731	0.748	0.715	0.746	0.768	0.748	0.794	0.735	0.734	0.680	0.790	0.722	0.626	0.685	0.733	0.730
	Wikipedia10	0.741	0.749	0.699	0.724	0.747	0.754	0.743	0.740	0.707	0.740	0.748	0.760	0.646	0.780	0.629	0.775	0.777	0.770	0.741	0.751	0.736
	Wikipedia11	0.723	0.725	0.734	0.713	0.656	0.724	0.725	0.725	0.655	0.713	0.725	0.755	0.778	0.756	0.691	0.769	0.746	0.759	0.715	0.713	0.725
	Wikipedia12	0.726	0.716	0.692	0.766	0.708	0.715	0.734	0.709	0.723	0.726	0.681	0.792	0.735	0.705	0.723	0.766	0.743	0.750	0.729	0.668	0.725
	Wikipedia13	0.784	0.786	0.700	0.713	0.749	0.711	0.714	0.647	0.755	0.764	0.638	0.771	0.692	0.743	0.664	0.727	0.728	0.754	0.729	0.737	0.725
	Wikipedia14	0.779	0.743	0.747	0.711	0.703	0.693	0.747	0.731	0.686	0.727	0.709	0.711	0.644	0.737	0.668	0.749	0.702	0.743	0.656	0.718	0.715
	Wikipedia15	0.769	0.783	0.684	0.713	0.710	0.699	0.716	0.690	0.723	0.741	0.695	0.803	0.749	0.676	0.705	0.745	0.743	0.765	0.708	0.742	0.728
	Wikipedia16	0.749	0.751	0.695	0.759	0.701	0.726	0.693	0.714	0.737	0.704	0.740	0.727	0.714	0.751	0.662	0.755	0.666	0.764	0.720	0.733	0.723
	Wikipedia17	0.761	0.764	0.700	0.703	0.735	0.711	0.746	0.681	0.737	0.759	0.698	0.685	0.664	0.733	0.665	0.762	0.682	0.734	0.729	0.716	0.718
	Wikipedia18	0.758	0.780	0.686	0.732	0.705	0.681	0.735	0.703	0.744	0.736	0.743	0.707	0.686	0.715	0.678	0.791	0.785	0.736	0.733	0.642	0.724
	Wikipedia19	0.733	0.748	0.681	0.735	0.644	0.750	0.675	0.692	0.727	0.690	0.674	0.704	0.745	0.726	0.684	0.799	0.736	0.747	0.705	0.739	0.717
	Wikipedia20	0.761	0.725	0.676	0.718	0.671	0.743	0.698	0.704	0.722	0.727	0.703	0.748	0.751	0.755	0.698	0.765	0.728	0.751	0.738	0.735	0.726
	Wikipedia21	0.743	0.759	0.735	0.691	0.648	0.731	0.742	0.697	0.774	0.729	0.755	0.697	0.763	0.715	0.700	0.745	0.711	0.765	0.672	0.752	0.726
	Wikipedia22	0.759	0.764	0.692	0.683	0.706	0.707	0.691	0.694	0.681	0.744	0.762	0.726	0.709	0.749	0.681	0.769	0.750	0.734	0.741	0.766	0.725
	Wikipedia23	0.753	0.752	0.701	0.719	0.661	0.733	0.703	0.688	0.763	0.718	0.705	0.749	0.716	0.756	0.641	0.794	0.790	0.743	0.720	0.738	0.727
	Wikipedia24	0.738	0.759	0.723	0.728	0.708	0.756	0.718	0.713	0.734	0.737	0.705	0.664	0.719	0.682	0.657	0.729	0.737	0.746	0.731	0.700	0.719
	Wikipedia25	0.731	0.740	0.743	0.770	0.766	0.688	0.740	0.702	0.737	0.657	0.743	0.737	0.719	0.703	0.730	0.779	0.718	0.716	0.732	0.726	0.729
	Wikipedia26	0.760	0.680	0.691	0.731	0.709	0.680	0.734	0.735	0.766	0.734	0.659	0.724	0.725	0.689	0.671	0.787	0.722	0.736	0.642	0.646	0.711
	Wikipedia27	0.734	0.742	0.694	0.718	0.739	0.728	0.737	0.655	0.718	0.734	0.741	0.685	0.777	0.783	0.685	0.774	0.756	0.769	0.719	0.721	0.730
	Wikipedia28	0.752	0.792	0.696	0.732	0.703	0.746	0.738	0.700	0.729	0.767	0.767	0.759	0.725	0.723	0.685	0.792	0.669	0.759	0.701	0.740	0.734
	Wikipedia29	0.765	0.756	0.678	0.741	0.712	0.768	0.711	0.715	0.722	0.729	0.747	0.757	0.746	0.766	0.723	0.777	0.698	0.750	0.743	0.722	0.736
	Average of **Wikipedia**	0.748	0.748	0.703	0.725	0.709	0.721	0.722	0.700	0.727	0.735	0.721	0.736	0.725	0.733	0.681	0.769	0.727	0.745	0.717	0.722	0.726

Table 11: Detailed BERTScore on **PubMedx**(We use **Pub** to refer the **PubMed** in the columns)

Automatic Text Simplification for People with Cognitive Disabilities: Resource Creation within the ClearText Project

Isabel Espinosa-Zaragoza[1], José Abreu-Salas[2], Paloma Moreda[3] and Manuel Palomar[3]
[1] Centre of Digital Intelligence, University of Alicante
isabel.espinosa@ua.es
[2] University Institute for Computing Research, University of Alicante
ji.abreu@ua.es
[3] Department of Computing and Information Systems, University of Alicante
{paloma,mpalomar}@dlsi.ua.es

Abstract

This paper presents the ongoing work conducted within the ClearText project, specifically focusing on the resource creation for the simplification of Spanish for people with cognitive disabilities. These resources include the CLEARSIM corpus and the Simple.Text tool. On the one hand, a description of the corpus compilation process with the help of APSA is detailed along with information regarding whether these texts are bronze, silver or gold standard simplification versions from the original text. The goal to reach is 18,000 texts in total by the end of the project. On the other hand, we aim to explore Large Language Models (LLMs) in a sequence-to-sequence setup for text simplification at the document level. Therefore, the tool's objectives, technical aspects, and the preliminary results derived from early experimentation are also presented. The initial results are subject to improvement, given that experimentation is in a very preliminary stage. Despite showcasing flaws inherent to generative models (e.g. hallucinations, repetitive text), we examine the resolutions (or lack thereof) of complex linguistic phenomena that can be learned from the corpus. These issues will be addressed throughout the remainder of this project. The expected positive results from this project that will impact society are threefold in nature: scientific-technical, social, and economic.

1 Introduction

People with cognitive disabilities have significant limitations in their intellectual functioning and/or may also lack the ability to adapt to everyday situations. In fact, they have spoken and written word comprehension deficits that may include misinterpretation of literal meanings and difficulty understanding complex instructions, to name a few. Among the different language phenomena they struggle with, there are idioms, figures of speech, abstractions, uncommon words, lack of precision, and complex syntax, among other aspects.

Currently, Natural Language Processing (NLP) technologies are developed and mature enough to provide a sound basis for (1) developing components to automatically detect and remove obstacles to reading comprehension and (2) generate additional content to facilitate reading comprehension. Thus, we begin this project with the main hypothesis that the research, development, and deployment of NLP technology can support the authoring of accessible content in Spanish for people with cognitive disabilities with the aim of increasing both their inclusion and empowerment in Europe.

With this hypothesis in mind, the ClearText project[1], funded by the Spanish Government and the European Union (grant reference TED2021-130707B-I00) and developed by the GPLSI research group[2] of the University of Alicante, focuses on researching, implementing, deploying, evaluating, and ultimately providing robust technologies for NLP to support the authoring of accessible Spanish content for public sector organisations —at local, regional, and national levels— that is intelligible to people with cognitive disabilities, thereby widening their inclusion and empowerment in Europe. This, in turn, will improve the ability to access written information for everyone, thereby reducing the risk of exclusion for those with cognitive disabilities. The project is expected to positively impact the quality of life of people with cognitive disabilities, by facilitating their access to educational, vocational, cultural, and social opportunities in public sector organisations.

This paper is structured as follows: Section 2 includes a literature review covering automatic text simplification and focusing on related work

[1]https://cleartext.gplsi.es/
[2]https://gplsi.dlsi.ua.es/

Proceedings of the Second Workshop on Text Simplification, Accessibility and Readability associated with RANLP-2023, pages 68–77,
held in Varna Bulgaria, Sept 7, 2023.
https://doi.org/10.26615/978-954-452-086-1_007

tackling corpora and tools; Section 3 presents the scientific and technological objectives of the project; Section 4 delves into the composition of the project's members; Section 5 describes the different resources created in this project, namely the CLEARSIM corpus and the Simple.Text tool; Section 6 details the expected scientific-technical and socio-economic impact of this project, while Section 7 concludes with the future work ahead.

2 Automatic Text Simplification: Review of Literature

Automatic Text Simplification (henceforth ATS) can be defined as "the process of reducing the linguistic complexity of a text to improve its understandability and readability, while still maintaining its original information content and meaning" (Al-Thanyyan and Azmi, 2022).

ATS can be achieved by following different approaches, namely rule-based, data-driven, or hybrid approaches, and by simplifying some or all language levels (i.e. lexical, syntactic, semantic, and stylistic). The more language levels and language phenomena tackled in the simplification, the more refined the simplified text will be. Specific domains are also an aspect to take into account when simplifying texts.

The audience for which these simplifications are created is diverse (e.g. children, non-native speakers, poor readers, and cognitively impaired individuals) although it is sometimes left unspecified. Hence, the importance of the current focus on customisation, as a given simplification solution may not work for all audiences (Alva-Manchego et al., 2020; Scarton et al., 2018).

Sections 2.1 and 2.2 cover a brief review of the main corpora and tools for ATS in Spanish in more detail.

2.1 ATS Corpora

According to Martin et al. (2023), there are 10 corpora for simplification in Spanish: FIRST (Štajner and Saggion, 2013), Automatic Noticias Fácil (Štajner et al., 2014), IrekiaLF (Gonzalez-Dios et al., 2022), CLARAMED (Campillos-Llanos et al., 2022) and some others which remain unnamed by Bott and Saggion (2011; 2014), Mitkov and Štajner (2014) and Štajner et al. (2019). Additionally, there are two English-Spanish: Newsela (Xu et al., 2015) and SIMPLETICO (Shardlow and Alva-Manchego, 2022).

The corpora review carried out by Martin et al. (2023) presented the following conclusions: (1) the majority of the corpora produced for ATS is in English, and only 7 out of the 24 official languages of the European Union are present, namely, Danish, English, French, German, Italian, Portuguese, and Spanish; (2) there is a scarcity of resources that address ATS aimed at domains that are important for social inclusion, such as health and public administration; (3) there is a lack of parallel corpora whose target is people with mild-to-moderate cognitive impairment; (4) there is a lack of experiments where the target audience was directly involved in the development of the corpus; and, lastly, (5) more than half of these corpora lack adequate documentation of how the simplification was performed, or at the very least, fail to identify the linguistic phenomenon tackled by the simplification.

Additionally, the domain is usually general information, like Wikipedia or news media, with the exception of CLARA-MED (Campillos-Llanos et al., 2022) and SIMPLETICO (Shardlow and Alva-Manchego, 2022) belonging to the health domain and IrekiaLF (Gonzalez-Dios et al., 2022) for the public administration. For more detailed information regarding aspects like language, domain, audience, alignment, size, and metadata, consult Martin et al.'s (2023) work.

2.2 ATS Tools

Regarding simplification tools, Espinosa-Zaragoza et al. (2023) concludes that (1) many languages are still not represented in ATS tools; (2) all language levels should be borne in mind; (3) multiplicity of options or, in other words, NLP solutions, should be presented to the user, as well as (4) customised simplifications to fulfil the need(s) of the varied targets users and, lastly, (5) the need for these tools to be fully accessible and operational for the public.

According to Espinosa-Zaragoza et al. (2023), there are 7 ATS tools for Spanish: arText (da Cunha Fanego et al., 2017), Simplext (Saggion et al., 2015), DysWebxia (Rello et al., 2013), EASIER (Alarcón et al., 2021), LexSIS (Bott et al., 2012), NavegaFácil (Bautista et al., 2018) and Open Book (Barbu et al., 2015). From those, only three are operational at the moment (i.e. accessible for people to simplify text): arText[3], EASIER[4], and Simplext[5]. The first one helps in the identification

[3]http://sistema-artext.com/

[4]http://163.117.129.208:8080/

[5]http://simplext.taln.upf.edu/

of complex language phenomena in a given text; the second one highlights complex vocabulary and provides a simpler substitute; and the last one allows for the simplification of sentences, as it has a character limitation.

3 Scientific and Technological Objectives

The main objective of the ClearText project can be divided into the following specific objectives:

- O1. To analyse the main comprehension obstacles posed by the language used in the web content of Spanish public sector organisations, such as ministries and other government agencies, for people with cognitive disabilities.
- O2. To analyse the needs of people with cognitive disabilities.
- O3. To research and adapt the COMPENDIUM System developed by Lloret et al. (2013) to the needs of public sector documentation.
- O4. To research, implement, deploy, and ultimately provide robust technologies to support the processing of structural complexity.
- O5. To research, implement, deploy, and ultimately provide robust technologies to support the processing of ambiguity in meaning.
- O6. To research, implement, deploy, and ultimately provide a robust text simplification system oriented toward public administration documentation.
- O7. To evaluate the simplification system.
- O8. To promote and disseminate the research results obtained from the project through different national and international media including well-indexed journals, conferences, seminars, etc., as well as exploit the potential for transferring this technology to society.

4 Human Resources

A multidisciplinary research team consisting of five computer science experts and three linguists, with seven of them holding doctorate degrees and one serving as a technician, is in charge of the project. All members belong to the GPLSI research group. The composition of the team reflects a slight positive gender imbalance with five women and three men. The team has extensive experience in technological research and development in NLP, spanning more than 30 years, and, more specifically, in relation to the requested project in word sense disambiguation, anaphora resolution, coreference, named entity, lexical and syntactic analysis, text summarisation and text simplification.

5 Tool and Corpus: Work in Progress

We are currently contemplating and developing both a traditional or conventional approach and also one with the training of a language model. For both of them, this project's aim includes the creation of two resources: (1) the CLEARSIM corpus of simplified texts in Spanish and (2) the Simple.Text tool.

5.1 CLEARSIM Corpus

The compilation process is determined to take place during the first year of the project, that is, 2023. As previously mentioned, the language used is Spanish and the domain pertains to public administration texts. Our target audience consist of people with cognitive disabilities and our alignment approach is document to document. Regarding the size of the corpus, the estimation of texts compiled by the end of the project is 18,000 texts, including 15,000 silver standard texts and 3,000 golden standard texts. The different compilation stages are described below:

- **Stage 1. Original text compilation:** The texts selected are published articles dealing with sports, leisure activities, and culture. These articles are sourced from the websites of town halls within the Alicante province, more specifically, from the following cities: Elche, Benidorm, Alicante, Alcoy, Elda, Torrevieja, and Orihuela.
- **Stage 2. Automatic text summarisation and simplification with ChatGPT:** Since the automatic summarisation task deals with the reduction of content to maintain the most important ideas and text simplification involves removing unnecessary information, this common ground led us to summarise the original text using ChatGPT, which yielded the RGPT texts (i.e. resumen GPT). Additionally, we also prompted a simplification from ChatGPT to compare the results from the summarisation and the simplification process and iden-

tify which processes this generative AI employs depending on the provided instructions. This ultimately generates the simplified version from ChatGPT (SGPT, i.e. simplificación GPT). Both summarisation and simplification processes were applied to the original text.

- **Stage 3. ChatGPT revised versions:** Subsequently, a human revision is manually carried out to ensure that the simplifications are properly performed. Due to time constraints, a set of easy-to-read guidelines is being considered and applied to the ChatGPT texts generated in the previous stage. Additionally, the summarisation helps the reviser check that no crucial information is deleted (e.g. dates, locations, and other pieces of information) in the simplified version. This stage was crucial for refining the prompt, which iterated and began with a simpler version (e.g. *Can you simplify this text?*) which, however, lacked conciseness. Although we still obtained simplified texts, manual revision was time-consuming due to the subjective nature of simplification. Nevertheless, a more refined prompt that explicitly indicated which language phenomena we consider difficult and required replacements generated better simplified outputs. This, in turn, accelerated the manual revision stage.

- **Stage 4. Easy-to-read and facilitated versions:** This stage is conducted by our collaborators, APSA[6], a Non-Governmental Organisation (NGO) which comprises a group of individuals with cognitive disabilities who possess expertise in the adaptation of texts in adherence to the easy-to-read guidelines. In this stage, our collaborators are provided with the original text and our revised simplified version (i.e. SUA, see Table 1) to create both an easy-to-read version (LF, i.e. lectura fácil) following all the easy-to-read guidelines (AENOR, 2018) and a "facilitated" version (FAC, i.e. facilitada), which yields a simplified version according to the legislation but disregarding outlay aspects (e.g. font type, size, color, and others). We utilise Google Drive for text interchange and provision, and APSA creates 50 texts weekly in both versions.

[6] `https://www.asociacionapsa.com/`

This compilation of different texts provides a bronze, silver, and gold standard in simplification, respectively (see Table 1). As can be observed, 7 different text types are included: the original text; a summary and a simplification created with ChatGPT; a revision for each of those versions created by ChatGPT made by our institution; and two manually simplified texts by our collaborator, one following all the easy-to-read guidelines and another disregarding some presentation guidelines. To date, we have compiled approximately 2,000 texts classified as silver standard and 400 texts classified as gold standard.

5.2 Simple.Text Tool

This section describes the tool's objectives, some technical aspects, and the preliminary results derived from early experimentation.

As commented before, text simplification implies solving different language phenomena such as co-references, complex words, or sentence structure. An automatic simplification system may address all or only a subset of these problems. Also, it may work at the sentence or document level. The first setup expects a sentence as input and outputs the simplified version. As Cripwell et al. (2023) noted, sentence-level systems may be leveraged for document-level simplification by iteratively processing the sentences. However, this approach may present problems such as failing to preserve the discourse structure.

Pure document-level simplification may pose challenges, such as the scarcity of datasets aligned at document level (Sun et al., 2021). In addition, the approaches to teaching the system to simplify full documents by simultaneously solving the different linguistic phenomena seem to be at an early stage (Sun et al., 2021; Cripwell et al., 2023). These issues are particularly relevant in the context of data-driven neural generative models.

We aim to explore LLMs in sequence-to-sequence setup for text simplification at the document level. In Sections 5.2.1 and 5.2.2 we cover the technical details of the implementation of Simple.Text tool. Section 5.2.3 discusses early findings from ongoing experiments we are carrying out at the moment.

5.2.1 Technical Details

Simple.Text Tool core is a T5 (small) model (Raffel et al., 2020) fine-tuned using the current version of SUA (see Table 1). The data comprises 925

Code	Description	Stage	Standard
TXT	Original texts	1	
RGPT	Summaries created with ChatGPT	2	Bronze
SGPT	Simplifications created with ChatGPT	2	Bronze
RUA	Summarised texts validated by our institution	3	Silver
SUA	Simplified texts validated by our institution	3	Silver
LF	Easy-to-read documents created by APSA	4	Gold
FAC	Facilitated texts created by APSA	4	Gold

Table 1: Summary of the Texts Created for the CLEARSIM Corpus

instances, which were split into 749 for training, 83 for validation and hyper-parameter tuning, and 93 for testing.

As the base model, we utilise *flax-community/spanish-t5-small*[7]. This model was trained on the large Spanish corpus provided by Cañete et al. (2020). Hyper-parameters were set taking into consideration *oskrmiguel/mt5-simplification-spanish*[8], which is a model for text simplification, although at sentence-level. We employed a learning rate of $2e-5$, weight decay of 0.01, and per device batch size of 8. The other hyper-parameters were set to defaults, training up to 10 epochs.

Evaluation over the validation set using a default generation strategy yielded SARI of 30.45, and BERT score F1 (average) of 0.66 for the best model (9th epoch).

When using the models for generation, we set beam search with 10 beams, with a repetition penalty of 1.2 as in Keskar et al. (2019) to generate from 0.8 to 1.1 the original text length.

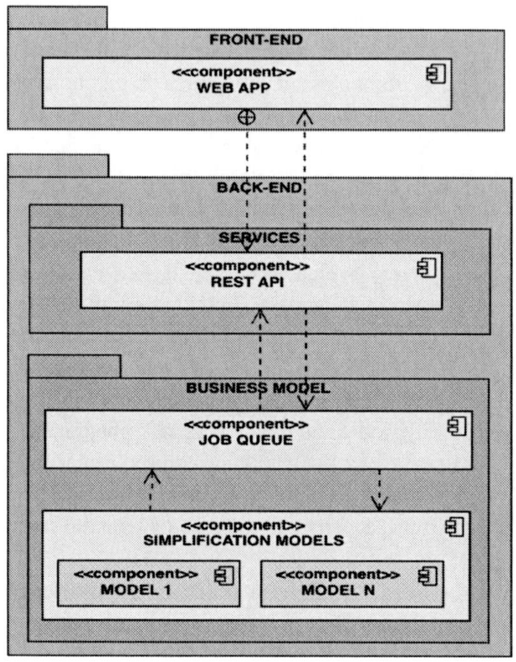

Figure 1: Architecture of Simple.Text Tool

5.2.2 Implementation Details

The tool implements a server-client architecture with the primary objective of providing text simplification services that can be queried from different front-ends or other applications. Figure 1 depicts the main components of the architecture.

The Services component is implemented using Flask[9] as well as Celery[10] for the Job Queue. The Simplification Models component is backed by Hugging Face Transformers Library[11]. Currently, the Web App is a prototype allowing users to select the simplification model and subsequently submit the text for simplification. Figure 2 shows the interface.

5.2.3 Preliminary Tool Testing and Assessment

Experimentation is in a very preliminary stage. Despite presenting different flaws inherent to generative models, such as hallucinations or repetitive text, that need to be addressed, we are currently examining the resolutions (or lack thereof) of the different linguistic phenomena that can be learned from the corpus. It must be pointed out that the language phenomena identified do not have a single NLP solution but several simplification options.

Figure 2 presents the results from imputing

[7]https://huggingface.co/flax-community/spanish-t5-small

[8]https://huggingface.co/oskrmiguel/mt5-simplification-spanish

[9]https://flask.palletsprojects.com

[10]https://docs.celeryq.dev

[11]https://huggingface.co

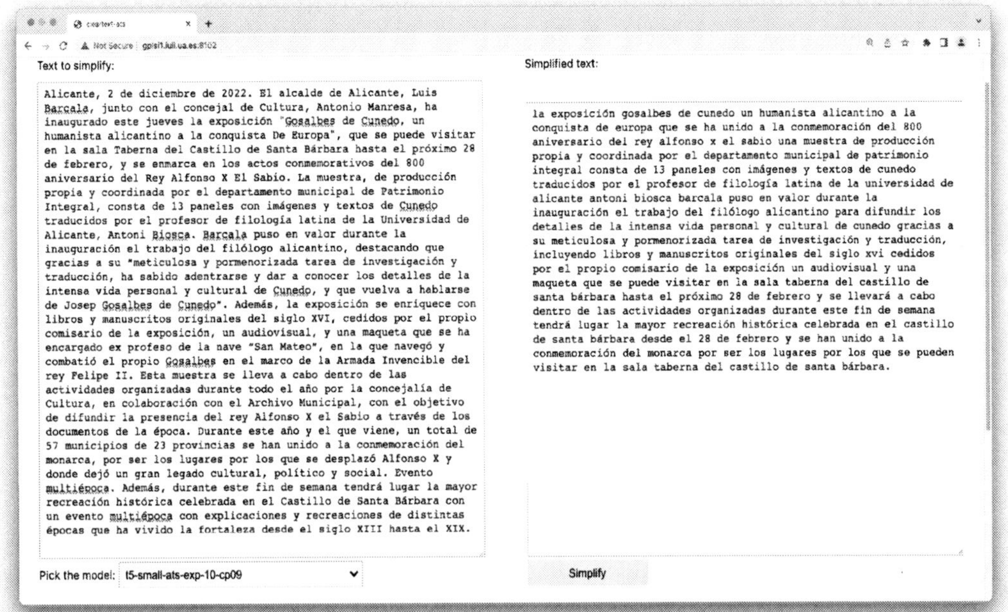

Figure 2: Simple.Text Tool Front End

text 65 from the corpus —which was randomly selected— and the output created by the system. The original text contains several complicated language phenomena identified in the easy-to-read guidelines. The examples presented below showcase some of them, but by no means are those the only complex language phenomena that could be found in that text:

- **Complex sentences:** sentence complexity is often derived from its length, due to the inclusion of appositions, relative clauses, coordinations and other constructions. This complexity can be remedied by splitting the sentence and, as a result, having less information per sentence. An example of a complex sentence from text 65 is the following: *El alcalde de Alicante, Luis Barcala, junto con el concejal de Cultura, Antonio Manresa, ha inaugurado este jueves la exposición "Gosalbes de Cunedo, un humanista alicantino a la conquista De Europa", que se puede visitar en la sala Taberna del Castillo de Santa Bárbara hasta el próximo 28 de febrero, y se enmarca en los actos conmemorativos del 800 aniversario del Rey Alfonso X El Sabio.*

- **Complex enumerations:** In the following example, even though there are not many elements enumerated (i.e. not more than three), additional information is included per each element enumerated. This aspect also increases the complexity level of the enumeration. *[...] se enriquece con libros y manuscritos originales del siglo XVI, cedidos por el propio comisario de la exposición, un audiovisual, y una maqueta que se ha encargado ex profeso de la nave "San Mateo", en la que navegó y combatió el propio Gosalbes en el marco de la Armada Invencible del rey Felipe II.* A potential solution could involve including that additional information in separate sentences, thereby simplifying the enumeration and enhancing the overall readability of the text.

- **Complex vocabulary:** Expressions such as *poner en valor* or *llevar a cabo* could be substituted by more direct verbs such as *valorar/reivindicar* and *realizarse/hacerse*, respectively.

At the moment, as illustrated in Figure 2, the output is far from perfect and presents several issues. Even though there is a reorganisation of the information (e.g. the information about when the event is going to take place appears at the end), there is a total failure in maintaining punctuation and capitalisation in the output text (e.g. the entire text has no full stops and only one comma is present. Additionally, no capitalisations are maintained for entities). Furthermore, there is a loss of information (e.g. entities) and a patent repetition of source sentences without undergoing any simplification operation. Some sort of simplification has occurred in the first sentence: *la exposición gosalbes de cunedo un humanista alicantino a la conquista de europa que se ha unido a la conmemoración del 800 aniversario del rey alfonso x el sabio*. The subject and the additional information from the appositions, rather than being presented in an independent sentence, are elided.

This preliminary evaluation of the output was performed by the linguists in the group. Nonetheless, a comprehensive evaluation campaign, involving both human validators with cognitive disabilities and a control group of laypeople, will be conducted to assess the effectiveness of the Simple.Text tool once the project is more advanced. It is apparent that a significant amount of work remains to be done, given the preliminary nature of this test. However, this presents an opportunity for substantial improvements to be attained throughout the remaining duration of this project.

6 Expected future impact

The expected positive results from this project that will impact society are three-fold in nature: (1) scientific-technical, (2) social, and (3) economic.

6.1 Scientific-Technical Impact

Language technologies are at the cornerstone of Artificial Intelligence (AI) and are among those tools for which there will be the greatest demand in the next decade. Concerning the scientific and technical impact, our project focuses on researching and developing technologies for NLP to support the authoring of accessible Spanish content for public sector organisations that is intelligible to people with cognitive disabilities. Among the resources developed, which will pique the interest of NLP and AI research communities, are the following:

- Text summarisation, text simplification, lexical analysis, syntactic analysis, anaphora resolution, word sense disambiguation, and summarisation reports.
- The methods, models, resources, and systems that will be researched, developed, and deployed in the project.

6.2 Social Impact

The following positive social impacts for people with cognitive disabilities can be attributed to the fulfilment of this project:

- Facilitation of access to digital information to promote social, and educational inclusion.
- Reduction of the digital divide by identifying barriers that prevent people with disabilities from accessing information on equal terms.
- Promotion of cooperation between the technological and social fields, fostering the design of technological solutions that consider the needs of people with disabilities.
- Facilitation of the daily actions of people with disabilities and widening of inclusion and empowerment in Europe.
- Improvement in the quality of life of those with cognitive disabilities, more specifically, their access to educational, vocational, cultural, and social opportunities in Europe.
- Promotion of an independent life and the capability to realise personal goals.
- Facilitation of equitable access to a meaningful education.
- Promotion of active engagement of individuals in all decisions that have an impact on their future.
- Encouragement of participation in the benefits offered by cultural, recreational, and sporting activities.

6.3 Economic Impact

The development of this project yields the following positive economic impacts for individuals with cognitive disabilities:

- Facilitation of access to digital information to promote economic and political inclusion.
- Promotion of full labor inclusion within the 2040 goal by access to employment for those with cognitive disabilities, and improving productivity via facilitating the performance of work-related functions for those with cognitive disabilities.

- Inclusion and empowerment increase for people with cognitive disabilities in Europe
- Enabling participation in the services provided for promoting effective management of personal finances.
- Provision of equal access to and use of all facilities, services, and activities in the public sector organisations at local, regional, and national levels, such as filing tax returns, paying fines, and managing community charges, among others.

7 Conclusion and Future Work

As a preliminary conclusion, we are currently developing a simplification system in Spanish for people with cognitive disabilities. We are collaborating with APSA, an NGO comprising a group of experts in text simplification, in the creation of a corpus of simplified texts in Spanish. The outcomes of our project will not only contribute to the development of resources for public administration but also facilitate the simplification process for our collaborator, by enabling automated workflows, thereby eliminating the need for manual simplification in the first stage of the simplification-validation process. The resources created by this project will be available on Huggingface[12] and the group's GitHub[13].

Future work is planned in several directions. On the one hand, by improving the corpus. This can be done by increasing its size, the domains as well as the universe of linguistic phenomena covered in it. This may benefit the development of data-driven solutions for ATS at the document level. Also, more research is needed to either validate or reject our hypothesis. Building an automatic document-level text simplification system based on large language models appears to be a challenging task given the scarce number of antecedents. Besides the corpus, other strategies need to be explored such as pre-training the model for specific simplification operations or reinforcement learning from human feedback. On the other hand, concerning the tool, a more advanced user interface needs to be developed so as to provide the user with automatic-to-fine-grained control of the simplification process. For instance, allowing the user to adjust the level of simplification. Additionally, the tool also needs to comply with accessibility recommendations.

[12]https://huggingface.co/gplsi
[13]https://github.com/gplsi

Lay Summary

People with cognitive disabilities face challenges in understanding written language, such as grasping the real meanings of words, phrases, and expressions, as well as retaining information in lengthy sentences, to mention a few. In order to improve their situation, promote their autonomy, and offer unrestricted access to information, Natural Language Processing (NLP) technologies provide ways to automatically simplify texts for these individuals.

In the ClearText project, we are undertaking two important actions to help with the understanding of Spanish texts from the Spanish administration. Specifically, we are creating two resources: the CLEARSIM corpus and the Clear.Text tool.

Firstly, we are putting together a collection of texts —a corpus—, called CLEARSIM, and transforming them into simpler versions with the help of a non-governmental organisation called APSA. These simplified versions have simpler vocabulary and syntax than the original. We are aiming to have approximately 18,000 of these simplified texts by the time the project concludes.

Secondly, we are using a Large Language Models (LLM), a resource that identifies complicated language aspects and automatically simplifies them to create the Clear.Text tool. This model is trained and assessed using the CLEARSIM corpus we are compiling.

We are currently in the process of learning and testing to fine-tune the tool's performance. However, like many LLMs, it frequently makes mistakes such as repeating sentences from the original text without simplifying the complex aspects that we want. Additionally, it may even invent information that was not present in the original text, a phenomenon known as 'hallucination'. We plan to solve these issues and perfect the output text as the the project evolves.

This project has three main goals: first, advancing our understanding of language and technology; second, helping people with cognitive disabilities be more included in society; and third, making the simplification of texts more efficient economically.

Acknowledgments

This research was conducted as part of the ClearText project (TED2021- 130707B-I00), funded by MCIN/AEI/10.13039/501100011033 and the European Union NextGenerationEU/PRTR.

References

AENOR. 2018. Norma Española Experimental UNE 153101 ex. Lectura Fácil: Pautas y recomendaciones para la elaboración de documentos.

Suha Al-Thanyyan and Aqil M. Azmi. 2022. Automated Text Simplification: A survey. *ACM Computing Surveys*, 54(2):43:1–43:36.

Rodrigo Alarcón, Lourdes Moreno, and Paloma Martínez. 2021. Lexical simplification system to improve web accessibility. *IEEE Access*, 9:58755–58767.

Fernando Alva-Manchego, Louis Martin, Antoine Bordes, Carolina Scarton, Benoît Sagot, and Lucia Specia. 2020. ASSET: A dataset for tuning and evaluation of sentence simplification models with multiple rewriting transformations. In *Proceedings of the 58th Annual Meeting of the Association for Computational Linguistics*, pages 4668–4679, Online. Association for Computational Linguistics.

Eduard Barbu, María Teresa Martín-Valdivia, Eugenio Martínez-Cámara, and Luis Alfonso Ureña López. 2015. Language technologies applied to document simplification for helping autistic people. *Expert Systems with Applications*, 42(12):5076–5086.

Susana Bautista, Raquel Hervás, Pablo Gervás, Axel Bagó, and Javier García-Ortiz. 2018. Taking text simplification to the user: Integrating automated modules into a web browser. In *Proceedings of the 8th International Conference on Software Development and Technologies for Enhancing Accessibility and Fighting Info-exclusion*, pages 88–96.

Stefan Bott, Luz Rello, Biljana Drndarevic, and Horacio Saggion. 2012. Can Spanish be simpler? LexSiS: Lexical simplification for Spanish. In *COLING 2012, 24th International Conference on Computational Linguistics, Proceedings of the Conference: Technical Papers, 8-15 December 2012, Mumbai, India*, pages 357–374. Indian Institute of Technology Bombay.

Stefan Bott and Horacio Saggion. 2011. An unsupervised alignment algorithm for text simplification corpus construction. In *Proceedings of the Workshop on Monolingual Text-To-Text Generation*, pages 20–26.

Stefan Bott and Horacio Saggion. 2014. Text simplification resources for Spanish. *Language Resources and Evaluation*, 48(1):93–120.

Leonardo Campillos-Llanos, Ana R Terroba Reinares, Sofía Zakhir Puig, Ana Valverde-Mateos, and Adrián Capllonch-Carrión. 2022. Building a comparable corpus and a benchmark for Spanish medical text simplification. *Procesamiento del Lenguaje Natural*, 69:189–196.

José Cañete, Gabriel Chaperon, Rodrigo Fuentes, Jou-Hui Ho, Hojin Kang, and Jorge Pérez. 2020. Spanish pre-trained BERT model and evaluation data. In *PML4DC at ICLR 2020*.

Liam Cripwell, Joël Legrand, and Claire Gardent. 2023. Document-level planning for text simplification. In *Proceedings of the 17th Conference of the European Chapter of the Association for Computational Linguistics*, pages 993–1006.

Iria da Cunha Fanego, M Amor Montané March, and Luis Hysa. 2017. The arText prototype: An automatic system for writing specialized texts. In *Martins A, Peñas A, editors. EACL 2017. 15th Conference of the European Chapter of the Association for Computatinal Linguistics. Proceedings of the Software Demonstrations; 2017 Apr 3-7; Valencia, Spain. Stroudsburg (PA): ACL; 2017. p. 57-60.*

Isabel Espinosa-Zaragoza, José Ignacio Abreu Salas, Elena Lloret, Paloma Moreda, and Manuel Palomar. 2023. A review of research-based automatic text simplification tools. In *Proceedings of the International Conference RANLP-2023*. Accepted for publication.

Itziar Gonzalez-Dios, Iker Gutiérrez-Fandiño, Oscar M Cumbicus-Pineda, and Aitor Soroa. 2022. IrekiaLFes: A new open benchmark and baseline systems for Spanish automatic text simplification. In *Proceedings of the Workshop on Text Simplification, Accessibility, and Readability (TSAR-2022)*, pages 86–97.

Nitish Shirish Keskar, Bryan McCann, Lav R Varshney, Caiming Xiong, and Richard Socher. 2019. Ctrl: A conditional transformer language model for controllable generation. *arXiv preprint arXiv:1909.05858*.

Elena Lloret, María Teresa Romá-Ferri, and Manuel Palomar. 2013. Compendium: A text summarization system for generating abstracts of research papers. *Data & Knowledge Engineering*, 88:164–175.

Tania Josephine Martin, José Ignacio Abreu Salas, and Paloma Moreda Pozo. 2023. A review of parallel corpora for automatic text simplification. key challenges moving forward. In *International Conference on Applications of Natural Language to Information Systems*, pages 62–78. Springer.

Ruslan Mitkov and Sanja Štajner. 2014. The fewer, the better? A contrastive study about ways to simplify. In *Proceedings of the Workshop on Automatic Text Simplification-Methods and Applications in the Multilingual Society (ATS-MA 2014)*, pages 30–40.

Colin Raffel, Noam Shazeer, Adam Roberts, Katherine Lee, Sharan Narang, Michael Matena, Yanqi Zhou, Wei Li, and Peter J Liu. 2020. Exploring the limits of transfer learning with a unified text-to-text transformer. *The Journal of Machine Learning Research*, 21(1):5485–5551.

Luz Rello, Ricardo Baeza-Yates, and Horacio Saggion. 2013. DysWebxia: Textos más accesibles para personas con dislexia * DysWebxia: Making texts more accessible for people with dyslexia. *Procesamiento del Lenguaje Natural*, 51:205–208.

Horacio Saggion, Montserrat Marimon, and Daniel Ferrés. 2015. Simplificación automática de textos para la accesibilidad de colectivos con discapacidad: experiencias para el Español y el Inglés. *IX Jornadas Científicas Internacionales de Inverstigación sobre Personas con Discapacidad.*

Carolina Scarton, Gustavo Paetzold, and Lucia Specia. 2018. SimPA: A sentence-level simplification corpus for the public administration domain. In *Proceedings of the Eleventh International Conference on Language Resources and Evaluation (LREC 2018)*. European Language Resources Association (ELRA).

Matthew Shardlow and Fernando Alva-Manchego. 2022. Simple TICO-19: A dataset for joint translation and simplification of COVID-19 texts. In *Proceedings of the Thirteenth Language Resources and Evaluation Conference*, pages 3093–3102.

Sanja Štajner, Ruslan Mitkov, and Gloria Corpas Pastor. 2014. Simple or not simple? A readability question. *Language Production, Cognition, and the Lexicon*, 48:379.

Sanja Štajner and Horacio Saggion. 2013. Adapting text simplification decisions to different text genres and target users. *Procesamiento del Lenguaje Natural*, 51:135–142.

Sanja Štajner, Horacio Saggion, and Simone Paolo Ponzetto. 2019. Improving lexical coverage of text simplification systems for Spanish. *Expert Systems with Applications*, 118:80–91.

Renliang Sun, Hanqi Jin, and Xiaojun Wan. 2021. Document-Level Text Simplification: Dataset, criteria and baseline. In *Proceedings of the 2021 Conference on Empirical Methods in Natural Language Processing*, pages 7997–8013.

Wei Xu, Chris Callison-Burch, and Courtney Napoles. 2015. Problems in current text simplification research: New data can help. *Transactions of the Association for Computational Linguistics*, 3:283–297.

Towards Sentence-level Text Readability Assessment for French

Duy Van Ngo
CNRS - LORIA
Vandœuvre-Lès-Nancy, France
van-duy.ngo@loria.fr

Yannick Parmentier[1,2]
(1) Université de Lorraine - LORIA
Vandœuvre-Lès-Nancy, France
(2) Université d'Orléans - LIFO
yannick.parmentier@loria.fr

Abstract

In this paper, we report on some experiments aimed at exploring the relation between document-level and sentence-level readability assessment for French. These were run on an open-source tailored corpus, which was automatically created by aggregating various sources from children's literature. On top of providing the research community with a freely available corpus, we report on sentence readability scores obtained when applying both classical approaches (aka readability formulas) and state-of-the-art deep learning techniques (e.g. fine-tuning of large language models). Results show a relatively strong correlation between document-level and sentence-level readability, suggesting ways to reduce the cost of building annotated sentence-level readability datasets.

1 Introduction

Text readability assessment can be defined as the ability to automatically estimate the difficulty for someone to understand a given text. While it was primarily designed for selecting materials for textbooks (Dale and Chall, 1948) and based on statistical formulas modelling lexical and syntactic complexity, it has proved useful in many other contexts, such as evaluation of text simplification systems (Štajner and Saggion, 2013; Alva-Manchego et al., 2019), and has been extended to modern neural architectures (Martinc et al., 2021).

Depending on the context, estimating readability can take different forms (and rely on different scales)[1]. When aiming at assigning a textbook to pupils, a common scale corresponds to pupils' age. When aiming at assigning learning materials to second-language learners, a common scale corresponds to the Common European Framework of Reference (CEFR) for Languages (Council of Europe, 2002). In some contexts, assessing readability amounts to classifying a given text as simple or complex (e.g. when learning to assess readability on binary corpora such as the Geo-Geolino corpus for German (Hancke et al., 2012)).

Linear regression models developed for English (such as that of Flesch (1948)) were capable of capturing some degree of lexical and syntactic complexity. Some of these were later adapted to other languages such as French (Kandel and Moles, 1958). Still, some studies (e.g. (Richaudeau and Staats, 1981)) showed that they do not always correlate with field data.

Various attempts at using machine learning techniques for (mainly English) text readability assessment have been carried out since the seminal work of Si and Callan (2001), who combined statistical language models with surface linguistic features extracted from large datasets. One may cite in particular the work of Filighera et al. (2019) in deep machine learning, where authors developed specific word embeddings and neural architecture.

Readability assessment for French was revisited by François and Fairon (2012), who explored various statistical algorithms and experimented with several linguistic features. Recent advances in this domain include work by Blandin et al. (2020) who considered psycholinguistic features (e.g. emotional impact of texts), and by Martinc et al. (2021) who fine-tuned a pretrained BERT model for CEFR classification for French (Yancey et al., 2021).

As pointed out by Hernandez et al. (2022), a common bottleneck in machine learning-based French text readability assessment lies in the scarcity of useful (e.g. labelled) resources. We build upon their work to provide researchers with a tailored and open-source corpus while studying the relation between sentence-level and document-level readability assessment.

[1]Following the terminology used in machine learning / classification, we will refer to values of these scales as *classes*.

Proceedings of the Second Workshop on Text Simplification, Accessibility and Readability associated with RANLP-2023, pages 78–84,
held in Varna Bulgaria, Sept 7, 2023.
https://doi.org/10.26615/978-954-452-086-1_008

The main contribution of this work is thus the compilation of an average size (1,228 documents) freely available corpus for French as a first language readability assessment, which has been preprocessed to remove noisy data and used to perform sentence-level automatic readability assessment with state-of-the-art BERT architectures, giving results in line with those obtained at the document level (Hernandez et al., 2022).[2]

2 Existing Models and Datasets

In this section, we briefly discuss the existing readability models and datasets related to our work. These models belong to two main categories: readability formulas and (deep and non-deep) machine learning-based approaches.

2.1 Readability Formulas

There have been plenty of approaches to measure the reading difficulty of a text such as Flesch Reading Ease (FRE) (Flesch, 1948), Kincaid Grade Level (KGL) (Kincaid et al., 1975), and Gunning Fog Index (GFI) (Gunning, 1969), to mention a few. The mutual simplicity-centric characteristic of these methods comes directly from the authors as they called the formulas "yardsticks" (Flesch, 1948; Gunning, 1969). Being rather arithmetic, these methods hold on to constants and self-defined coefficients in the effort of fitting the outcome in a fixed range of values while making use of similar variables (e.g. number of syllables).

2.2 Machine Learning-based Approaches

Text readability assessment can be viewed as a classification problem (François and Fairon, 2012; Hancke et al., 2012; Vajjala and Lučić, 2018). While statistical models can be employed upon the extraction and quantification of linguistic features of a text for reading difficulty evaluation (François and Fairon, 2012), approaches using Large Language Models (LLMs) require less symbolisation of linguistic features and yet demonstrate dominant performance amongst the rest (Hernandez et al., 2022). LLMs, especially pretrained LLMs with BERT-like architecture have drawn attentions of users from a wide range of fields and practical usages. Having been pretrained on massive datasets, these LLMs with fine-tuning techniques achieved state-of-the-art results in many Natural Language Understanding tasks (Devlin et al., 2018) where the text readability assessment task manifests itself. The prospect of utilising fine-tuned pre-trained LLMs for text readability assessment is noticeable (Hou et al., 2022). Recent prominent encoders are proven to store linguistic features without explicit guidelines. Since the readability of a text is correlated with such features (including but not limited to lexical, syntactic, and semantic features), features contained in document embeddings are definitely valuable in the understanding of text complexity.

2.3 Datasets

Despite the fact that labelled datasets are crucial for classification tasks, the French language has experienced a shortage of such datasets for readability assessment under the L1 learner-centric theme.

Still, some French corpora dedicated to this task do exist. One may cite the corpus collected by Daoust et al. (1996) within the SATO-CALIBRAGE project aiming at assisting teachers in the selection and creation of adapted learning materials, and which consits of 679 texts from textbooks from primary and secondary schools in Quebec. François et al. (2014) developed AMESURE, a collection of 105 administrative texts automatically annotated into 5 readability classes. More recently, Wilkens et al. (2022) compiled FLM-CORP, a carefully curated corpora gathering 334 texts from Belgian textbooks of French literature, history, and sciences. Unfortunately, these corpora are not openly accessible due to copyright constraints.

Regarding open corpora supporting French, Hernandez et al. (2022) created three open corpora by collecting free books on the internet from the following sources: Je Lis Libre[3] (JLL), Litterature de Jeunesse Libre[4] (LJL), and Bibebook[5] (BB). Each of these corpora uses specific readability scales (having 3 to 4 classes). Altogether these corpora contain 998 texts. Classifications conducted using the corpora provision promising results, showing that document-level text readability assessment can be achieved using a fine-tuned BERT model with a macro F1 score from 69% on LJL to 92% on JLL, depending on the characteristics of each corpus.

[2]This work was financially supported by the French Scientific Research Center (CNRS) within the GramEx project.

[3]http://www.crdp-strasbourg.fr/je_lis_libre/

[4]https://litterature-jeunesse-libre.fr/bbs/

[5]http://www.bibebook.com/

3 Experimental Framework

In this work, we are studying sentence-level readability assessment for French. The readability scale we are using comes from the context of this work, namely the implementation of a computer assisted language learning environment for French L1 learners. We consider the five following levels (classes):

0 emergent readers
1 short and easy texts
2 long and easy texts
3 lower-intermediate texts
4 upper-intermediate texts

These levels are loosely related to the French primary school curriculum, and match the categories available in the online resource used to create our corpus (namely StoryWeaver, see below).

3.1 Corpus Construction

The target corpus is designated to be the consolidation of contents from French books available on the StoryWeaver[6] website under a creative commons licence. The website lists 1257 children stories in French language that belong to 5 readability levels, categorised as described in Table 1 (and which, as mentioned above, match our readability classes).

Level	Word count	Other descriptions
0	< 50	Familiar words, word rep.
1	$50 - 250$	Easy words, word rep.
2	$250 - 600$	Simple concepts
3	$600 - 1500$	Longer sentences
4	> 1500	Long & nuanced stories

Table 1: StoryWeaver level description

To back up the claim that simpler texts tend to be more repetitive, we computed repetition rates for each of these levels. Results are given in Table 2 below (level 4's lower repetition rate comes from its relatively small number of tokens).

Level	#uniq. lemmas	#tokens	Rep. rate(%)
0	852	4,076	20.90
1	4,919	63,255	7.78
2	8,776	157,372	5.58
3	10,318	192,137	5.37
4	9,014	128,440	7.02

Table 2: Repetition rate of unique lemmas

[6]https://storyweaver.org.in/en/

Data Retrieval The books are filtered by readability levels before their ID and level are extracted and stored in a PolaRS[7] dataframe. Afterwards, the URL to each story is constructed by concatenating the path with its ID. Thanks to Selenium[8] on Python, each story with its basic information, including title, author, level, and translator (optional, only applicable if the story is not originally written in French) are automatically scraped from the HTML documents and stored along with a local path to the downloaded PDF file.

Pre-processing After the removal of duplicated stories, there are a total number of 1256 stories of five readability levels downloaded. The PyPDF2 library is used to extract texts from the PDF files. To minimise the presence of unwanted texts such as authors' name, acknowledgements, credits, etc., the cover page of every book is ignored along with the last four pages since these pages do not contribute to the individual content of the book. Besides, to ensure the lowest rate of noises possible for the corpus, page numbers are excluded, along with sentences whose length is smaller than 4 tokens or greater than 28 tokens. Table 3 outlines key properties of the corpus as a result of the pre-processing step. We used the SpaCy library and its `fr_core_news_md` pipeline[9] for sentence segmentation and tokenization.

Level	#documents	#sentences	#tokens
All	1,228	52,168	545,280
0	84	700	4,076
1	424	7,903	63,255
2	421	16,672	157,372
3	215	16,748	192,137
4	84	10,145	128,440

Table 3: Corpus level-based x-counts

The resulting corpus, named FSW (for French StoryWeaver), is freely available under a Creative Commons CCBY4.0 license.[10]

3.2 Readability Assessment

We applied both traditional readability formulas and deep learning classification models to our tai-

[7]https://pola-rs.github.io/polars/polars/index.html
[8]https://www.selenium.dev/
[9]https://spacy.io/models/fr/
[10]https://gitlab.inria.fr/vngo/fsw-corpus

lored corpus as described below.[11]

Traditional Metrics Though French is not the target language for the KGL and FRE metrics, the scores do depict the complexity with regards to the average words per sentence and syllables per word. For the statistics concerning the mean KGL scores, FRE scores, token counts, and syllable counts, see Table 4 below.

Level	KGL	FRE	tokcount	sylcount
0	-3.23	127.69	48.52	48.19
1	-0.50	113.60	149.19	152.54
2	1.05	105.25	373.80	404.34
3	2.19	100.46	893.66	995.62
4	2.76	97.50	1529.05	1772.29

Table 4: Basic metrics of each readability class

These results confirm that there exists a strong correlation between each pre-existing text readability level and the KGL and FRE metrics.

Fine-tuned CamemBERT for Classification To examine the distinctiveness of documents from different readability levels from a LLM perspective, we consider fine-tuning and evaluating CamemBERT models (Martin et al., 2020) with the corpus we obtained. We conduct two experiments using the `camembert-base` model[12], attempting to decipher the correlation between document-level and sentence-level readability (keeping in mind that the distinctiveness of classes is a key factor). Due to the insignificant volume of data compared to other classes, the documents with level 0 are ignored. If not explicitly mentioned, we fine-tune pretrained CamemBERT models with 5 epochs and the batch size of 64 using the `grele` cluster of Grid5000[13]. The fine-tuning process on this cluster with a single GTX 1080Ti GPU takes approximately 30 minutes.

Randomly Split Datasets In this first experiment, we examine the performance of a fine-tuned CamemBERT model for classification. We use SpaCy to collect the sentences from each document. These sentences are assigned the level from the document they are originally from. The dataset made of sentences labelled with their level is then randomly split into two subsets: train and test sets. We finetune the CamemBERT model on the train set and evaluate it on the balanced test set. The classification result is illustrated in Figure 1.

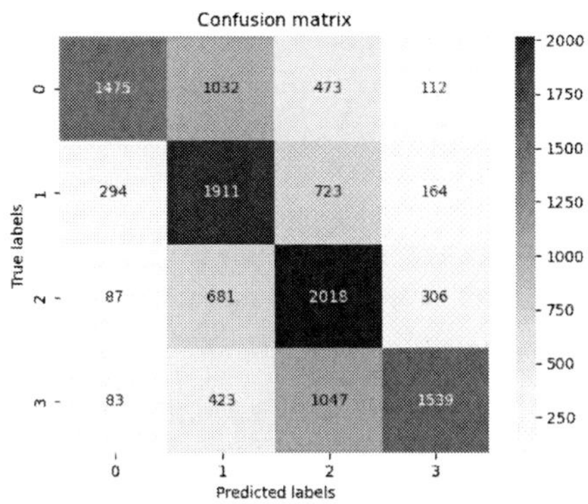

Figure 1: Classification results on randomly split test set

The fine-tuned model performs relatively well on the test set, and is able to classify most of the sentences to the readability level of the documents where they are extracted from. Indeed F1 scores range from 53% to 59% depending on the level (recall that document-level readability assessment on LJL, that is, a corpus of children's book comparable to ours, made by Hernandez et al. (2022) reached 69%). Table 5 shows the details of our classification attempt.

Level	Precision	Recall	F1 Score
1	76.07	47.70	58.64
2	47.22	61.80	53.54
3	47.36	65.27	54.89
4	72.56	49.77	59.04

Table 5: Classification scores on randomly split test set

When compared with the application of neural transformer-based models to document-level text readability assessment in English using datasets such as WeeBit, whose performance reaches an F1 score of 85% (Martinc et al., 2021),[14] these results may seem somehow limited, suggesting that our corpus is still relatively noisy. Another reason for our scores may come from the model itself. Indeed Martinc et al. (2021) used a model which was

[11]For a more exhaustive evaluation of comparable corpora against non-deep machine learning-based approaches such as SVM, see (Hernandez et al., 2022).

[12]`https://huggingface.co/camembert-base`

[13]`https://www.grid5000.fr/`

[14]Even better performances (99% classification accuracy) have been obtained for English by mixing handcrafted linguistic features with transformer-based models (Lee et al., 2021). We could not experiment with these hybrid models as they do not support French.

pretrained on documents of a somehow homogeneous type (books and wikipedia articles) while we used CamemBERT whose pretraining relied on much diverse documents (coming from Common Crawl). Furthermore our corpus is mainly made of children's books, whose content may be less close to the pretraining data. To put these results into perspective, one can note that Martinc et al. (2021) also applied BERT-like architectures on Slovenian school books, and obtained a F1 score of 41%. Eventually, the size of the model's input data (document-level vs sentence-level assessment) may also impact its performance.

Disjoint Datasets This experiment is conducted to test the generalisability of the model and eliminate the possible cross contamination that may lead to the model trying to identify documents using the given sentences rather than the readability level of the sentence itself. We split the dataset into two subsets, train and test sets, in which the documents in each set are disjoint. In other words, all the sentences in the train set belong to none of the documents in the test set. We fine-tune the CamemBERT model on the train set and evaluate its performance on the balanced test set. The classification result with regards to the confusion matrix is displayed in Figure 2.

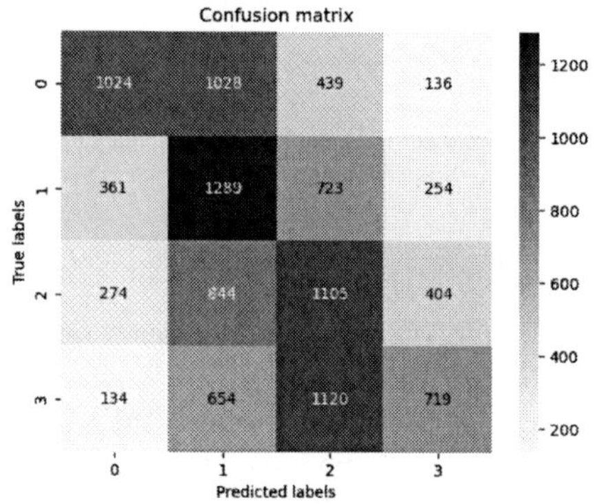

Figure 2: Classification results on disjoint test set

Furthermore, for the detailed classification results with regards to the precision, recall, and F1 scores, see Table 6.

Despite the lower scores compared to the model fine-tuned on the randomly split dataset, the model in this experiment reveals interesting common phenomena, such as significantly higher precision scores for level 1 and level 4 while maintaining

Level	Precision	Recall	F1 Score
1	57.11	38.98	46.33
2	33.79	49.07	40.02
3	32.62	42.06	36.75
4	47.52	27.37	34.73

Table 6: Classification scores on disjoint test set

relatively high recall scores for the two middle levels. Besides, there exists a higher confusion rate between sentences of adjacent classes than that of distant classes.[15] Except the prediction that labels many level 4 sentences as level 3, the model does portray a distinctiveness between levels, and maintains a consistent reduction of confusion rate as the differences between levels increase.

About Sentence-level Readability Assessment In these experiments, we took the document's level as a reliable level for the sentences contained in the said document. This may seem unreasonable as texts cannot be expected to contain only sentences of a given level. Recall that we performed some preprocessing on the input data to remove very short and very long sentences, and that our input data belong to a specific domain, namely children's stories. We think that in this context, the impact of this sentence labelling is weaker than in a general setting (i.e., when more diverse texts are used). Furthermore, we aim at studying the performance of readability assessment under such a heuristic. Our results tend to show than it remains reasonable considering the prediction performances on adjacent classes (i.e., when allowing for "minor" errors).

4 Conclusion

In this paper, we presented a freely available corpus for French sentence-level text readability, which was automatically extracted from online resources and evaluated against state-of-the art deep-learning techniques. Results show some correlation between document-level and sentence-level readability assessment, which suggests that extending training corpora could be done by considering labelled documents, thus saving annotation costs.

Acknowledgments

We are grateful to Claire Gardent and anonymous reviewers for their valuable comments on this work.

[15]Considering adjacent levels is also done by François and Fairon (2012) to distinguish minor errors from more serious ones.

Lay Summary

"Is it possible to automatically assign a given text a readability score, which would reflect the difficulty for someone to understand this text ?" is a question which has been discussed by researchers from various fields including linguistics, science of education, or computer science for decades. Being able to compute such scores could for instance help teachers to select learning materials depending on their target audience. First attempts at computing such scores were based on so-called readability formulas, where readability was a function of various linguistic properties (e.g. sentence length).

More recent work applied techniques borrowed from the field of machine learning to this task, reaching state-of-the-art results. Such approaches require labelled data, that is, texts whose content has been labelled with a readability score by a human annotator. Freely available such labelled data is still relatively rare for other languages than English, especially French.

With the growing availability of texts (and computing power), new techniques of machine learning called deep learning (or sometimes simply AI) arose. Such techniques use so-called deep neural networks, which correspond to very large parameterized networks capable of learning implicit patterns from input data. These techniques were in particular used to create large language models (LLMs) which are trained on extremely large datasets and can be adapted to specific tasks via an additional training phase called fine-tuning.

In this work, our objective is (1) to create an average size open dataset for French, which would associate sentences with a readability score, and (2) to study how well would a LLM fine-tuned with this dataset would perform.

While a similar study has already been done at the document level reaching relatively good results (80% in terms of average accuracy), here we focus on the sentence level. We aim at finding whether assigning sentences with their document readability level (e.g. in case of lacking sentence-labelled data) would still be a viable option. The experiments we ran tend to show that such an assignment does not prevent the fine-tuned LLM from performing well, in so far as the LLM makes relatively few strong errors (i.e., it rarely computes readability scores which are not close to the target scores).

References

Fernando Alva-Manchego, Louis Martin, Carolina Scarton, and Lucia Specia. 2019. EASSE: Easier automatic sentence simplification evaluation. In *Proceedings of the 2019 Conference on Empirical Methods in Natural Language Processing and the 9th International Joint Conference on Natural Language Processing (EMNLP-IJCNLP): System Demonstrations*, pages 49–54, Hong Kong, China. Association for Computational Linguistics.

Alexis Blandin, Gwénolé Lecorvé, Delphine Battistelli, and Aline Étienne. 2020. Recommandation d'âge pour des textes. In *Actes de la Conférence sur le Traitement Automatique des Langues Naturelles. Volume 2 : Traitement Automatique des Langues Naturelles (Articles courts)*, pages 164–171, Nancy, France. Association pour le Traitement Automatique des Langues. Age recommendation for texts.

Council of Europe. 2002. *Common European Framework of Reference for Languages: Learning, Teaching, Assessment : Case Studies*. Language Learning. Council of Europe Publishing/Éditions du Conseil de l'Europe.

Edgar Dale and Jeanne Sternlicht Chall. 1948. A formula for predicting readability. *Educational research bulletin*, 27(1):11–28.

François Daoust, Léo Laroche, and Lise Ouellet. 1996. Sato-calibrage : présentation d'un outil d'assistance au choix et à la rédaction de textes pour l'enseignement. *Revue québécoise de linguistique*, 25(1):205–234.

Jacob Devlin, Ming-Wei Chang, Kenton Lee, and Kristina Toutanova. 2018. BERT: pre-training of deep bidirectional transformers for language understanding. *CoRR*, abs/1810.04805.

Anna Filighera, Tim Steuer, and Christoph Rensing. 2019. Automatic text difficulty estimation using embeddings and neural networks. In *Transforming Learning with Meaningful Technologies: 14th European Conference on Technology Enhanced Learning, EC-TEL 2019, Delft, The Netherlands, September 16–19, 2019, Proceedings*, page 335–348, Berlin, Heidelberg. Springer-Verlag.

Rudolph Flesch. 1948. A new readability yardstick. *Journal of applied psychology*, 32(3):221.

Thomas François, Laetitia Brouwers, Hubert Naets, and Cédrick Fairon. 2014. AMesure: a readability formula for administrative texts (AMESURE: une plateforme de lisibilité pour les textes administratifs) [in French]. In *Proceedings of TALN 2014 (Volume 2: Short Papers)*, pages 467–472, Marseille, France. Association pour le Traitement Automatique des Langues.

Thomas François and Cédrick Fairon. 2012. An "ai readability" formula for french as a foreign language.

In *Proceedings of the 2012 joint conference on empirical methods in natural language processing and computational natural language learning*, pages 466–477.

Robert Gunning. 1969. The fog index after twenty years. *Journal of Business Communication*, 6(2):3–13.

Julia Hancke, Sowmya Vajjala, and Detmar Meurers. 2012. Readability classification for German using lexical, syntactic, and morphological features. In *Proceedings of COLING 2012*, pages 1063–1080, Mumbai, India. The COLING 2012 Organizing Committee.

Nicolas Hernandez, Nabil Oulbaz, and Tristan Faine. 2022. Open corpora and toolkit for assessing text readability in french. In *Proceedings of the 2nd Workshop on Tools and Resources to Empower People with REAding DIfficulties (READI) within the 13th Language Resources and Evaluation Conference*, pages 54–61.

Shudi Hou, Simin Rao, Yu Xia, and Sujian Li. 2022. Promoting pre-trained lm with linguistic features on automatic readability assessment. In *Proceedings of the 2nd Conference of the Asia-Pacific Chapter of the Association for Computational Linguistics and the 12th International Joint Conference on Natural Language Processing*, pages 430–436.

Liliane Kandel and Abraham Moles. 1958. Application de l'indice de flesch à la langue française. *Cahiers Etudes de Radio-Télévision*, 19(1958):253–274.

J Peter Kincaid, Robert P Fishburne Jr, Richard L Rogers, and Brad S Chissom. 1975. Derivation of new readability formulas (automated readability index, fog count and flesch reading ease formula) for navy enlisted personnel. Technical report, Naval Technical Training Command Millington TN Research Branch.

Bruce W. Lee, Yoo Sung Jang, and Jason Lee. 2021. Pushing on text readability assessment: A transformer meets handcrafted linguistic features. In *Proceedings of the 2021 Conference on Empirical Methods in Natural Language Processing*, pages 10669–10686, Online and Punta Cana, Dominican Republic. Association for Computational Linguistics.

Louis Martin, Benjamin Muller, Pedro Javier Ortiz Suárez, Yoann Dupont, Laurent Romary, Éric de la Clergerie, Djamé Seddah, and Benoît Sagot. 2020. CamemBERT: a tasty French language model. In *Proceedings of the 58th Annual Meeting of the Association for Computational Linguistics*, pages 7203–7219, Online. Association for Computational Linguistics.

Matej Martinc, Senja Pollak, and Marko Robnik-Šikonja. 2021. Supervised and unsupervised neural approaches to text readability. *Computational Linguistics*, 47(1):141–179.

François Richaudeau and Donna M. Staats. 1981. Some French Work on Prose Readability and Syntax. *Journal of Reading*, 24(6):503–508.

Luo Si and Jamie Callan. 2001. A statistical model for scientific readability. In *Proceedings of the Tenth International Conference on Information and Knowledge Management*, CIKM '01, page 574–576, New York, NY, USA. Association for Computing Machinery.

Sanja Štajner and Horacio Saggion. 2013. Readability indices for automatic evaluation of text simplification systems: A feasibility study for Spanish. In *Proceedings of the Sixth International Joint Conference on Natural Language Processing*, pages 374–382, Nagoya, Japan. Asian Federation of Natural Language Processing.

Sowmya Vajjala and Ivana Lučić. 2018. OneStopEnglish corpus: A new corpus for automatic readability assessment and text simplification. In *Proceedings of the thirteenth workshop on innovative use of NLP for building educational applications*, pages 297–304.

Rodrigo Wilkens, David Alfter, Xiaoou Wang, Alice Pintard, Anaïs Tack, Kevin P Yancey, and Thomas François. 2022. Fabra: French aggregator-based readability assessment toolkit. In *Proceedings of the Thirteenth Language Resources and Evaluation Conference*, pages 1217–1233.

Kevin Yancey, Alice Pintard, and Thomas Francois. 2021. Investigating readability of french as a foreign language with deep learning and cognitive and pedagogical features. *Lingue e linguaggio, Rivista semestrale*, 2021(2):229–258.

Document-level Text Simplification with Coherence Evaluation

Laura Vásquez-Rodríguez[1,2,*], **Matthew Shardlow**[4],
Piotr Przybyła[5,6], **Sophia Ananiadou**[2,3]
[1]Idiap Research Institute, Martigny, Switzerland
[2]National Centre for Text Mining, Department of Computer Science,
The University of Manchester, Manchester, UK
[3]Artificial Intelligence Research Center (AIRC), Tokyo, Japan
[4]Department of Computing and Mathematics, Manchester Metropolitan University, UK
[5]Universitat Pompeu Fabra, Barcelona, Spain
[6]Institute of Computer Science, Polish Academy of Sciences, Warsaw, Poland
laura.vasquez@idiap.ch, m.shardlow@mmu.ac.uk
piotr.przybyla@upf.edu, sophia.ananiadou@manchester.ac.uk

Abstract

We present a coherence-aware evaluation of document-level Text Simplification (TS), an approach that has not been considered in TS so far. We improve current TS sentence-based models to support a multi-sentence setting and the implementation of a state-of-the-art neural coherence model for simplification quality assessment. We enhanced English sentence simplification neural models for document-level simplification using 136,113 paragraph-level samples from both the general and medical domains to generate multiple sentences. Additionally, we use document-level simplification, readability and coherence metrics for evaluation. Our contributions include the introduction of coherence assessment into simplification evaluation with the automatic evaluation of 34,052 simplifications, a fine-tuned state-of-the-art model for document-level simplification, a coherence-based analysis of our results and a human evaluation of 300 samples that demonstrates the challenges encountered when moving towards document-level simplification.

1 Introduction

Text Simplification (TS) is the process of transforming text into a simpler variant that is easier to understand for wider audiences (Rello et al., 2013a; Collantes et al., 2015; Xu et al., 2015; Paetzold and Specia, 2016; Scarton et al., 2018; Cao et al., 2020). Simplifications can vary depending on the audiences' needs and expertise. For example, people with disabilities, such as dyslexia, have a better understanding of content with shorter word lengths (Rello et al., 2013b), however, this aspect is not necessarily relevant for non-native speakers (Paetzold and Specia, 2016).

In the past decade, most of the research efforts in automatic TS have focused on simplification at the sentence level, without considering the impact of TS at a document level. When multiple sentences in text are simplified, the overall quality of the text is affected (Siddharthan, 2003). Incorrect simplifications impact the overall text meaning and create disruptions to its structure (e.g., a sentence split without using adequate sentence connectors). Sentence simplification usually does not take into account the wider context to which sentences belong. Nevertheless, most of the practical applications of TS are motivated by the target audience needing to understand complete documents rather than isolated sentences. In general, sentences are evaluated within the scope of the sentence that is being simplified without considering possible disruptions that can happen between the nearby context (e.g., sentences left unconnected or unrelated sentences).

The generation and evaluation of document-level simplification[1] have been explored to a limited extent (Section 2). Meanwhile, the discourse features, such as cohesion, coherence and anaphora, have been widely considered in related fields (Maruf et al., 2021). We choose coherence to measure the relatedness of sentences in document-level TS, because of the availability of annotated data.[2]

Coherence is a logical and structured relationship between co-located sentences. This relationship can be at a local level between nearby sentences. This is called local coherence. In contrast,

*Work done as a PhD student at the University of Manchester, United Kingdom.

[1]We refer to "document-level simplification" to multiple sentences or paragraphs, given the nature of existing TS datasets beyond sentence level. We report average numbers per document in Table 1.

[2]In the future, the support of additional evaluation metrics could be needed. These would address possible issues that arise in a document-level scenario such as the overdeletion and reordering of sentences, which could also affect the coherent aspects of the text.

Proceedings of the Second Workshop on Text Simplification, Accessibility and Readability associated with RANLP-2023, pages 85–101,
held in Varna Bulgaria, Sept 7, 2023.
https://doi.org/10.26615/978-954-452-086-1_009

this relation could be observed at a broader level, such as sentences in each section of a scientific paper, where they belong to a common topic. We refer to this scenario as global coherence (Jurafsky and Martin, 2021). When a sentence is incoherent, the logical relationship between the events is disrupted, such as in Example 1 (Li and Jurafsky, 2017). This example is readable, simple, and grammatically correct, but there is no logical sequence of events or discourse elements.

Hui went to a restaurant
She ordered a pizza (1)
She read a menu and sat down

In this paper, we contribute to the transition from sentence-level to document-level TS (DocS), carrying out experiments at a paragraph level to understand the possible challenges of this setting. To achieve this, we enhance a state-of-the-art sentence simplification model to perform DocS with paragraph-level data from the general and medical domains. In addition, we evaluate our system outputs using DocS metrics, such as coherence, readability, and simplicity, to validate the suitability of simplifications when multiple sentences are present. We summarise our main contributions as follows:

1. The evaluation of local coherence at the document level using state-of-the-art neural models. This task has not been explored before in the field of TS.

2. A state-of-the-art model for simplification generation at the document level, fine-tuned with paraphrasing data.

3. A manual analysis of the results and a human evaluation of simplifications that highlights the challenges and limitations faced when performing TS at the document level, including the evaluation of coherence.

2 Related Work

In the past, TS at the document level has scarcely been explored despite the known need for simplification methods and evaluation metrics beyond sentence-level (Alva-Manchego et al., 2019). Nevertheless, recently, new directions have been explored leveraging existing methods and resources from sentence-level domain (Siddharthan, 2003; Alva-Manchego et al., 2019; Sun et al., 2021; Cripwell et al., 2023b; Sun et al., 2023; Cripwell et al., 2023a; Joseph et al., 2023).

Similarly for document-level corpora, there have been limited efforts to alleviate the lack of parallel texts at a document level (Xu et al., 2015; Vajjala and Lučić, 2018). Recently, datasets for the general (Sun et al., 2020; Laban et al., 2023) and medical (Devaraj et al., 2021; Joseph et al., 2023) domains have been proposed, aligning existing corpora such as Wikipedia and Cochrane reviews.[3] These resources include complex and simpler variants of a text, which are leveraged for TS. The creation of new parallel corpora for document-level simplification is also increasing beyond English (Rios et al., 2021; Hauser et al., 2022; Trienes et al., 2022; Aumiller and Gertz, 2022), which enhances opportunities for cross-lingual settings.

In relation to the evaluation metrics, sentence-level research has typically relied on the following automatic metrics: SARI (Xu et al., 2016) for simplicity, Flesch–Kincaid Grade Level (FKGL) (Kincaid et al., 1975) for readability and BLEU (Papineni et al., 2002) for grammaticality. However, BLEU, typically used in TS and summarisation, has been discouraged due to its poor performance in simplification operations, such as sentence splitting, and its negative correlation with simplicity (Sulem et al., 2018). Similarly, there are also limitations considered for FKGL (Tanprasert and Kauchak, 2021). However, we still use this metric in our work to compare with previous work. At a document level, Sun et al. (2021) proposed D-SARI evaluation metric that considers additional document-level penalties for system outputs (e.g., simplifications that outnumber the gold standard in sentence count).

2.1 Coherence as a Metric for Evaluation

Document-level evaluation is used for several NLP applications (e.g., machine translation (Maruf et al., 2021), summarisation (Fabbri et al., 2021) and simplification (Devaraj et al., 2022)), covering a wide range of discourse phenomena, such as anaphora, cohesion and coherence. In particular, coherence has been considered for applications including summarisation and essay rating, where the relationship (e.g., common entities and topics) between sentences is relevant.

[3] https://www.cochranelibrary.com/cdsr/reviews

The evaluation of coherence has typically been analysed using methods, such as entity-grids (Barzilay and Lapata, 2008; Joty et al., 2018), graphs (Mesgar and Strube, 2015, 2016) and Rhetorical Structure Theory (Šnajder et al., 2019; Guz et al., 2020). Unfortunately, manual assessment of coherence is challenging and laborious. Therefore, artificially augmented data have been used, where an ordered paragraph is considered coherent, but its randomly reordered counterpart is assumed not to be (Mohiuddin et al., 2021). To improve this practice, Lai and Tetreault (2018) proposed the Grammarly Corpus of Discourse Coherence (GCDC), which is manually annotated by experts and non-experts (i.e., MTurk workers).

Overall, TS at a document level has been barely explored, mainly because of the low corpora availability and challenges in evaluation. We introduce coherence as an automatic metric for the first time in TS, using existing state-of-the-art coherence models trained on professionally-created corpora. Furthermore, beyond the limitations of the existing evaluation resources for DocS and the difficulty it represents for evaluators to assess coherence, we share a detailed analysis of challenges encountered when using coherence as an evaluation metric.

3 Methods

We describe the adaptation of sentence-level TS methods into a document-level setting. We trained a sentence-level state-of-the-art TS model using paragraphs (Section 3.1) for discourse generation (i.e., longer, well-structured and logically simplified texts). There is no limitation on the simplifications that can occur at the document level, which means that we can expect modifications at a lexical, syntactic or semantic level, inferred from the training data. After texts are generated, we evaluate our simplifications (Section 3.2) through document-level metrics for simplicity, readability and coherence. We demonstrate our selected methods in Figure 1.

3.1 Model

Our proposed coherence-aware TS approach extends sentence simplification models for document-level simplification. We generate simplification of multiple sentences by retraining the sentence simplification model on longer passages (i.e., paragraph-level or document-level data). We select the Multilingual Unsupervised Sentence Simplification by Mining Paraphrases (MUSS) model (Martin et al., 2022), a multilingual model designed for sentence simplification. Although MUSS was designed to output individual sentences, its underlying architecture is the language generation model BART (Lewis et al., 2020). BART is capable of generating longer outputs if trained for a specific task (e.g., summarisation (Goldsack et al., 2022)) by changing its constraints, such as the number of tokens in the output.

3.2 Evaluation

One of the main challenges of document-level TS is evaluation. When simplification of multiple sentences of text is performed, the continuity of the discourse can be disrupted, affecting the semantic narrative of the text. Since there is no single evaluation metric to capture all possible variations caused by simplification, we relied on different metrics to approximate the performance of our model.

We measured readability using FKGL (Kincaid et al., 1975), simplicity using D-SARI metric (Sun et al., 2021) and coherence using a neural approach (Section 3.2.1). We clarify that despite the well-known criticism of simplification evaluation metrics, we used D-SARI and FKGL as a baseline for comparison with previous work. Also, we discarded SARI (Xu et al., 2016) and BLEU (Papineni et al., 2002) as evaluation baselines since they only deal with sentence-level TS. We expect that our initial efforts towards evaluation at a document level contribute to the development of TS.

3.2.1 Coherence

Since the aforementioned metrics (i.e., FKGL and D-SARI) do not measure any semantic component of the discourse structure, we selected coherence as a complementary evaluation metric. For the evaluation of coherence, we have selected a neural model trained on data annotated by experts as proposed by Lai and Tetreault (2018). We measured the coherence of the original text, the predicted simplification, and the gold-standard simplification to understand how coherence is affected during simplification. For this task, we selected the Paragraph Sequence (ParSeq) model (Lai and Tetreault, 2018). Its architecture consists of 3 stacked LSTMs. Each layer consists of sequences of word embeddings that represent sentences (layer 1), paragraphs (layer 2) and documents (layer 3).

The document represented in the last layer will be scored with a coherence label. This model con-

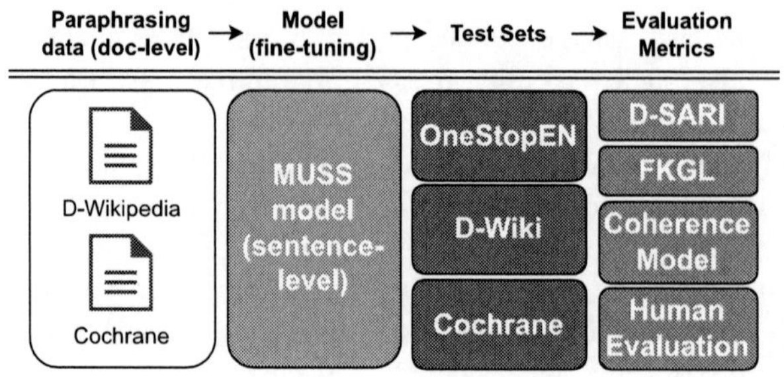

Figure 1: MUSS model fine-tuning with coherence evaluation.

siders the natural division of paragraphs (i.e. paragraph breaks) as an element to consider for the evaluation of coherence. The model was trained on the GCDC dataset (Lai and Tetreault, 2018), individually for each data source (i.e., Clinton, Enron, Yahoo and Yelp).

We adapted the model provided by the authors to our setting in order to evaluate our simplified outputs. We did not perform major modifications to the model; our changes were focused on the data processing stage to align with the expected format in the original model. The goal of this coherence model was to evaluate our predictions by assigning values to determine the quality of simplification in terms of coherence using the following scale: -1 (low coherence), 0 (medium coherence), and 1 (high coherence). Once the coherence model was trained, we scored the system outputs generated from our proposed baselines (Section 4.2).

The main limitation of these models is that although their training procedure is straightforward, the accuracy of the model is not high (Table 2). However, assessing coherence is challenging, even for humans (Lai and Tetreault, 2018). We still find coherence assessment valuable, especially when these models can help to discriminate between extremes (i.e., high or low coherence).

4 Experiments

We adapted three sentence simplification models (Section 4.2) for DocS by training them with paragraph-level data (Section 4.1). We evaluated our models with metrics that consider discourse factors to understand the impact on simplification when multiple sentences are involved (Section 4.3).

4.1 Datasets

We trained our sentence simplification models using corpora from the general and medical domains. These simplification models were trained using the training and validation sets. For the general domain, we used D-Wikipedia[4] dataset and for the medical domain, we used Cochrane[5], a paragraph-level dataset built by aligning the relevant sections of the Cochrane Database of Systematic Reviews (CDSR) abstracts and their plain language summaries. We show statistics of the selected datasets in Table 1.

With respect to the availability of datasets, document-level simplification resources are scarce. To alleviate this, we use "plain language"[6] as an alternative to the simple language. For Cochrane dataset, the plain language summary is a simpler version of the original, however, it may not be simple enough for many audiences. Tailoring simplification to a specific audience will require an additional step of personalisation, which is beyond this work.

Given our selected datasets and our training stage, we evaluated our model with the test sets available for D-Wikipedia and Cochrane. We also tested the models using the OneStopEnglish Corpus[7] to understand how well the model can generalise to external data. This dataset is divided into levels of complexity: Advanced, Intermediate and Elementary. We selected the samples from the Elementary level and Advanced level articles where the difference in complexity is more considerable.

For the evaluation of coherence, we used the released code and the dataset by Lai and Tetreault (2018) to train the proposed models since no trained models were made available. Lai and Tetreault (2018) introduced several coherence mod-

[4] https://github.com/RLSNLP/Document-level-text-simplification

[5] https://github.com/AshOlogn/Paragraph-level-Simplification-of-Medical-Texts

[6] As defined by Cochrane in their guide: https://training.cochrane.org/guidance-writing-cochrane-plain-language-summary.pdf

[7] https://github.com/nishkalavallabhi/OneStopEnglishCorpus

Dataset	Subset	Samples	Sentences	Sent/Doc	Words (W)	W/Sent
Cochrane	train	3 568	51 280	14.37	1 478 770	28.84
	valid	411	5 788	14.08	168 365	29.09
	test	480	6 984	14.55	197 480	28.28
D-Wikipedia	train	132 546	652 644	4.92	18 776 870	28.77
	valid	3 000	14 764	4.92	425 317	28.81
	test	8 000	40 062	5.01	1 155 679	28.85
OneStopEN	all	2 623	7 115	2.71	182 224	25.61

Table 1: Datasets statistics. We report the total number of documents, sentences and words.

Dataset	Train Samples	Test Samples	Accuracy
Clinton	1000	200	42.00%
Enron	1000	200	48.50%
Yahoo	1000	200	52.00%
Yelp	1000	200	48.00%
All	4000	800	40.50%

Table 2: Coherence datasets statistics and classification task accuracy for the ParSeq Model

els, trained on four datasets: Yahoo[8], Clinton[9], Enron[10] and Yelp[11]. We selected the Yahoo dataset of the GCDC corpus[12], which consists of 369 texts for training and 76 texts for testing. This corpus was created using the Yahoo Questions and Answers dataset, which is freely available upon request for research purposes. We also performed experiments using all datasets combined. However, we did not get any improvement with respect to the Yahoo dataset, which initially performed well on the original paper benchmarks. For the replication of this experiment, we trained the ParSeq model with the original train split and tested it on the held-out dataset. For the "All" category, we created a combined dataset with all the available train and test splits. We present the results in Table 2 with the coherence evaluation for each dataset. These coherence models were trained to classify texts in low, medium and high coherence. For our experiments, we classified the outputs of the simplification models and report the normalised scores for simplification assessment as described in Section 4.3.

4.2 Models

We adapted the MUSS model (Martin et al., 2022) to generate document-level simplifications by removing sentence-level constraints (i.e., token limits for the output). We also updated the existing sentence-level evaluation of the original model to document-level, using the document-level evaluation metric D-SARI and the test sets from D-Wikipedia and Cochrane instead of SARI metric and ASSET (Alva-Manchego et al., 2020).[13]

The original MUSS model was fine-tuned in multiple datasets and languages. Among these available models, we selected the *Mined* model as a baseline, which was trained using mined paraphrases from the CCNet (Wenzek et al., 2020), a subset of an open source snapshot of the WWW. The model was trained with multiple sequences (i.e., groups of sentences with less than 300 characters) and it was designed to perform at a sentence level, which will make it a useful reference to compare to the document-level counterparts. This model is openly available,[14] avoiding the need to replicate the training stage. We decided not to use the *Mined+WikiLarge* model, since it was trained on a sentence-level dataset Wikilarge (Zhang and Lapata, 2017), which diverges from our objective of document-level TS.

On the basis of these resources, we tested the following combinations:

- **Mined+D-Wikipedia**: *Mined* model fine-tuned with D-Wikipedia train and validation sets.
- **Mined+Cochrane**: *Mined* model fine-tuned with Cochrane train and validation sets.

[8] L6 - Yahoo! Answers Comprehensive Questions and Answers version 1.0 (multi part):https://webscope.sandbox.yahoo.com/catalog.php?datatype=l

[9] https://foia.state.gov/Search/Results.aspx?collection=Clinton_Email

[10] https://www.cs.cmu.edu/~./enron/

[11] https://www.yelp.com/dataset

[12] https://github.com/aylai/GCDC-corpus

[13] We make our code available in Github: https://github.com/lmvasque/ts-coherence

[14] https://github.com/facebookresearch/muss

- **Mined+D-Wikipedia+Cochrane**: *Mined+D-Wikipedia* model fine-tuned with Cochrane train and validation sets.

4.2.1 Training Details

We performed our training using 1 NVIDIA HGX A100 SXM4 80GB GPU and the same hyperparameters as in the original work by Martin et al. (2022). Training for the Cochrane and D-Wikipedia datasets took 1.3 days and 4 hours respectively. We used this hardware for convenience and due to time constraints, but these jobs can be replicated using a GPU with 32 GB of RAM.

4.3 Evaluation

We evaluated our models using readability, simplicity and coherence evaluation metrics. To calculate FKGL scores, we used the textstat[15] Python package. For D-SARI, we adapted the available code to score our simplification outputs, since the original code evaluates a single text and its gold standard at the same time. In addition, we also analysed the lengths of our predictions and references to further understand the impact on the D-SARI evaluation metric.

Finally, we evaluated coherence before and after simplification. The original GCDC corpus coherence ratings were given using the values of 1 (high), 2 (medium), or 3 (low). We used normalised coherence scores as follows: 1 for high coherence, 0 for medium coherence and -1 for low coherence. We used this scale to make it easier to understand by humans, as it seemed more natural for us. This however does not affect any of the computational aspects of the work. The coherence scores were calculated individually for each sample, and we report the average value for all the samples in the test set as shown in Table 3.

5 Results

We evaluated the results for simplification quality (D-SARI) and readability (FKGL) in Table 4 and Table 5, respectively. We also included D-SARI underlying scores related to three simplification operations: keep (D_{keep}), delete (D_{del}) and add (D_{add}). Since D-SARI is a relatively recent simplification metric, we performed a detailed analysis of the impact of the difference in lengths between predictions and references in the calculation of this metric. We aim to understand the underlying penalties from D-SARI, demonstrating how document-level TS models are likely to generate an output of different lengths, affecting the reliability of this metric. As a reference, we include our analysis in Appendix A.

In terms of readability, the FGKL metric (lower is better) in the model *Mined+D-Wikipedia+Cochrane*, showed the worst performance when evaluated using the Cochrane test set, with a score of 12.69. This result is mainly because the Cochrane articles are in the medical domain, where the vocabulary tends to be more complex and the sentences are longer. We also calculated the FKGL score of the gold reference corresponding to this simplification and we achieved a similar value of 12.43 for the Cochrane test set. The *Mined+D-Wikipedia* model showed the best readability results.

We selected the OneStopEnglish dataset as an external dataset for model generalisation. As shown in Figure 2f in the Appendix, almost all predictions are shorter than the gold standard simplification. Therefore, all values for D_{add} are low, due to the penalty of LP_1. In terms of readability, all models evaluated with OneStopEnglish test set showed better performance compared to Cochrane test set.

We evaluated our selected measure of coherence in our models' predictions, including comparisons between the inputs (complex), predictions (simple) and gold-standard simplifications. As shown in Table 3, our coherence predictions in OneStopEnglish, D-Wikipedia and Cochrane texts are affected by simplification. For OneStopEnglish and Cochrane, the coherence scores in all our predictions were lower than the complex text. In the D-Wikipedia test set, coherence values were lower only for the complex text for the model *Mined+Cochrane*. Since this test set was automatically aligned from Wikipedia, it may already have coherence limitations resulting from its original text.

Also, we note that for professionally written samples (OneStopEnglish) the coherence is significantly high, especially for the complex texts, which are more elaborated. Cochrane and OneStopEnglish gold-standard have a higher coherence, which may be related to the fact that these are written by professional authors, rather than created by crowdsourcing community as the D-Wikipedia dataset. Overall, gold-standard values

[15]`https://pypi.org/project/textstat/`

Model	Simple (prediction)	Simple (gold-reference)	Complex	Test Set
Mined	**0.167**	0.056	**0.222**	OneStopEnglish
Mined+D-Wikipedia	0.019			
Mined+Cochrane	0.0			
Mined+D-Wikipedia+Cochrane	-0.037			
Mined	0.041	-0.005	0.031	D-Wikipedia
Mined+D-Wikipedia	**0.098**			
Mined+Cochrane	0.028			
Mined+D-Wikipedia+Cochrane	0.041			
Mined	**0.047**	**0.061**	0.055	Cochrane
Mined+D-Wikipedia	-0.013			
Mined+Cochrane	-0.07			
Mined+D-Wikipedia+Cochrane	-0.053			

Table 3: Document level TS Models coherence evaluation. We evaluated each text with the following value of coherence: 1 (high), 0 (medium) and -1 (low). We report the average value for each model and test set.

Model	Test	D-SARI↑	D_{keep} ↑	D_{del} ↑	D_{add} ↑
Mined	OneStopEnglish	25.46	14.77	61.46	0.16
Mined+D-Wikipedia		24.67	11.71	61.85	0.46
Mined+Cochrane		**26.05**	**14.88**	**62.74**	**0.53**
Mined+D-Wikipedia+Cochrane		23.14	7.21	61.91	0.32
Mined	D-Wikipedia	26.67	19.56	**59.78**	0.68
Mined+D-Wikipedia		**32.51**	**27.43**	59.31	**10.77**
Mined+Cochrane		22.87	18.1	49.22	1.30
Mined+D-Wikipedia+Cochrane		22.39	12.74	53.27	1.17
Mined	Cochrane	**33.16**	17.09	**82.07**	0.33
Mined+D-Wikipedia		30.53	13.12	77.75	0.71
Mined+Cochrane		32.98	**18.06**	78.55	**2.32**
Mined+D-Wikipedia+Cochrane		32.14	16.20	78.55	1.68

Table 4: Document-level evaluation using D-SARI (complex, simple and reference).

are also higher than most of our predictions, except for D-Wikipedia, which again, is likely to have noisy alignments (e.g., no simplification, incorrect complex-simple pairs), affecting its coherence.

5.1 Manual Analysis of Coherence

To analyse complex, reference, and simplified sentences, we automatically scored 34,052 simplifications from all baselines using our selected coherence model. We summarised the scores of the evaluated texts in Table 3. Then, we performed a manual review of ~50 samples with the goal of evidencing possible coherence issues. We selected texts that were negatively affected by the simplification process. A total of 12,585 samples were ranked as "Low" coherence. Additionally, we verified that their complex counterparts had a "Medium" or "High" coherence to ensure that it was not originally incoherent. This analysis was manually performed by the first author of this paper.

Our analysis confirmed the difficulty of distinguishing outputs between high coherence and medium coherence, as explained by Lai and Tetreault (2018). In some cases, the models may also assign low scores to complex sentences and references. This may be due to the fact that most of these texts are automatically aligned (except for OneStopEnglish) and also, because of the fair accuracy of the coherence model as shown in Table 2. Additionally, to support our findings, we analysed a set of low-coherence samples to highlight the potential issues related to coherence that can occur after simplification. We compared a set of complex sentences with their simple counterparts generated by the proposed simplification systems. We report below our analysis of the selected samples, including a summary of the coherence issues found, as shown in Table 6.

1. **Unconnected content:** content that differs from the original topic of the complex text. In Example 1 there is a 'review' or 'evaluation' which has no connection with the biography of the Nepalese actor. Also, in the first sentence in Example 3 it is not clear whether males earn more than women (when the original and remaining text state otherwise). These pitfalls are also referred to in TS research as factuality

Model	Test	$FKGL_c \downarrow$	$FKGL_s \downarrow$	$FKGL_r \downarrow$
Mined	OneStopEnglish	10.71	10.84	7.89
Mined+D-Wikipedia			10.51	
Mined+Cochrane			**9.84**	
Mined+D-Wikipedia+Cochrane			9.91	
Mined	D-Wikipedia	**10.14**	9.60	**7.10**
Mined+D-Wikipedia			**7.95**	
Mined+Cochrane			9.81	
Mined+D-Wikipedia+Cochrane			9.53	
Mined	Cochrane	10.40	12.24	12.43
Mined+D-Wikipedia			**11.37**	
Mined+Cochrane			12.00	
Mined+D-Wikipedia+Cochrane			12.69	

Table 5: Document-level evaluation using FKGL (complex, simple and reference).

Example #	Issue	Model	Test Set
1	unconnected ideas, words or phrase repetition	Mined+D-Wiki+Cochrane	D-Wikipedia
2	change in sentence order	Mined+D-Wiki	
3	unconnected ideas, words or phrase repetition	Mined+D-Wiki+Cochrane	OneStopEnglish
4	words or phrase repetition	Mined+D-Wiki+Cochrane	
5	unconnected ideas, lack of connectives, non-logical entities	Mined+D-Wiki	Cochrane
6	lack of connectives, words or phrase repetition	Mined+D-Wiki+Cochrane	

Table 6: Summary of coherence issues present in the manual analysis. We report the most representative issues found in Table 8 and 9, including information about the trained model and the test set used for evaluation.

evaluation (Devaraj et al., 2022) before and after simplification.

2. **Words or phrase repetition:** words or phrases can also show nonsense repetitions, such as "film film film" or "performed and performed" in Example 1 or 'in-human-induced climate' in Example 4. Similar situation for Example 6.

3. **Lack of connectives:** although sentences can have a related topic (i.e., topically coherent), they lack adequate connections between sentences. In Example 5 most of the sentences are introduced by "this is done", or sentences starting with "this". There is no fluent narrative in this text.

4. **Non-logical entities:** subjects or entities could be completely disconnected from the context, such as the word "motorage" in a clinical study (Example 5), lacking lexical coherence.

5. **Change in sentence order:** sentences in a text can keep their same content, but changing their original order and extracting them from the original context leads to less coherent ideas, such as in Example 2.

6 Human Evaluation

Due to the limitations of the coherence neural models, we further evaluate their performance against human criteria to better understand the existing gap with respect to automatic metrics. We performed a human evaluation of 300 samples of automatically simplified text, divided into 5 sets of 20 paragraphs; each set was annotated by 3 evaluators. For the evaluation, we recruited 15 annotators working within the NLP domain (staff and PhD students from the University of Manchester and Manchester Metropolitan University). We selected the *Mined+Cochrane* model evaluated in the Cochrane dataset and the *Mined+D-Wikipedia* model evaluated in the D-Wikipedia. We had a total of 50 unique texts for each model. We selected these models to measure coherence in both domains (medical and general) in their best setting (within their own test sets).[16]

As a result of our human evaluation, we noticed that texts from the general domain were perceived as more coherent than those from the medical domain. While some of our annotators had experience with texts from the medical domain, these are still significantly technical and seem incoherent for some of them. However, most of the texts from both domains were rated as high coherence. We also correlated the automatic scores for each of

[16]We explain in detail the proposed task in Appendix B

the evaluated texts. The correlation between automatic metrics and human evaluation was 0.029 and -0.085 for the general and medical domains.

The correlation between the coherence estimation of human annotators and the trained model is clearly weak.[17] The main reason is that the model has to operate outside its original domain: it was trained on documents written by human authors but was evaluated on the machine-generated text of simplifications. Designing architectures and training strategies for coherence assessment models that operate with good performance on substantially different data is a direction for future research.

7 Discussion

We trained the sentence-level MUSS model using paragraph-level data, evaluated with TS metrics and coherence. In our results, we observed the generation of longer sentences, in comparison to the original model. In addition, we saw an improvement in readability for the *Mined+D-Wikipedia* model using the D-Wikipedia test set compared to the other baselines. The *Mined+Cochrane* had the lowest performance, most likely since it belongs to the medical domain.

The reliable evaluation of TS remains a challenge. We noticed that the use of D-SARI evaluation is significantly affected by the penalties from differences in the number of words and sentences. This leaves other aspects of simplification unattended, mainly at a discourse level such as the generation of coherent, topically-related simplifications. When simplification is performed at the document level, there are more opportunities for elaboration (Srikanth and Li, 2021), but also, for shortening the content when it is explained in simpler words. Due to this, it is unlikely to find a strong correlation (i.e., equality in length) between the size of the predictions and the gold standard. This is one of the main weaknesses of traditional TS metrics (e.g., FKGL, D-SARI), which rely mostly on length aspect. Our analysis was done to demonstrate this limitation further and as a motivation for discourse-level evaluation metrics for TS.

The evaluation of coherence has shown new directions that could be explored to address this need. When simplification is performed beyond the sentence level, it disrupts the flow of ideas in the text and leaves sentences in paragraphs unconnected. As shown in Table 3, there is a decrease in coherence for both professionally and non-professionally written corpora for most of the models, which means simplification cannot be done without considering this aspect. In general, our samples were classified from medium to low coherence. Thereby, there is an opportunity to improve the coherence models to have more notable gaps and a more fine-grained analysis between the proposed categories. These coherence models could have alternative neural architectures, including larger annotated datasets by professional annotators.

As we mentioned earlier, coherence itself is a challenging factor to assess. This applies not only to automated evaluation methods but also to humans, especially to non-trained experts (Lai and Tetreault, 2018) when classifying average samples (e.g., medium level of coherence). However, there is value in classifying simplifications as an additional aspect to consider for document-level TS. By performing a comparison between our inputs, predictions and the gold standard we obtain a valuable notion of coherence in model evaluation. The evaluation of coherence is a first step, among the possible discourse elements that must be assessed during simplification, such as better readability (Martinc et al., 2021) and factuality (Devaraj et al., 2022).

8 Conclusion

In this study, we demonstrated that with the models and resources available, implementing discourse-aware simplification models becomes possible. We implemented a document-level model by extending a state-of-the-art sentence TS model and included different evaluations from a document-level perspective. The evaluation of DocS based on coherence is necessary, but it remains a challenge due to the subjective nature of this task. Nevertheless, the assessment of coherence represents a viable tool for detecting those simplifications that are unclear, inconsistent or lack a consistent narrative.

In the future, we expect to explore additional directions towards discourse elements such as cohesion and anaphora to support coherence evaluation for TS. We will also consider the implementation of alternative coherence models to improve coherence assessment and its generalisation for other domains within TS. Finally, we will consider baselines in which documents are simplified sentence-by-sentence to compare against our DocS systems, which consider context in the generation step.

[17]We include our annotator agreement analysis and their feedback in Appendix C.

9 Lay Summary

Text Simplification (TS) is a research area that makes text more understandable for wider audiences. A complex text can be transformed into a more simple variety, based on the needs of specific populations. These audiences include people with disabilities, non-native speakers or people with minimum expertise in areas such as healthcare, law and news. Text is simplified by changing difficult words, writing sentences in a more simple structure (e.g., shorter, avoiding passive voice) and explaining technical terms.

In recent years, simplification research has only been limited to the transformation of sentences. However, we could also make documents more accessible to the general public, such as the simplification of scientific papers, legal contracts and news, rather than just individual sentences. This is a challenging step, as there is limited annotated data by people trained to simplify documents. Also, the evaluation requires a lot of time and effort, and the automatic evaluation metrics are not reliable.

In this work, we proposed the SimDoc simplification system. This model combines different aspects of language such as simplicity, readability and coherence to achieve the simplification of documents. The aspect of coherence expresses the logical relationships between sentences from the same topic (e.g., a story or a news article). We contribute with our research by including a professionally annotated dataset adapted to different levels of readability. We also include a benchmark that evaluates large language models incrementally, starting with no data to larger sets of simplification examples. These large language models have been trained to automatically generate text, but they do not know how to simplify text until we show similar examples. Finally, we carry out a detailed analysis of the system outputs showing the limitations and future work of our solution.

The simplification of text considering simplicity, readability and coherence is encouraging, which motivates the research community to continue towards the direction of document-level simplification. Eventually, this will make knowledge more accessible and universal to wider communities. However, the simplification of documents is a challenging area of research. The evaluation of coherence can be improved using more professionally annotated data and from multiple domains. Although our method is tested in the news domain, it would not necessarily perform well in the medical domain. Also, the evaluation of coherence beyond the existing classification (low, medium and high) could be more granular, opening an opportunity to expand the benefit of this research to more audiences.

Acknowledgments

We would like to thank Nhung T.H. Nguyen for her valuable discussions and comments. Also, we thank Joel Tetreault for sharing the GCDC dataset and the related code. Laura Vásquez-Rodríguez's work was funded by the Kilburn Scholarship from the University of Manchester. Piotr Przybyła's work was supported by the Polish National Agency for Academic Exchange through a Polish Returns grant number PPN/PPO/2018/1/00006.

References

Fernando Alva-Manchego, Louis Martin, Antoine Bordes, Carolina Scarton, Benoît Sagot, and Lucia Specia. 2020. ASSET: A dataset for tuning and evaluation of sentence simplification models with multiple rewriting transformations. In *Proceedings of the 58th Annual Meeting of the Association for Computational Linguistics*, pages 4668–4679, Online. Association for Computational Linguistics.

Fernando Alva-Manchego, Carolina Scarton, and Lucia Specia. 2019. Cross-sentence transformations in text simplification. In *Proceedings of the 2019 Workshop on Widening NLP*, pages 181–184, Florence, Italy. Association for Computational Linguistics.

Dennis Aumiller and Michael Gertz. 2022. Klexikon: A German dataset for joint summarization and simplification. In *Proceedings of the Thirteenth Language Resources and Evaluation Conference*, pages 2693–2701, Marseille, France. European Language Resources Association.

Regina Barzilay and Mirella Lapata. 2008. Modeling local coherence: An entity-based approach. *Computational Linguistics*, 34(1):1–34.

Yixin Cao, Ruihao Shui, Liangming Pan, Min-Yen Kan, Zhiyuan Liu, and Tat-Seng Chua. 2020. Expertise style transfer: A new task towards better communication between experts and laymen. In *Proceedings of the 58th Annual Meeting of the Association for Computational Linguistics*, pages 1061–1071, Online. Association for Computational Linguistics.

Miguel Collantes, Maureen Hipe, Juan Sorilla, Laurenz Tolentino, and Briane Paul Samson. 2015. Simpatico: A text simplification system for senate and house bills. In *Proceedings of the 11th National Natural Language Processing Research Symposium*, pages 26–32, Manila, Philippines. National University.

Liam Cripwell, Joël Legrand, and Claire Gardent. 2023a. Context-aware document simplification. In *Findings of the Association for Computational Linguistics: ACL 2023*, pages 13190–13206, Toronto, Canada. Association for Computational Linguistics.

Liam Cripwell, Joël Legrand, and Claire Gardent. 2023b. Document-level planning for text simplification. In *Proceedings of the 17th Conference of the European Chapter of the Association for Computational Linguistics*, pages 993–1006, Dubrovnik, Croatia. Association for Computational Linguistics.

Ashwin Devaraj, Iain Marshall, Byron Wallace, and Junyi Jessy Li. 2021. Paragraph-level simplification of medical texts. In *Proceedings of the 2021 Conference of the North American Chapter of the Association for Computational Linguistics: Human Language Technologies*, pages 4972–4984, Online. Association for Computational Linguistics.

Ashwin Devaraj, William Sheffield, Byron Wallace, and Junyi Jessy Li. 2022. Evaluating factuality in text simplification. In *Proceedings of the 60th Annual Meeting of the Association for Computational Linguistics (Volume 1: Long Papers)*, pages 7331–7345, Dublin, Ireland. Association for Computational Linguistics.

Alexander R. Fabbri, Wojciech Kryściński, Bryan McCann, Caiming Xiong, Richard Socher, and Dragomir Radev. 2021. SummEval: Re-evaluating Summarization Evaluation. *Transactions of the Association for Computational Linguistics*, 9:391–409.

Tomas Goldsack, Zhihao Zhang, Chenghua Lin, and Carolina Scarton. 2022. Making science simple: Corpora for the lay summarisation of scientific literature. *In Proceedings of the 2022 Conference on Empirical Methods in Natural Language Processing*, page 10589–10604.

Grigorii Guz, Peyman Bateni, Darius Muglich, and Giuseppe Carenini. 2020. Neural RST-based evaluation of discourse coherence. In *Proceedings of the 1st Conference of the Asia-Pacific Chapter of the Association for Computational Linguistics and the 10th International Joint Conference on Natural Language Processing*, pages 664–671, Suzhou, China. Association for Computational Linguistics.

Renate Hauser, Jannis Vamvas, Sarah Ebling, and Martin Volk. 2022. A multilingual simplified language news corpus. In *Proceedings of the 2nd Workshop on Tools and Resources to Empower People with REAding DIfficulties (READI) within the 13th Language Resources and Evaluation Conference*, pages 25–30, Marseille, France. European Language Resources Association.

Sebastian Joseph, Kathryn Kazanas, Keziah Reina, Vishnesh J. Ramanathan, Wei Xu, Byron C. Wallace, and Junyi Jessy Li. 2023. Multilingual simplification of medical texts.

Shafiq Joty, Muhammad Tasnim Mohiuddin, and Dat Tien Nguyen. 2018. Coherence modeling of asynchronous conversations: A neural entity grid approach. In *Proceedings of the 56th Annual Meeting of the Association for Computational Linguistics (Volume 1: Long Papers)*, pages 558–568, Melbourne, Australia. Association for Computational Linguistics.

Daniel Jurafsky and James H. Martin. 2021. Discourse Coherence. *Draft of December 29, 2021*, pages 1–25.

J. Peter Kincaid, Robert P. Fishburne, R L Rogers, and Brad S. Chissom. 1975. Derivation of new readability formulas (automated readability index, fog count and flesch reading ease formula) for navy enlisted personnel. In *Institute for Simulation and Training*, pages 1–49.

Philippe Laban, Jesse Vig, Wojciech Kryscinski, Shafiq Joty, Caiming Xiong, and Chien-Sheng Wu. 2023. SWiPE: A dataset for document-level simplification of Wikipedia pages. In *Proceedings of the 61st Annual Meeting of the Association for Computational Linguistics (Volume 1: Long Papers)*, pages 10674–10695, Toronto, Canada. Association for Computational Linguistics.

Alice Lai and Joel Tetreault. 2018. Discourse coherence in the wild: A dataset, evaluation and methods. In *Proceedings of the 19th Annual SIGdial Meeting on Discourse and Dialogue*, pages 214–223, Melbourne, Australia. Association for Computational Linguistics.

Mike Lewis, Yinhan Liu, Naman Goyal, Marjan Ghazvininejad, Abdelrahman Mohamed, Omer Levy, Veselin Stoyanov, and Luke Zettlemoyer. 2020. BART: Denoising sequence-to-sequence pre-training for natural language generation, translation, and comprehension. In *Proceedings of the 58th Annual Meeting of the Association for Computational Linguistics*, pages 7871–7880, Online. Association for Computational Linguistics.

Jiwei Li and Dan Jurafsky. 2017. Neural net models of open-domain discourse coherence. In *Proceedings of the 2017 Conference on Empirical Methods in Natural Language Processing*, pages 198–209, Copenhagen, Denmark. Association for Computational Linguistics.

Louis Martin, Angela Fan, de la Clergerie, Antoine Bordes, and Benoit Sagot. 2022. Muss: Multilingual unsupervised sentence simplification by mining paraphrases. In *Proceedings of the Language Resources and Evaluation Conference*, pages 1651–1664, Marseille, France. European Language Resources Association.

Matej Martinc, Senja Pollak, and Marko Robnik-Šikonja. 2021. Supervised and unsupervised neural approaches to text readability. *Computational Linguistics*, 47(1):141–179.

Sameen Maruf, Fahimeh Saleh, and Gholamreza Haffari. 2021. A survey on document-level neural machine translation: Methods and evaluation. *ACM Computing Surveys*, 54(2).

Mohsen Mesgar and Michael Strube. 2015. Graph-based coherence modeling for assessing readability. In *Proceedings of the Fourth Joint Conference on Lexical and Computational Semantics*, pages 309–318, Denver, Colorado. Association for Computational Linguistics.

Mohsen Mesgar and Michael Strube. 2016. Lexical coherence graph modeling using word embeddings. In *Proceedings of the 2016 Conference of the North American Chapter of the Association for Computational Linguistics: Human Language Technologies*, pages 1414–1423, San Diego, California. Association for Computational Linguistics.

Tasnim Mohiuddin, Prathyusha Jwalapuram, Xiang Lin, and Shafiq Joty. 2021. Rethinking coherence modeling: Synthetic vs. downstream tasks. In *Proceedings of the 16th Conference of the European Chapter of the Association for Computational Linguistics: Main Volume*, pages 3528–3539, Online. Association for Computational Linguistics.

Gustavo Paetzold and Lucia Specia. 2016. Understanding the lexical simplification needs of non-native speakers of English. In *Proceedings of COLING 2016, the 26th International Conference on Computational Linguistics: Technical Papers*, pages 717–727, Osaka, Japan. The COLING 2016 Organizing Committee.

Kishore Papineni, Salim Roukos, Todd Ward, and Wei-Jing Zhu. 2002. Bleu: a method for automatic evaluation of machine translation. In *Proceedings of the 40th Annual Meeting of the Association for Computational Linguistics*, pages 311–318, Philadelphia, Pennsylvania, USA. Association for Computational Linguistics.

Luz Rello, Ricardo Baeza-Yates, Stefan Bott, and Horacio Saggion. 2013a. Simplify or help? text simplification strategies for people with dyslexia. In *Proceedings of the 10th International Cross-Disciplinary Conference on Web Accessibility*, W4A '13, pages 1–10, New York, USA. Association for Computing Machinery.

Luz Rello, Ricardo Baeza-Yates, Laura Dempere-Marco, and Horacio Saggion. 2013b. Frequent words improve readability and short words improve understandability for people with dyslexia. In *Human-Computer Interaction – INTERACT 2013*, pages 203–219, Berlin, Heidelberg. Springer Berlin Heidelberg.

Annette Rios, Nicolas Spring, Tannon Kew, Marek Kostrzewa, Andreas Säuberli, Mathias Müller, and Sarah Ebling. 2021. A new dataset and efficient baselines for document-level text simplification in German. In *Proceedings of the Third Workshop on New Frontiers in Summarization*, pages 152–161, Online and in Dominican Republic. Association for Computational Linguistics.

Carolina Scarton, Gustavo Paetzold, and Lucia Specia. 2018. SimPA: A sentence-level simplification corpus for the public administration domain. In *Proceedings of the Eleventh International Conference on Language Resources and Evaluation (LREC 2018)*, Miyazaki, Japan. European Language Resources Association (ELRA).

Advaith Siddharthan. 2003. Preserving discourse structure when simplifying text. In *Proceedings of the 9th European Workshop on Natural Language Generation (ENLG-2003) at EACL 2003*, pages 103–110, Budapest, Hungary. Association for Computational Linguistics.

Jan Šnajder, Tamara Sladoljev-Agejev, and Svjetlana Kolić Vehovec. 2019. Analysing rhetorical structure as a key feature of summary coherence. In *Proceedings of the Fourteenth Workshop on Innovative Use of NLP for Building Educational Applications*, pages 46–51, Florence, Italy. Association for Computational Linguistics.

Neha Srikanth and Junyi Jessy Li. 2021. Elaborative simplification: Content addition and explanation generation in text simplification. In *Findings of the Association for Computational Linguistics: ACL-IJCNLP 2021*, pages 5123–5137, Online. Association for Computational Linguistics.

Elior Sulem, Omri Abend, and Ari Rappoport. 2018. BLEU is not suitable for the evaluation of text simplification. In *Proceedings of the 2018 Conference on Empirical Methods in Natural Language Processing*, pages 738–744, Brussels, Belgium. Association for Computational Linguistics.

Renliang Sun, Hanqi Jin, and Xiaojun Wan. 2021. Document-level text simplification: Dataset, criteria and baseline. In *Proceedings of the 2021 Conference on Empirical Methods in Natural Language Processing*, pages 7997–8013, Online and Punta Cana, Dominican Republic. Association for Computational Linguistics.

Renliang Sun, Zhe Lin, and Xiaojun Wan. 2020. On the helpfulness of document context to sentence simplification. In *Proceedings of the 28th International Conference on Computational Linguistics*, pages 1411–1423, Barcelona, Spain (Online). International Committee on Computational Linguistics.

Renliang Sun, Wei Xu, and Xiaojun Wan. 2023. Teaching the pre-trained model to generate simple texts for text simplification. In *Findings of the Association for Computational Linguistics: ACL 2023*, pages 9345–9355, Toronto, Canada. Association for Computational Linguistics.

Teerapaun Tanprasert and David Kauchak. 2021. Flesch-kincaid is not a text simplification evaluation metric. In *Proceedings of the 1st Workshop on Natural Language Generation, Evaluation, and Metrics (GEM 2021)*, pages 1–14, Online. Association for Computational Linguistics.

Jan Trienes, Jörg Schlötterer, Hans-Ulrich Schildhaus, and Christin Seifert. 2022. Patient-friendly clinical notes: Towards a new text simplification dataset. In *Proceedings of the Workshop on Text Simplification, Accessibility, and Readability (TSAR-2022)*, pages 19–27, Abu Dhabi, United Arab Emirates (Virtual). Association for Computational Linguistics.

Sowmya Vajjala and Ivana Lučić. 2018. OneStopEnglish corpus: A new corpus for automatic readability assessment and text simplification. In *Proceedings of the Thirteenth Workshop on Innovative Use of NLP for Building Educational Applications*, pages 297–304, New Orleans, Louisiana. Association for Computational Linguistics.

Guillaume Wenzek, Marie-Anne Lachaux, Alexis Conneau, Vishrav Chaudhary, Francisco Guzmán, Armand Joulin, and Edouard Grave. 2020. CCNet: Extracting high quality monolingual datasets from web crawl data. In *Proceedings of the Twelfth Language Resources and Evaluation Conference*, pages 4003–4012, Marseille, France. European Language Resources Association.

Wei Xu, Chris Callison-Burch, and Courtney Napoles. 2015. Problems in current text simplification research: New data can help. *Transactions of the Association for Computational Linguistics*, 3:283–297.

Wei Xu, Courtney Napoles, Ellie Pavlick, Quanze Chen, and Chris Callison-Burch. 2016. Optimizing statistical machine translation for text simplification. *Transactions of the Association for Computational Linguistics*, 4:401–415.

Xingxing Zhang and Mirella Lapata. 2017. Sentence simplification with deep reinforcement learning. In *Proceedings of the 2017 Conference on Empirical Methods in Natural Language Processing*, pages 584–594, Copenhagen, Denmark. Association for Computational Linguistics.

A Analysis of D-SARI penalties

In the Cochrane test set (Figure 2d), we noticed an increase in the length of the majority predictions (mostly between 100 and 200 words), compared the observations of the D-Wikipedia dataset (Figure 2e), in which the length range is more variable (from 0 to 200 words). In the D-Wikipedia test set (Figure 2e), there is a large group of predictions that are longer than the reference, but the majority are shown on the right of the red line, which means that the predictions are still shorter than the reference. This behaviour is even more evident in the OneStopEnglish (Figure 2f) test set, which has longer input articles, therefore, no predictions are longer than the reference. These patterns are also consistently repeated in the sentence-based analysis as well in Figures 2b, 2a and 2c.

With respect to Table 4 results, for D-SARI (where 0 is the lowest and 100 the highest value), we found that the *Mined* model has the highest score of 33.16 using the Cochrane (C) test set. As shown in Figure 2d, the *Mined* model predictions are even shorter than the gold standard simplifications, relative to other models. This leads to significant penalties (LP_1) in D_{add}, with a score of 0.33. Nonetheless, D_{keep} and D_{del} scores, 17.09 and 82.07, respectively, are less affected for the inverse case, where the gold standard is longer than the predictions (LP_2). Additionally, we can see that most of the datasets show a low score for D_{add}, for having smaller predictions than the reference. In the case of the OneStopEnglish corpus, the D-SARI scores are lower for all the models. This dataset has a larger difference between the simple and complex versions and the content is completely new to the models.

Regarding the sentence count, there is no clear correlation between the number of sentences in the gold standard and the predictions (i.e., they do not have the same number of sentences), directly affecting D_{keep} with SLP penalty in the difference in sentence numbers. The difference in sentence count affects the Cochrane test set for the *Mined+Cochrane* model (18.06) than the D-Wikipedia test set for *Mined+D-Wikipedia* (27.43) in D_{keep} scores. The Cochrane dataset is created from the alignment of an extended abstract (with multiple sections, e.g., background, objectives, results), whereas their plain language summaries may consist of a few paragraphs or a less structured format (Devaraj et al., 2021). Since its content may differ significantly, more penalties (SLP) are present in D_{keep} due to the high variability in the number of sentences.

Model	Test Set	Human	Auto	Corr.
Mined+ D-Wiki	D-Wikipedia	0.613	-0.060	0.029
Mined+ Cochrane	Cochrane	0.147	-0.100	-0.085

Table 7: Human Evaluation for general and medical domain, including automatic scores from the neural coherence models. The coherence score values range from 1 (high) to -1 (low). *Corr* stands for Correlation.

B Human Evaluation: Task Definition

The proposed task consisted in classifying texts into two categories. Unlike the automatic evaluation of coherence, we performed the evaluation using 2 categories (low, high) rather than 3 categories (low, medium, high). Previous research (Lai and Tetreault, 2018) has demonstrated the difficulty of modelling an intermediate class in human evaluation, leading to the inaccurate classification of texts, especially for those annotators that are not professionally trained. We requested our annotators to evaluate the coherence of 20 texts each in a spreadsheet. Similarly to Lai and Tetreault (2018), we also provided a definition for coherence to the annotators.

The annotators could ask questions anytime and provide feedback once the evaluation was completed, if any. We present our results in Table 7. While the evaluation was done using categorical values (high, low), we normalised our evaluation as with the automatic evaluation (1 for high and -1 for low coherence). We report the average values of each model.

C Annotator Agreement

We calculated the Fleiss' kappa values to measure the agreement between the annotators, using the pyirr[18] Python package. For the general domain, we had an agreement of 0.402 (*Mined+D-Wikipedia*), while in the medical domain, it scored 0.019 (*Mined+Cochrane*).

For *Mined+D-Wiki* texts, the agreement was fair, while Cochrane showed slight agreement between annotators. As mentioned in Section 6, the varied experience of the annotators in the different domains may have affected the final agreement on

[18]`https://pypi.org/project/pyirr/`

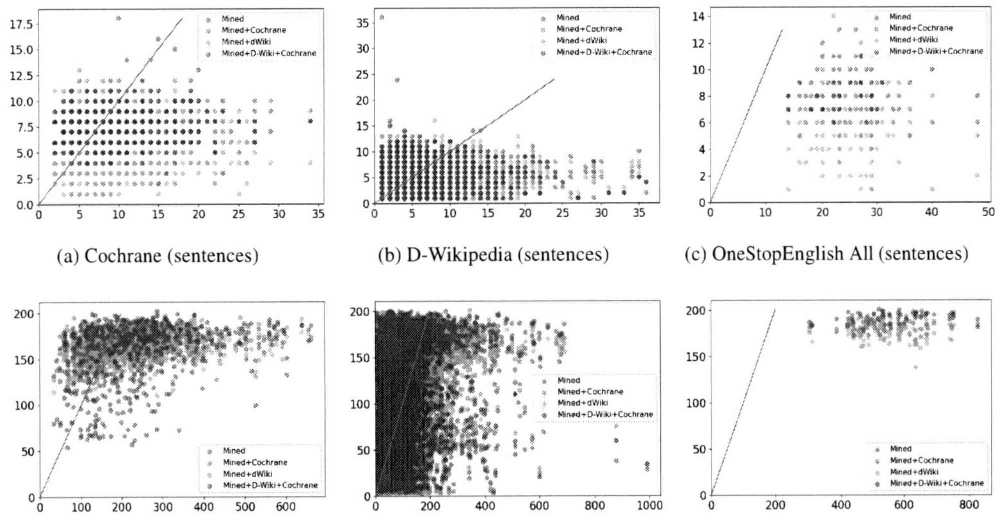

(a) Cochrane (sentences) (b) D-Wikipedia (sentences) (c) OneStopEnglish All (sentences)

(d) Cochrane (words) (e) D-Wikipedia (words) (f) OneStopEnglish All (words)

Figure 2: D-SARI metric is affected by this length of sentences and words in their predictions and gold-standard. In this Figure, we analysed the difference in the count of words and sentences between predictions (*y-axis*) vs gold-standard simplifications (*x-axis*). The red line marks the limit where observations have the same number of words or sentences. Predictions that are smaller than their gold-standard are shown to the right of the line.

the evaluations. A more segregated and detailed definition of the task (i.e., with examples) could also have helped on better annotators' accuracy.

While our human evaluation may have some limitations, we have learned lessons for the improvement of future evaluation. Overall, the annotators' feedback can be summarised as follows:

1. Provide concrete examples of high and low coherence texts with the coherence definition.
2. Include additional post-processing steps, which could help the annotators to focus on coherence only and not other aspects of language (e.g., grammar).
3. Give a more strict definition for coherence since different people can consider different coherence levels as satisfactory.
4. Keep texts short, since longer texts could be more difficult to evaluate.

We understand that coherence is challenging to evaluate. When using the current coherence model, we often see cases in which the differences in coherence scores are not significant between each other in our model outputs. Hence, with a minimal difference, untrained readers could be confused on defining coherence in a subjective way. Therefore, the evaluation and quality of the simplifications should be supported with a human evaluation.[19]

D Error Analysis

We performed a manual inspection of the evaluated samples to further understand the limitations of the automatic evaluation in comparison with the human evaluation. To that end, we split the samples into 2 groups: where automatic metrics agreed with humans and also, the cases in which they differ.

Since our systems are sentence-based pre-trained models, some of the outputs were quite short (1-2 sentences). These samples, such as Example 2, were mostly categorised as incoherent by the automatic metrics, although they formed coherent sentences (which was also confirmed with the human evaluation).

john caspar wild (1804-1846) was a swiss-american artist . he was a lithographer and painter . (2)

However, when collections of multiple short sentences were gathered together, there was an agree-

[19]We have included an error analysis of the evaluated samples in the Appendix D

Table 8: Simplification samples from evaluations, examples 1 to 3

Example 1: Complex vs system (Mined+DWiki+Cochrane) - D-Wikipedia test set
Complex: hari bansha acharya ( ) is a nepalese actor , comedian , singer and writer . he is known for his method acting . he is one half of the comedy duo maha jodi along with fellow comedian madan krishna shrestha . he is known for his performance as arjun in the 1997 patriotic drama film " balidaan " . he also wrote and performed in the film " shatru gatey " .
System: the purpose of this review was to evaluate **the role of hari bansha acharya in the 1997** film film film **balidaan and** performed and performed **in the film shatruy . he is known for his performance as arjun in the 1997 review** film film **balidaan was** performed and performed **in the film shatru gatey .**
Example 2: Complex vs system (Mined+DWiki) - D-Wikipedia test set
Complex: **tapestry is a form of textile art , traditionally woven by hand on a loom . tapestry is weft-faced weaving , in which all the warp threads are hidden in the completed work ,** unlike cloth weaving where both the warp and the weft threads may be visible . in tapestry weaving , weft yarns are typically discontinuous ; **the artisan interlaces each coloured weft back and forth in its own small pattern area .** it is a plain weft-faced weave having weft threads of different colors worked over portions of the warp to form the design.**most weavers use a natural warp thread , such as wool , linen or cotton . the weft threads are usually wool or cotton but may include silk , gold , silver , or other alternatives .**
System: it is a plain weft-faced weave having weft threads of different colors worked over portions of the warp to form the design . unlike cloth weaving where both the warp and the weft threads may be visible in the completed work , in tapestry weaving the weft threads are typically discontinuous .
Example 3: Complex vs system (Mined+DWiki+Cochrane) - OneStopCorpus test set
Complex: **male bosses are being paid bonuses double the size of those given to female colleagues in identical jobs – a disparity that means men enjoy salary top-ups of £141,500 more than women over the course of a working lifetime . the figures , released by the chartered management institute (cmi) , reveal that men in uk management roles earned average bonuses of £6,442 in 2012 compared with £3,029 for women . in the most senior roles , female directors received bonuses of £36,270 over the past 12 months , compared with £63,700 awarded to male directors .**
System: this review found that men in uk management roles earned average less of £3,029 for women **over the course of a working lifetime . in the most senior roles , female directors received greater rates of £36,270 over the past 12 months , compared with £63,700 given with male directors . however , men enjoy salary top-ups of £141 ,** more than women over the course of a working lifetime than women over the course of a working lifetime .

ment between the system and humans, such as Example 3. This case was mostly present in general domain test sets.

> the 1917 south american championship of nations was the second south american championship of nations tournament . it was held in montevideo , uruguay from september 30 to october 14 , 1917 . uruguay won the title after winning 1-0 over argentina . ángel romano was the top scorer of the tournament with 4 goals . uruguay was the defending champions . (3)

Finally, grammar and punctuation can also affect the coherence outcome. Texts such as Example 4, have an automatic rating of -1 (low), while the human evaluation had a full agreement of 1 (high).

> lionel blair (born henry lionel ogus ; 12 december 1928) is a british actor , choreographer , tap dancer and television presenter . he is best known for presenting " name that tune " in the united kingdom . (4)

For the medical domain, there was a significant disagreement between annotations. Texts can vary in complexity and length and the experience of the annotators as well. We did not find any specific pattern for coherence in the Cochrane test set, except for those already mentioned.

Table 9: Simplification samples from evaluations, examples 4 to 6)

Example 4: Complex vs system (Mined+DWiki+Cochrane) - OneStopCorpus test
Complex: low-income countries will remain on the front line of human-induced climate change over the next century , experiencing gradual sea-level rises , stronger cyclones , warmer days and nights , more unpredictable rainfall , and larger and longer heatwaves , according to the most thorough assessment of the issue yet . the last major united nations (un) assessment , in 2007 , predicted runaway temperature rises of 6°c or more by the end of the century . that is now thought unlikely by scientists , but average land and sea temperatures are expected to continue rising throughout this century , possibly reaching 4°c above present levels – enough to devastate crops and make life in many cities unbearably hot .
System: the aim of this review was to assess the evidence from randomised controlled trials to determine the effects of human-induced climate change in human-induced climate change over the next century , experiencing gradual sea-level rises , stronger cyclones , warmer days and nights , more unpredictable rainfall , and larger and longer heat groups according to the most thorough assessment of the intervention yet . the evidence is current to august 2013. the review concludes that there is now thought unlikely by scientists , but average land and sea temperatures are expected to continue through rising throughout this century , possibly reaching 4°c above present levels – enough to allow life in many cities involving hot .
Example 5: Complex vs system (Mined+DWiki) - Cochrane test set
Complex: we included two trials (116 women) comparing planned home versus hospital management for pprom . overall , the number of included women in each trial was too small to allow adequate assessment of pre-specified outcomes . investigators used strict inclusion criteria and in both studies relatively few of the women presenting with pprom were eligible for inclusion . women were monitored for 48 to 72 hours before randomisation . perinatal mortality was reported in one trial and there was insufficient evidence to determine whether it differed between the two groups (risk ratio (rr) 1.93 , 95 % confidence interval (ci) 0.19 to 20.05) . there was no evidence of differences between groups for serious neonatal morbidity , chorioamnionitis , gestational age at delivery , birthweight and admission to neonatal intensive care . there was no information on serious maternal morbidity or mortality . there was some evidence that women managed in hospital were more likely to be delivered by caesarean section (rr (random-effects) 0.28 , 95 % ci 0.07 to 1.15) . however , results should be interpreted cautiously as there is moderate heterogeneity for this outcome (i^2 = 35 %) . mothers randomised to care at home spent approximately 10 fewer days as inpatients (mean difference -9.60 , 95 % ci -14.59 to -4.61) and were more satisfied with their care . furthermore , home care was associated with reduced costs . the review included two relatively small studies that did not have sufficient statistical power to detect meaningful differences between groups . future large and adequately powered randomised controlled trials are required to measure differences between groups for relevant pre-specified outcomes . special attention should be given to the assessment of maternal satisfaction with care and cost analysis as they will have social and economic implications in both developed and developing countries .
System: motorage is a term used to describe a condition that affects two trials . it is a type of problem that affects two trials . this is done by putting a lot of conditions in a certain area . this is done to make a lot of changes in a certain area . this is done by looking at a certain number of places where they have to do not have to have a problem . this means that they have to do not have to be able to do with a problem . this is because it is not possible to have a problem that they have to do not have to have a problem . this is because it is not possible to have a lot of conditions that are not caused by people who have to do not have to have a problem . this is because it is not possible that some people have to do not have to know what they have to do . this is because people who have to do not have to know what they have to do .
Example 6: Complex vs system (Mined+Cochrane) - Cochrane test
Complex: six studies (including 142 participants) were eligible for inclusion . two compared three-times-a-week prophylactic administration with on-demand treatment in children with hemophilia . pooled results from these two studies showed a rate ratio of 0.30 (95 % confidence interval ; 0.12 to 0.76) for all bleedings and 0.22 (95 % confidence interval 0.08 to 0.63) for joint bleedings favouring prophylaxis . results on the number of patients with preserved joints after three to seven years of follow-up were not pooled due to significant heterogeneity . three of the remaining four studies evaluated hemophilia a ; one showed a statistically significant decrease in frequency of joint bleeds with prophylaxis compared to placebo , with a rate difference of -10.73 (95 % confidence interval -16.55 to -4.91) bleeds per year . two studies compared two prophylaxis regimens , failing to demonstrate an advantage of one regimen over the other in terms of bleeding frequency . the fourth study evaluated hemophilia b and showed fewer joint bleeds with weekly (15 iu/kg) versus bi-weekly (7.5 iu/kg) prophylaxis , rate difference -3.30 (95 % confidence interval -5.50 to -1.10) bleeds per year . non-significant increases in both inhibitor and infectious complications were observed in patients on prophylaxis , which occurred more often when using long-term venous access . there is strong evidence from randomised controlled trials and observational trials that prophylaxis preserves joint function in children with hemophilia as compared to on-demand treatment . there is insufficient evidence from randomised controlled trials to confirm the observational evidence that prophylaxis decreases bleeding and related complications in patients with existing joint damage . well-designed randomised controlled trials and prospective observational controlled studies are needed to establish the best prophylactic regimen and to assess the effectiveness of prophylactic clotting factor concentrates in adult patients .
System: this review included six studies (including 142 participants) comparing three-times-a-week prophylactic administration with on-demand treatment in children with hemophilia . the review includes six studies with a total of 142 participants . two studies evaluated the effects of prophylactic treatment on the frequency of joint bleeds with on-demand treatment in children with hemophilia . two studies compared two prophylaxis regimens , failing to demonstrate an advantage of one regimen over the other in terms of bleeding frequency . the fourth study evaluated hemophilia b and showed fewer joint bleeds with weekly . in the number of patients with preserved joints after three to seven years of follow-up were not pooled due to significant heterogeneity . three of the remaining four studies evaluated hemophilia a ; one showed a statistically significant decrease in frequency of joint bleeds with prophylaxis compared to placebo.

LSLlama: Fine-Tuned LLaMA for Lexical Simplification

Anthony Baez
Massachusetts Institute of Technology
Cambridge, MA, USA
acbaez@mit.edu

Horacio Saggion
LaSTUS / TALN / DTIC
Universitat Pompeu Fabra
Barcelona, Spain
horacio.saggion@upf.edu

Abstract

Generative Large Language Models (LLMs), such as GPT-3, have become increasingly effective and versatile in natural language processing (NLP) tasks. One such task is Lexical Simplification, where state-of-the-art methods involve complex, multi-step processes which can use both deep learning and non-deep learning processes (Sheang et al., 2022). LLaMA, an LLM with full research access, holds unique potential for the adaption of the entire LS pipeline. This paper details the process of fine-tuning LLaMA to create LSLlama, which performs comparably to previous LS baseline models LSBert and UniHD.

1 Introduction

Lexical Simplification (LS) is a sub-task within the field of Text Simplification (Saggion, 2017) in which complex words are substituted with simpler words while maintaining the meaning of the surrounding sentence (Shardlow, 2014). This is done to improve the comprehension of text for those who do not have sufficient reading proficiency, such as a language learner, young child, or someone with a learning disability (Saggion et al., 2022). Current LS models usually involve a multi-step process, including 1) the identification of complex words; 2) the generation of substitution words; 3) the selection of the substitutes based on context; 4) ranking substitutes by their simplicity; and 5) further context adaptation (Saggion et al., 2022). Recently, deep learning has been incorporated into some of these steps, such as a method that adapted BERT (Devlin et al., 2019), a bidirectional encoder, to generate substitution words (Qiang et al., 2020).

However, the development of generative LLMs, such as GPT-3 (Brown et al., 2020), presents an opportunity to drastically simplify this multi-step process by utilizing their ability to process and evaluate natural language. While these LLMs have significantly more parameters (110M for BERT vs. 175B for GPT3), and their training requires a substantially greater amount of computation than BERT-based models, this cost could be mitigated by fine-tuning a pre-trained LLM on a selected task. This fine-tuning could enable the model size to be drastically reduced while maintaining similar performance.

Large Language Model Meta AI (LLaMA) is a recently released generative LLM (Touvron et al., 2023). The size of its smallest variant, at 7B parameters, and its full research access provide a unique potential for adapting it to perform the LS task.

This paper details the novel fine-tuning of LLaMA on a Lexical Simplification task to create LSLlama. In order to determine if LSLlama is effective at the task, its performance was evaluated and compared to previously existing benchmark LS models that use deep learning, such as LSBert (Qiang et al., 2020) and UniHD (Aumiller and Gertz, 2022) using three testing datasets [1].

The structure of the following sections is as follows: Section 2 details related work in LS and deep learning. Section 3 details the method used to fine-tune LSLlama and evaluate the models. Section 4 details the results of this evaluation, and Section 5 discusses the implications of these results, error analysis, and limitations of the method. Section 6 concludes the paper and points to possible future work.

2 Related Work

The first method to incorporate deep learning into LS involved the use of neural networks to rank substitution candidates after being generated by a word embeddings model (Paetzold and Specia, 2017).

[1]The data and code are available at https://github.com/acbaez9/LSLlama/tree/main

Proceedings of the Second Workshop on Text Simplification, Accessibility and Readability associated with RANLP-2023, pages 102–108,
held in Varna Bulgaria, Sept 7, 2023.
https://doi.org/10.26615/978-954-452-086-1_010

A later implementation (Qiang et al., 2020) used BERT, a bidirectional encoder transformer model. BERT was used as a masked language model to predict the masked word in a sample sentence for simplification. The proposed substitution candidates were then ranked using a combination of LSBert, semantic similarity, and a frequency feature.

Recently developed generative LLMs such as GPT-3 (Brown et al., 2020) can be trained on billions of tokens and can process and respond in natural language. In the TSAR-2022 Shared Task on Lexical Simplification (Saggion et al., 2022), the highest scoring model on the English language task, called UniHD, used GPT-3 inference with six prompt variations to generate substitution candidates and a ranking algorithm that combined these candidate lists (Aumiller and Gertz, 2022). While this method outperformed all other BERT-based models, GPT-3 is not fully publicly available, and inference had to be done using paid API requests.

A recent generative LLM, LLaMA, (Touvron et al., 2023) was shown to achieve similar performance to GPT-3 in various NLP tasks at a fraction of the size with architecture improvements and a 1T token training set. Alpaca, a model that was created by fine-tuning LLaMA on 52K question-answer prompts, was also found to often behave similarly to ChatGPT in answering broad sets of questions (Taori et al., 2023).

3 Method

In order to evaluate LSLlama and compare it to LSBert and UniHD, LLaMA was first fine-tuned on an LS task to produce LSLlama. The specific version of LSBert used was adapted from its original version to act as a benchmark of an LS task (Štajner et al., 2022). All three models were then used to propose substitution candidates on three different datasets and evaluated on performance metrics.

3.1 Datasets

The dataset used to fine-tune LLaMA was the TSAR-2022 English gold standard dataset (TSAR) from Saggion et al. (2022), a multilingual shared LS task. There were three test datasets used to compare the three models: NNSeval (Paetzold and Specia, 2016b), BenchLS (Paetzold and Specia, 2016a), and LexMTurk (Horn et al., 2014). All datasets each contained hundreds of instances of a sentence, target word, and list of substitution candidates created using human annotators. While LexMTurk was sourced from Wikipedia, BenchLS was created by combining two other datasets, and NNSeval is a refined version of BenchLS.

All datasets were processed slightly to create ranked lists of candidate substitutes. For the TSAR dataset, repeated words were removed from its lists of candidates. In BenchLS and NNSeval, each candidate substitute had a number denoting the frequency that it was chosen by annotators, and this was removed.

3.2 Training

The 7B parameter variant of LLaMA was fine-tuned on the TSAR dataset using a modified version of the fine-tuning method of Alpaca (Taori et al., 2023). The fine-tuning involved feeding a prompt to the model which instructs it to respond with a list of synonyms that fit the context of the sentence. The target given was the corresponding list of substitution candidates, ranked by frequency, for that instance. This was done so the model could directly respond with ranked lists. The exact wording of the prompt went through multiple alterations to improve performance. The final version of the prompt used for fine-tuning, along with a example instance of an target word, sentence, and candidate list is in Table 1.

Prompt:
Respond with a list of different, simpler synonyms of the complex word in the given context. ### Complex Word: ***prototype*** ### Sentence: *This discovery helped to establish yet another spectral class even cooler than L dwarfs, known as "T dwarfs", for which Gliese 229B is the **prototype**.* ### Response:
Ranked Candidate List:
['model', 'sample', 'original', 'example', 'template', 'base', 'archetype', 'test', 'first']

Table 1: An example instance of the prompt and corresponding substitution candidate list used to fine-tune LSLlama

3.3 Inference

The generation parameters of the LSLlama inference were manually tuned. The most extensively tuned parameter was repetition penalty, which had considerable impact on the quality and nature of the output of LSLlama. When the repetition penalty

Dataset	Model	ACC@1	ACC@1@Top1	ACC@2@Top1	ACC@3@Top1
NNSeval	LSBert	0.4310	0.2469	0.3766	0.4519
	UniHD	**0.5732**	0.2803	**0.3849**	0.4435
	LSLlama	0.4519	**0.3096**	0.3808	**0.4686**
BenchLS	LSBert	0.6631	0.3703	0.5016	0.5748
	UniHD	0.7234	0.3057	0.4564	0.5436
	LSLlama	**0.7820**	**0.4700**	**0.5700**	**0.6460**
LexMTurk	LSBert	0.8300	0.3200	0.4300	0.4920
	UniHD	**0.8480**	0.4060	0.5560	0.6260
	LSLlama	0.8060	**0.4680**	**0.5740**	**0.6440**

Table 2: Results of models on the NNSeval, BenchLS, and LexMTurk datasets for Accuracy@1 and Accuracy@k@Top1

Dataset	Model	POT@3	POT@5	POT@10	MAP@3	MAP@5	MAP@10
NNSeval	LSBert	0.6946	0.7699	0.8619	0.2894	0.2180	0.1349
	UniHD	**0.7824**	**0.8619**	**0.9163**	**0.3661**	**0.2659**	**0.1629**
	LSLlama	0.7657	0.8536	0.8703	0.3233	0.2513	0.1425
BenchLS	LSBert	0.8396	0.8859	0.9225	0.4471	0.3341	0.2042
	UniHD	0.8751	0.9214	0.9483	0.4766	0.3552	0.2137
	LSLlama	**0.9420**	**0.9720**	**0.9760**	**0.5519**	**0.4329**	**0.2453**
LexMTurk	LSBert	0.9620	0.9680	0.9900	0.6044	0.4591	0.2865
	UniHD	**0.9700**	**0.9900**	**1.0000**	**0.6067**	**0.4638**	**0.2893**
	LSLlama	**0.9700**	0.9860	0.9880	0.5777	0.4556	0.2620

Table 3: Results of models on the NNSeval, BenchLS, and LexMTurk datasets for Potential@k and MAP@k

was too low, the model would respond with a long list of identical or very similar substitution candidates that would cause an error in the post-processing. When the repetition penalty was too high, the model would only output a few substitution candidates. Therefore, an optimal repetition penalty would not cause a post-processing error while allowing the responded list to reach a length of ten as frequently as possible. The optimal repetition penalty, to the nearest hundredth, was found by starting at a value of 1.00 and incrementally raising it until there was not an error in the post-processing after inference. If the repetition penalty for one dataset was found to be too low for another dataset, the tuning process was done again so the repetition penalty value did not cause an error for any dataset. The lowest repetition penalty value that did not cause an error was used for inference on all datasets, so that the same version of the model was used on all datasets. Regarding the prompt used for inference, it only differed from the prompt used in fine-tuning in that it asked specifically for a list of ten substitution candidates. LSLlama was eventually able to consistently output a single token that was a list of Python strings, so only minor post-processing was needed to correct occasional malformed strings and convert the output into a Python list. Other implementation details can be found in the Appendix.

3.4 Evaluation

Various metrics were calculated with the results of the tested models. These metrics were used in Saggion et al. (2022) to quantify the performance of models on the TSAR dataset.

Accuracy@1 (ACC@1): the percent of instances where the top-ranked substitute candidate is in the test dataset candidate list

Accuracy@k@Top1 (ACC@k@Top1): the percent of instances where at least one of the k top-ranked substitute candidates matched the top-ranked candidate of the test dataset

Potential@k (POT@k): the percent of instances where at least one of the k top-ranked substitute candidates is present in the test dataset candidate list

Mean Average Precision@k (MAP@k): a measure that incorporates the percent of k top-ranked substitute candidates that are present in the test dataset candidate list and the relative ranking of the proposed substitute candidate list

Values of k $\in \{1, 2, 3\}$ were used for ACC@k@top1, and values of k $\in \{3, 5, 10\}$ were used for Potential@k and MAP@k

4 Results

After evaluating LSBert, UniHD, and LSLlama on the test datasets, the results of the Accuracy@1 and Accuracy@k@Top1 metrics were compiled in Table 2, and the Potential@k and MAP@k metrics were compiled in Table 3.

Table 2 shows that for ACC@1, on the NNSeval dataset, LSBert scored 0.4310, UniHD scored 0.5732, and LSLlama scored 0.4519. On the BenchLS dataset, LSBert scored 0.6631, UniHD scored 0.7234, and LSLlama scored 0.7820. On the LexMTurk dataset, LSBert scored 0.8300, UniHD scored 0.8480, and LSLlama scored 0.8060. For ACC@1, in the NNSeval and LexMTurk datasets, UniHD is the highest scoring model, and on the BenchLS dataset, LSLlama is the highest scoring model. This signifies that UniHD's top-ranked substitute candidate is better than those of LSBert and LSLlama for the NNSeval and LexMTurk datasets, while LSLlama's top-ranked substitute candidate is the best for the BenchLS dataset. However, for ACC@k@Top1, LSLlama outperforms LSBert and UniHD on eight of the nine trials over all datasets. This shows that among the first three top-ranked substitution candidates, LSLlama generated candidates more likely to match the top candidate in all test datasets nearly every time.

In the POT@k values in Table 3, UniHD performed better than LSBert and LSLlama for all k values in the NNSeval and LexMTurk datasets, except for one tie between UniHD and LSLlama in POT@3 in the LexMTurk dataset. In the BenchLS dataset, LSLlama performed better than LSBert and UniHD in all k values. This indicates that on the NNSeval and LexMTurk datasets, UniHD is almost always able to produce the best substitutes over the whole list, while for BenchLS, LSLlama is able to produce better substitutes over the whole candidate list.

With the MAP@k values in Table 3, UniHD performed better than LSBert and LSLlama in the NNSeval and LexMTurk datasets. In the BenchLS dataset, LSLlama performed better than LSBert and UniHD in all k values. This result shows that UniHD generally proposes more relevant and better ranked candidates on the NNSeval and LexMTurk datasets, while LSLlama does this best on the BenchLS dataset.

5 Discussion

On the BenchLS dataset, LSLlama achieved the best scores on all evaluation metrics, so LSLlama consistently outperformed LSBert and UniHD on this dataset. On NNSeval, there were more mixed results in the ACC@k@Top1 metrics, with both UniHD and LSLlama having the highest score in different trials. However, for all other metrics on NNSeval, UniHD performed the best. On LexMTurk, LSLlama performed the best in the ACC@k@Top1 metrics, while UniHD performed as well or better than LSLlama on the other metrics. LSBert was always outperformed by either UniHD or LSLlama.

UniHD was better able to identify the top-ranked substitution candidate, as evidenced in its highest Accuracy@1 value, have a better ranking of candidates, as evidenced by its highest MAP@k value, and propose more relevant candidates when having multiple attempts, as shown by its highest Potential@k values on the NNSeval and LexMTurk datasets. However, on these datasets, LSLlama usually best identifies the test dataset's top-ranked candidate in the first few substitution candidates, as evidenced by its highest ACC@k@Top1 values on all but one trial. On the BenchLS dataset, LSLlama was best able to identify the top-ranked substitution candidates, have a better ranking of candidates, and propose more relevant candidates when having multiple attempts.

When looking at results overall, LSLlama always outperformed UniHD on one dataset. With the other two datasets, LSLlama outperformed UniHD on some metrics, and UniHD outperformed LSLlama on some metrics, with UniHD outperforming LSLlama more often. This indicates that, overall, UniHD and LSLlama performed comparably when looking at all datasets as a whole. Additionally, for all trials, at least one of these two models, UniHD and LSLlama, always outperformed LSBert, as LSBert was never the top scoring model on any metric.

5.1 Error Analysis

While using a generative LLM allows for drastic simplification of the LS pipeline, it can also lead to difficulty getting the model to respond coherently and as intended. Some issues and errors that were encountered are detailed below.

Variation in Output Length Despite including the specification of a list of ten substitute words in the prompt used for inference, LSLlama did not respond with a consistent number of substitution candidates. This likely occurred due to the generation method used, in which the list of candidates was generated using a single token, so there was no parameter that could directly control the length of the substitute list. The fine-tuning dataset for LSLlama also did not have a consistent length of substitution candidate lists. However, the average length of the candidate lists was around ten, and the fine-tuning and generation parameters were able to regulate the length of the response enough so that there was a difference in the results between the metrics with k = 5 and k = 10.

Prompt Stability A commonly-encountered weakness of generative LLMs is how subtle changes of the prompt can lead to dramatic changes in the nature of the output. A process of modifying the prompt and then performing inference to qualitatively gauge its effect was done in order to improve the efficiency of the prompt. Two of the changes that yielded the most improvement was specifying "different" and "simpler" synonyms in the prompt, which is reflected in the final prompt in Table 1. The lack of intuitiveness of this process made it time consuming and imprecise. For example, "Respond with a list of words that can replace the complex word" was changed to "Respond with a list of synonyms of the complex word". In this specific LS task, using the first wording is more accurate, as depending on the context, the best substitution candidates are not necessarily exact synonyms to the complex word, and the best candidate to replace a word might be a phrase of two or more words. However, the second wording of the prompt noticeably outperformed the first wording. An explanation could be that asking for a "synonym" is a more clear and direct command than asking for "words to replace". Every time such a change to the inference prompt was made, the fine-tuning prompt also needed to be changed, as altering only the inference prompt led to incomprehensible responses from the model. This resulted in needing to fine-tune the model again to get the results of each prompt change, which added a substantial amount of time to the process.

5.2 Limitations

In working with LLMs, a significant amount of computational resources were needed for fine-tuning and inference. This computational cost resulted in longer times for fine-tuning and inference, limiting the extent to which the fine-tuning hyperparameters and the inference parameters could be optimized.

Additionally, the TSAR dataset used for fine-tuning only contained 373 instances, a very small number when compared to other fine-tuning datasets, such as the 52K instance dataset used in Alpaca. Whereas ChatGPT was used to generate these examples, the specificity needed for the LS task necessitates human annotators in the creation of a dataset.

6 Conclusion and Future Work

This paper compared a fine-tuned, generative LLM, LSLlama, to previously existing LS baseline models LSBert and UniHD. At evaluation, LSLlama outperformed UniHD in all metrics on one dataset, while on the other two datasets, UniHD outperformed LSLlama on most, but not all, metrics. LSBert also never scored the highest on any metric. Regarding their architectures, generative LLMs require more computational resources than BERT-based models, however LSLlama is able to simplify the multi-step process of LSBert. LSLlama generates and ranks substitution candidates at inference, whereas a separate ranking algorithm is used after inference from LSBert. A separate ranking algorithm is also used in UniHD. Even though UniHD and LSLlama are both generative LLMs, LSLlama takes advantage of fine-tuning to significantly reduce its size, from 175B parameters for GPT-3 to 7B parameters for LSLlama, while maintaining comparable performance on evaluation metrics. Despite some recorded challenges posed by their architecture, this research demonstrates the potential for LLaMA and other LLMs that are fine-tuned on a LS task to improve upon existing benchmarks in Lexical Simplification.

For future work, fine-tuning could be done using multiple datasets. This could improve the model's specificity, as it would increase the size of the training set used for fine-tuning. Testing then can be done on one dataset. In addition, further manipulation of the fine-tuning hyperparameters, inference parameters, and prompt wording could also be pursued to improve the performance of LSLlama.

7 Lay Summary

Lexical Simplification (LS) is a field which develops methods to simplify text by substituting complex words with simpler ones while maintaining the meaning of the surrounding sentence. This is done to improve the reading comprehension of text for those who do not have sufficient proficiency in a specific language.

Recently, methods involving deep learning, which use multi-layered neural networks, have improved upon the performance of previous methods that did not incorporate deep learning. There are two notable methods for LS that use deep learning: LSBert and UniHD. LSBert uses a combination of a deep learning model and other non-deep learning methods. UniHD uses a Large Language Model (LLM), a large neural network that runs on many powerful computer components called graphics processing units (GPUs), and ranks multiple outputs to propose candidates to substitute for a selected complex word.

Both of these models pose challenges. LSBert uses a multi-step process with multiple inputs to propose candidates, while UniHD uses a two-step process that needs a large network of GPUs. LSLlama, the proposed model, resolves these weaknesses by using a single-step process that can be run on four GPUs. The performance of LSBert, UniHD, and LSLlama on a LS task were compared to determine whether LSLlama is competitive with these previous baseline models.

After carrying out testing, LSLlama was found to perform comparably to LSBert and UniHD on the three test datasets. LSLlama outperformed UniHD on one dataset consistently, and UniHD outperformed LSLlama the majority of the time on the other two datasets. LSBert was never the highest performing model on any metric. This demonstrates that the improvements to LSLlama's design do not come at the cost of significant performance, indicating a promising direction for improvement in lexical simplification.

By simplifying text with LS, it becomes more accessible for readers such as new language learners, young children, or those with a learning disability. In order for someone to benefit from this research, LSLlama would need to be incorporated as a component in a text simplification system that can be used with natural language and that is available for free or commercial use.

References

Dennis Aumiller and Michael Gertz. 2022. UniHD at TSAR-2022 shared task: Is compute all we need for lexical simplification? In *Proceedings of the Workshop on Text Simplification, Accessibility, and Readability (TSAR-2022)*, pages 251–258, Abu Dhabi, United Arab Emirates (Virtual). Association for Computational Linguistics.

Tom Brown, Benjamin Mann, Nick Ryder, Melanie Subbiah, Jared D Kaplan, Prafulla Dhariwal, Arvind Neelakantan, Pranav Shyam, Girish Sastry, Amanda Askell, et al. 2020. Language models are few-shot learners. *Advances in neural information processing systems*, 33:1877–1901.

Jacob Devlin, Ming-Wei Chang, Kenton Lee, and Kristina Toutanova. 2019. BERT: Pre-training of deep bidirectional transformers for language understanding. In *Proceedings of the 2019 Conference of the North American Chapter of the Association for Computational Linguistics: Human Language Technologies, Volume 1 (Long and Short Papers)*, pages 4171–4186, Minneapolis, Minnesota. Association for Computational Linguistics.

Colby Horn, Cathryn Manduca, and David Kauchak. 2014. Learning a lexical simplifier using wikipedia. In *Proceedings of the 52nd Annual Meeting of the Association for Computational Linguistics (Volume 2: Short Papers)*, pages 458–463.

Gustavo Paetzold and Lucia Specia. 2016a. Benchmarking lexical simplification systems. In *Proceedings of the Tenth International Conference on Language Resources and Evaluation (LREC'16)*, pages 3074–3080.

Gustavo Paetzold and Lucia Specia. 2016b. Unsupervised lexical simplification for non-native speakers. In *Proceedings of the AAAI Conference on Artificial Intelligence*, volume 30.

Gustavo Paetzold and Lucia Specia. 2017. Lexical simplification with neural ranking. In *Proceedings of the 15th Conference of the European Chapter of the Association for Computational Linguistics: Volume 2, Short Papers*, pages 34–40.

Jipeng Qiang, Yun Li, Yi Zhu, Yunhao Yuan, and Xindong Wu. 2020. Lexical simplification with pretrained encoders. In *Proceedings of the AAAI Conference on Artificial Intelligence*, volume 34, pages 8649–8656.

Horacio Saggion. 2017. *Automatic Text Simplification*, volume 10 of *Synthesis Lectures on Human Language Technologies*. Morgan & Claypool Publishers.

Horacio Saggion, Sanja Štajner, Daniel Ferrés, Kim Cheng Sheang, Matthew Shardlow, Kai North, and Marcos Zampieri. 2022. Findings of the TSAR-2022 shared task on multilingual lexical simplification. In *Proceedings of the Workshop on Text Simplification, Accessibility, and Readability (TSAR-2022)*, pages 271–283, Abu Dhabi, United Arab Emirates (Virtual). Association for Computational Linguistics.

Matthew Shardlow. 2014. A survey of automated text simplification. *International Journal of Advanced Computer Science and Applications*, 4(1):58–70.

Kim Cheng Sheang, Daniel Ferrés, and Horacio Saggion. 2022. Controllable lexical simplification for English. In *Proceedings of the Workshop on Text Simplification, Accessibility, and Readability (TSAR-2022)*, pages 199–206, Abu Dhabi, United Arab Emirates (Virtual). Association for Computational Linguistics.

Sanja Štajner, Daniel Ferrés, Matthew Shardlow, Kai North, Marcos Zampieri, and Horacio Saggion. 2022. Lexical simplification benchmarks for english, portuguese, and spanish. *Frontiers in Artificial Intelligence*, 5:991242.

Rohan Taori, Ishaan Gulrajani, Tianyi Zhang, Yann Dubois, Xuechen Li, Carlos Guestrin, Percy Liang, and Tatsunori B. Hashimoto. 2023. Stanford alpaca: An instruction-following llama model. `https://github.com/tatsu-lab/stanford_alpaca`.

Hugo Touvron, Thibaut Lavril, Gautier Izacard, Xavier Martinet, Marie-Anne Lachaux, Timothée Lacroix, Baptiste Rozière, Naman Goyal, Eric Hambro, Faisal Azhar, et al. 2023. Llama: Open and efficient foundation language models. *arXiv preprint arXiv:2302.13971*.

A Appendix

Huggingface Transformers and Pytorch were used for implementation of the model. DeepSpeed was also implemented to optimize fine-tuning, which used the cpu_adam optimizer. The model was fine-tuned for 4 epochs. All other fine-tuning hyperparameters are identical to Alpaca (Taori et al., 2023). The fine-tuning and inference was done on 4 V100-32G GPUs.

Inference on LSLlama was performed using greedy decoding with a temperature of 0.1, top_k of 0.75, and a repetition penalty of 1.11.

B Acknowledgements

We would like to thank Kim Cheng Sheang, Euan McGill, and Ella Tubbs for their contributions. We would also like to thank the MISTI program at MIT for making this collaboration possible.

LC-Score: Reference-less estimation of Text Comprehension Difficulty

Paul Tardy
U31
https://u31.io
pltrdy@gmail.com

Charlotte Roze
U31
https://u31.io
charlotte.roze@u31.io

Paul Poupet
U31
https://u31.io
paul.poupet@u31.io

Abstract

Being able to read and understand written text is critical in a digital era. However, studies shows that a large fraction of the population experiences comprehension issues. In this context, further initiatives in accessibility are required to improve the audience text comprehension. However, writers are hardly assisted nor encouraged to produce easy-to-understand content. Moreover, Automatic Text Simplification (ATS) model development suffers from the lack of metric to accurately estimate comprehension difficulty We present LC-SCORE, a simple approach for training text comprehension metric for any French text without reference *i.e.* predicting how easy to understand a given text is on a $[0, 100]$ scale. Our objective with this scale is to quantitatively capture the extend to which a text suits to the *Langage Clair* (LC, *Clear Language*) guidelines, a French initiative closely related to English Plain Language. We explore two approaches: (i) using linguistically motivated indicators used to train statistical models, and (ii) neural learning directly from text leveraging pre-trained language models. We introduce a simple proxy task for comprehension difficulty training as a classification task. To evaluate our models, we run two distinct human annotation experiments, and find that both approaches (indicator based and neural) outperforms commonly used readability and comprehension metrics such as FKGL and SAMSA.

1 Introduction

The ability to understand text is essential for a wide range of daily tasks. It enables individuals to stay informed, understand administrative forms, and have a full, unimpeded access to social and medical care.

Studies shows that a large fraction of the population experiences comprehension issues in their daily life. Almost half of the OECD population shows reading and written information comprehension difficulties (OECD 2013; Štajner, 2021).

Such difficulties have a major impact in people's life. In France for example, the National Statistic Institute (INSEE 2012) reports that one person out of four has already abandoned an administrative procedure deemed too complicated to follow-along.

In order to improve written text accessibility, initiatives such as Plain Language[1] or *Language Clair* (LC, translates to *Clear Language*) defines writing guidelines to produce clearer texts. Moreover, comprehension makes its way into international standards and norms (ISO 24495; WCAG 2018) but still lacks of concrete solution and measurable objectives.

With the rise of deep-learning approaches in natural language processing, as well as its recent successes in a wide variety of tasks (transcription, translation, summarization, question answering), Automatic Text Simplification is an interesting candidate for accessibility improvements at scale. However, system performances are difficult to measure due to the limitations of current automatic metrics (Alva-Manchego et al., 2021).

We hypothesize that the development of better text comprehension metrics could provide Automatic Text Simplification researchers with a way of validating their models while also to giving measurable objectives for the content editors to write clearer texts.

In this context, we focus our work in developing models for reference-less text comprehension evaluation as a scoring function for French texts *i.e.* $s : \text{text} \mapsto [0, 100]$ reflecting how clearly written a text is.

In this paper, we present the following contributions:

[1]https://plainlanguagenetwork.org/plain-language/what-is-plain-language

Proceedings of the Second Workshop on Text Simplification, Accessibility and Readability associated with RANLP-2023, pages 109–115,
held in Varna Bulgaria, Sept 7, 2023.
https://doi.org/10.26615/978-954-452-086-1_011

- We introduce a simple approach to address comprehension evaluation as a classification task

- We introduce a set of linguistically motivated lexical, syntactic and structural indicators

- We train both indicator based models and text-based Neural Models

- We evaluate our experiments thanks to two human annotation experiments using crowd sourced human judgement for one and expert rating for the second.

2 Related Work

Defining what makes a text difficult to understand is a complex task by itself. Multiple approaches are explored, like studying the age at which children acquires complex syntactic constructions in French (Canut, 2014); or relying on standardized foreign language levels such as the Common European Framework of Reference (CEFR), ranging from A1 to C2. Wilkens et al. (2022) uses this scale to study French as a Foreign Language difficulty.

In order to improve texts clarity, some organizations produced redaction guidelines *i.e.* suggestions of good practices to write clear texts, such as Plain Language (PLAIN) and, in French, (Leys, 2011). Gala et al. (2020) also published guidelines for adapting French texts to increase readability and comprehension. More closely related to our work, Francois and Fairon (2012) introduced a readability formula for French as a foreign language.

Automatic Text Simplification aims at generating simpler versions of a source texts. In literature, such models are usually evaluated using automatic metrics. Therefore, standard language level and redaction guidelines are hardly suitable to evaluate simplification models since it would require an expert judgement. Automatic evaluation instead mostly rely on readability metrics such as FKGL (Kincaid et al., 1975), SMOG (McLaughlin, 1969) and Gunning fog Index (Gunning, 1952). Such metrics were designed with English in mind but can be used on French in practice. On the other hand, SAMSA (Sulem et al., 2018), a semantic metric, is currently not implemented for French, as discussed in section 3.1.

Other approach include learning regression and classification models (Martin et al., 2018) or pre-trained language models (Zhang et al., 2020). However, (Alva-Manchego et al., 2021) found that automatic metrics remains unsuitable to evaluate progress in Automatic Text Simplification.

3 Methods

3.1 Baseline metrics

In order to evaluate our work with respect to the literature we take the following existing readability metrics as baselines: FKGL (Kincaid et al., 1975), SMOG (McLaughlin, 1969), Gunning Fog (Gunning, 1952).

The SAMSA metric (Sulem et al., 2018) takes semantic into consideration. Even though it would be theoretically possible to adapt this metric for french, it is not yet implemented. We tried adapting existing implementation from EASSE (Alva-Manchego et al., 2019) based on CoreNLP (Manning et al., 2014) but it turned out to fail due to the lack of French lemmatization model.

3.2 Evaluate text comprehension difficulty as a classification task

Training a model to predict comprehension difficulty would require a text corpus annotated with comprehension scores. However, to the best of our knowledge, their is no such corpus for the general audience and of sufficient size to envision model training. In this context, we suggest to rely on a simpler proxy task consisting of a classification between *simple* and *complex* texts. Defining what makes a text simple or complex here is difficult. In order to bypass this question, we uses pairs of content sources such as one is roughly a simplified version of the other:

Encyclopedia articles based on French Wikipedia (*complex*) and its simpler alternative, Vikidia (*simple*), designed for 8-13 years old readers. We only took into consideration the introduction paragraph as it is a concise and synthetic presentation of the article. Articles are aligned *i.e.* the corpus consists in $(simple, complex)$ pairs.

International Radio Journal Transcriptions with *France Culture international press review* (*complex*) [2] and *RFI Journal En Français Facile* (*simple*), [3] aimed at french speakers that do not speak the language on a daily basis. Articles

[2] https://www.radiofrance.fr/franceculture/podcasts/revue-de-presse-internationale

[3] https://francaisfacile.rfi.fr/fr/podcasts/journal-en-fran%C3%A7ais-facile/

Corpus	#T	#W/#T	#W/#S
Wikipedia	25812	144	26.0
Vikidia	25812	80	18.9
France Culture	1402	1106	28.8
Journal en Français Facile	1555	1494	19.0

Table 1: Comprehension Classification Datasets: number of texts per corpus ($\#T$), average word per text ($\#W/\#T$) and average word per sentence $\#W/\#S$).

have similar subjects (international news) but are not aligned strictly speaking *i.e.* there is no $(complex, simple)$ pairs for a given article. We report statistics about this new corpus in table 1.

3.3 Linguistic Indicators

Deriving from works on Langage Clair we introduce a set of complexity indicators. Indicators varies from lexical difficulties (*i.e.* a word difficulty score) to syntactic difficulties or sentences parse tree height. Indicators are detailed below.

Indicators are detected based on our own rules implementation using SpaCy pipeline based on both dependency and constituency parsing respectively using `fr-dep-news-trf`[4] and `benepar`[5].

Lexical Indicators (5) These are indicators of difficulties at word level. We use a word difficulty score based on word frequencies in corpora of different difficulty levels: elementary school textbooks of various grades from Manulex (Lété et al., 2004) and French as a Foreign Language textbooks of various CEFR (Common European Framework of Reference for Languages) levels from FLELex (François et al., 2014). Lexical indicators also include abbreviations, acronyms, named entities and numerical expressions.

Sentence Length Indicators (3) We measure sentences lengths with averages of words per sentence; dependency and constituency tree heights.

Syntactic Indicators (17) Several difficulties on the syntactic level in sentences are identified, which are related to sentence structure: coordinate clauses, relative clauses, adverbial clauses, participle clauses, cleft structures, interpolated clauses, appositive phrases, enumerations, etc.). Information about verb forms are also detected: non-finite clauses, passive voice, complex verbal tenses, conditional mood. Negations marks, complex noun phrases and text spans between brackets are also included in syntactic indicators.

Structure Indicators (3) Two indicators are related to the presence of connectives and their potential complexity, estimated by syntactic information (*e.g.* clause position for conjunction connectives, sentence initial position for adverbial connectives) and information from a French connectives lexicon (Roze et al., 2010). A third indicator counts temporal breaks (*i.e.* a tense change) within text paragraphs.

We train models using `sklearn`: two linear models (Linear SVC and Ridge) for fairer comparison to linear readability metrics, and 2 non-linear (Random Forest and Multi Layer Perceptron)

3.4 Neural Methods based on Text

Even though indicator-based approaches rely on linguistic motivations, they lack the possibility to learn from deeper relationships throughout the text such as the subject, the context and the semantic that might carry essential information to infer comprehension difficulty. This is the reason why we chose to compare indicator-based methods with deep learning approaches directly relying on text.

We use two French pre-trained language models such as BARThez (Eddine et al., 2020) and CamemBERT (Martin et al., 2020) fine-tuned with a classification (C) or a regression objective (R).

4 Comprehension Difficulty Annotation

We ran two human annotation experiments in two different contexts: the first one using Mechanical Turk, a crowd-sourcing platform to receive annotations of French speakers from general audience (4.1); the second based on the feedback of Langage Clair experts in our team (4.2).

4.1 Crowd-sourced Human Annotation

In order to get the most reliable annotations we follow (Kiritchenko and Mohammad, 2017) and use a Best-Worst Scaling (BWS) technique. They recommend to use comparison task instead of direct assessment *i.e.* directly giving a note to a given text. More specifically, BWS compares k (typically $k =$

[4] `https://spacy.io/models/fr#fr_dep_news_trf`

[5] `https://github.com/nikitakit/self-attentive-parser`

4) simultaneous examples and asks the annotator to select the best one and the worst one with respect to the dimension of interest (text comprehension difficulty in our context).

When annotating texts of up to 200 words, preliminary experiments showed us that comparing $k = 4$ simultaneous texts was too long and fastidious. In this light, we reduce to $k = 3$.

The annotation counts $T = 48$ news articles (up to 200 words). Each text is present in $e = 12$ different examples of $k = 3$ texts. Examples are annotated by $a = 3$ separate annotators in a total of 26. We end up with a total of $E = (T \times e)/k = 192$ examples, and $E \times a$ annotation *i.e.* for any three texts $\{T_a; T_b; T_c\}$ the annotation task consist in submitting an ordered set *e.g.* $T_c > T_a > T_b$.

Each text T_i is associated with an annotation score by $score(i) = \#best\%(i) - \#worst\%(i)$ with $\#best\%(i)$ (resp. $\#worst\%(i)$) representing the frequency at which T_i was evaluated the best (resp. worst) text out of the 3.

In order to measure the reliability of an annotation experiment, a common practice is to measure inter-annotation agreement. However, in a BWS process, each annotators is presented with a different set of examples which makes the concept of annotator agreement less relevant. Moreover, disagreement is even beneficial to produce accurate annotation: for two items A and B of similar difficulty, we can expect half of the annotator to rate $A > B$ and the other half $B > A$. From this apparent disagreement emerges diversity that actually reinforce score accuracy. For this reason, BWS is instead evaluated in terms of reproductibility metrics like Split Half Reliability (SHR). SHR is the correlation between two randomly sampled half of the annotation. In practice, we average SHR over 1000 iterations to rule out randomness.

4.2 Expert Annotation

In addition to crowd-sourced corpus, our team built a small corpus of 74 texts annotated with difficulty scores. We selected 37 texts originating from news articles, literature, and customer support mails. In addition, we provide 37 manually simplified versions following Langage Clair methodology. Each of the 74 resulting texts were then scored on a $[0, 100]$ scale by 4 LC experts from our team.

To make sure we obtained good quality annotation, we measure annotator agreement with Intraclass Correlation Coefficient (ICC2, Shrout and Fleiss, 1979). ICC2 ranges from 0 (no agreement) to 1 (perfect agreeement).

5 Results

5.1 Annotation results

Annotations experiments text length metrics and reliability measure are reported in table 2.

Good reliability from MTurk and Expert even though our annotation experiments are very different in terms of annotators and process, both shows high reliability measures achieving respectively an SHR correlation of 64.7 (MTurk) and an Intraclass Correlation Coefficient of 74.6 (Experts).

Filtering MTurk workers does not increase reliability A common practice when involving crowd-sourced annotation is to filter-out users that shows the lowest agreement. Even though we discussed in 4.2 that agreement is not considered to be the most relevant metric for BWS annotation, we challenge this hypothesis by calculating worker agreement rate based on how often a given user submits the same result than another worker. Then, we suppose that workers with the lowest agreement rate might add noise to the experiment so we might want to exclude them. However, results showed the opposite: filtering out workers does not increase reliability in terms of SHR, no matter the agreement rate of each. This observation is in line with the hypothesis that annotator disagreement is expected and beneficial in a BWS annotation experiment.

	MTurk	**Expert**
#T	48	37 / 37
#W/#T	183	190 / 209
#W/#S	25	28 / 13
#Annotators	26	4
Type	BWS	RS
Reliability Measure	SHR	ICC2
Reliability	64.7	74.6

Table 2: Human Annotation Experiments. Corpus are reported with number of texts per corpus ($\#T$), average word per text ($\#W/\#T$) and average word per sentence $\#W/\#S$). Since Expert is aligned, metrics are reported for both sides. Experiments uses two different annotation processes (i) Best Worst Scaling (BWS) evaluated in term of Split Half Reliability (SHR) and (ii) Rating Scale in $[0, 100]$ (RS, 100 is best) evaluated with Intraclass Correlation Coefficient (ICC2).

Model	Valid $acc\%$	MTurk ρ	Expert ρ
SMOG	-	-18.68	-73.09
Gunning Fog	-	-12.59	**-82.14**
FKGL	-	**-19.66**	-77.54
Linear SVC	73.07	20.94	69.37
Ridge	-	27.58	86.44
MLP	75.31	32.56	85.73
Random Forest	**77.20**	**34.42**	**88.09**
BARThez	79.64	23.16	58.41
Camembert(R)	**91.01**	**28.35**	75.85
Camembert(C)	90.15	18.44	**84.73**

Table 3: Scoring models Spearman correlations (ρ) with human judgement. (C) and (R) respectively indicates classification and regression training objective.

5.2 Scoring results

First, we evaluate model performances with respect to their own training by measure accuracy on their validation set: a 10% held-out subset from the training set. Validation accuracy is used to select the best hyper-parameters and training iterations for each models.

Models are then evaluated against human annotations from MTurk and Experts using Spearman Rank Correlations (ρ).

Results are reported in Table 3. Our approaches show better correlations with the human judgement than readability metrics. Models trained from indicators achieves the highest correlations, with Random Forest being the best on both evaluation sets, MTurk and Expert.

It is also interesting that even simple linear statistical models based on our indicators outperforms readability metrics therefore arguing in favor of this indicator set. In particular, the Ridge Regression model outperform FKGL by 14.76 and 10.55 correlation point respectively on MTurk and Expert.

Readability metrics seems complementary in that FKGL achieve better correlation on MTurk evaluation while Gunning Fog does on Expert.

Similarly, we observe sensible differences between Camembert training objectives, with the regression (R) being better on MTurk and classification (C) on Expert.

6 Discussions

Results shows a large improvement of human judgement correlation in favor to our approaches over existing readability metrics. Moreover, indicator based method outperform neural models fine-tuned from pre-trained model. Neural models' results are promising and could be extended with longer training time and adapting their training objective to produce equally distributed scores.

In addition to outperforming neural models, indicator based model are far cheaper to train and predict with since they does not require GPU. Being indicator-based makes it easier to interpret and more predictable than neural models, and thus might deliver a better user experience. We observed Neural models we trained tend to produce very polarized output probabilities *i.e.* either very close to 0 or to 1. That's not a problem to quantitatively evaluate the resulting score, but it should probably be adapted to output equally distributed scores in order to be more intuitive.

7 Conclusion

Developing methods to accurately measure written text comprehension difficulty is a key challenge that would help better assessing the quality of Automatic Text Simplification models, and provide with a tool for editors to produce texts that are simpler to understand.

We explore multiple approaches for training a reference-less metric based on a simple classification task. Our systems rely either on linguistic indicators or directly from text.

To evaluate our models, we two human annotation experiments. The first involves crowd-sourced workers, asked to compare text based on their comprehension difficulties using Best Worst Scaling with $k = 3$. In the second experiment, texts are simplified then rated on a $[0, 100]$ scale by experts from our team.

Both neural and indicator based methods shows promising results and largely outperform other broadly used readability metrics, on both crowd-sourced and expert human annotations. Even simple linear models largely outperform readability metrics which adds an evidence against using it to estimate text comprehension complexity.

As further researches, we suggest exploring multi-lingual neural training. This would have the obvious benefit of overcoming the language restriction of our work while also mutualizing learning from each language and unifying comprehension difficulties estimation accross languages.

8 Lay Summary

Nowadays, most services use the Internet as their primary way of communicating. Therefore, being able to read and understand texts is really important. But a lot of people have difficulties reading and understanding so it is not simple for them to access information or complete administrative procedures.

We introduce a method to calculate a difficulty score for French texts. A score of 0 means that the text is really difficult to understand, whereas a score of 100 means it is really clear. We suggest that developing such a score is a first step toward helping people write easier texts. We gathered two categories of texts: some that we consider easy to understand and others that we consider difficult to understand. Then, we trained models to predict whether a text is categorized as "easy" or not. After training, we use the predictions as our scoring method: the score corresponds to the probability (multiplied by 100) that a text is categorized as easy by the model.

We explored two kinds of models. For the first one, we count different kinds of linguistic difficulties and give them to the model to predict the difficulty. The second kind of model is deep neural networks that have already been trained to learn French. We specialize it in predicting the difficulty based on the text by providing examples of texts and their difficulties.

To measure how relevant our models are, we asked people on the Internet as well as experts to give their opinions on texts. In particular, they were given texts and should determine how difficult they are. We found that people agreed more with our method's scores than with other existing scoring methods.

References

Fernando Alva-Manchego, Louis Martin, Carolina Scarton, and Lucia Specia. 2019. EASSE: Easier Automatic Sentence Simplification Evaluation. In *Proceedings of the 2019 Conference on Empirical Methods in Natural Language Processing and the 9th International Joint Conference on Natural Language Processing (EMNLP-IJCNLP): System Demonstrations*, pages 49–54, Stroudsburg, PA, USA. Association for Computational Linguistics.

Fernando Alva-Manchego, Carolina Scarton, and Lucia Specia. 2021. The (Un)Suitability of Automatic Evaluation Metrics for Text Simplification. *Computational Linguistics*, 47(4):861–889.

Emmanuelle Canut. 2014. Acquisition des constructions syntaxiques complexes chez l'enfant français entre 2 et 6 ans. *SHS Web of Conferences*, 8:1437–1452.

Moussa Kamal Eddine, Antoine J. P. Tixier, and Michalis Vazirgiannis. 2020. BARThez: a Skilled Pretrained French Sequence-to-Sequence Model.

Thomas Francois and Cedrick Fairon. 2012. An "AI readability" formula for French as a foreign language. In *EMNLP-CoNLL 2012 - 2012 Joint Conference on Empirical Methods in Natural Language Processing and Computational Natural Language Learning, Proceedings of the Conference*, pages 466–477.

Thomas François, Nùria Gala, Patrick Watrin, and Cédrick Fairon. 2014. FLELex: a graded lexical resource for French foreign learners. In *Proceedings of the Ninth International Conference on Language Resources and Evaluation (LREC'14)*, pages 3766–3773, Reykjavik, Iceland. European Language Resources Association (ELRA).

Núria Gala, Amalia Todirascu, Ludivine Javourey-Drevet, Delphine Bernhard, Rodrigo Wilkens, Jean-Paul Meyer, and Al Recommandations. 2020. Recommandations pour des transformations de textes français afin d'améliorer leur lisibilité et leur compréhension.

Robert Gunning. 1952. The technique of clear writing. *1952*, page 289.

INSEE 2012. 2012. Pour les générations les plus récentes, les difficultés des adultes diminuent à l'écrit, mais augmentent en calcul. Standard, INSEE.

ISO 24495. 2023. Plain language – Part 1: Governing principles and guidelines. Standard, International Organization for Standardization.

J. P. Kincaid, R. P Fishburne, R. L Rogers, and B. S Chissom. 1975. Derivation of new readability formulas for navy enlisted personnel. *Naval Technical Training Command Millington TN Research Branch.*

Svetlana Kiritchenko and Saif Mohammad. 2017. Best-Worst Scaling More Reliable than Rating Scales: A Case Study on Sentiment Intensity Annotation. In *Proceedings of the 55th Annual Meeting of the Association for Computational Linguistics (Volume 2: Short Papers)*, volume 2, pages 465–470, Stroudsburg, PA, USA. Association for Computational Linguistics.

Bernard Lété, Liliane Sprenger-Charolles, and Pascale Colé. 2004. MANULEX: a grade-level lexical database from French elementary school readers. *Behavior Research Methods Instruments and Computers*, 36(1):156–66.

Michel Leys. 2011. Écrire pour être lu : comment rédiger des textes administratifs faciles à comprendre? Technical report, Fédération Wallonie-Bruxelles.

Christopher D. Manning, Mihai Surdeanu, John Bauer, Jenny Finkel, Steven J. Bethard, and David McClosky. 2014. The stanford CoreNLP natural language processing toolkit. In *Proceedings of the Annual Meeting of the Association for Computational Linguistics*, volume 2014-June, pages 55–60. Association for Computational Linguistics (ACL).

Louis Martin, Samuel Humeau, Pierre Emmanuel Mazare, Antoine Bordes, Eric De La Clergerie, Sagot Benoit, Pierre-Emmanuel Mazaré, and Antoine Bordes. 2018. Reference-less Quality Estimation of Text Simplification Systems. In *ATA 2018 - 1st Workshop on Automatic Text Adaptation, Proceedings of the Workshop*, pages 29–38. Association for Computational Linguistics (ACL).

Louis Martin, Benjamin Muller, Pedro Javier Ortiz Suárez, Yoann Dupont, Laurent Romary, Éric Villemonte de la Clergerie, Djamé Seddah, and Benoît Sagot. 2020. CamemBERT: A tasty French language model. In *Proceedings of the Annual Meeting of the Association for Computational Linguistics*, pages 7203–7219. Association for Computational Linguistics (ACL).

G.H. McLaughlin. 1969. SMOG grading: A new readability formula. *Journal of reading*, 12(8):639–646.

OECD 2013. 2013. OECD Skills Outlook 2013 – First Results from the Survey of Adult Skills. Standard, OECD.

PLAIN. 2023. Federal Plain Language Guidelines. Standard, Plain Language Action and Information Network (PLAIN).

Charlotte Roze, Danlos Laurence, and Philippe Muller. 2010. LEXCONN: a French Lexicon of Discourse Connectives. In *MAD 2010 - 8th Workshop Multidisciplinary Approaches to Discourse*, Proceedings of the 8th Workshop Multidisciplinary Approaches to Discourse (MAD 2010), pages 114–125, Moissac, France.

Patrick E. Shrout and Joseph L. Fleiss. 1979. Intraclass correlations: Uses in assessing rater reliability. *Psychological Bulletin*, 86(2):420–428.

Sanja Štajner. 2021. Automatic Text Simplification for Social Good: Progress and Challenges. In *Findings of the Association for Computational Linguistics: ACL-IJCNLP 2021*, pages 2637–2652.

Elior Sulem, Omri Abend, and Ari Rappoport. 2018. Semantic structural evaluation for text simplification. In *NAACL HLT 2018 - 2018 Conference of the North American Chapter of the Association for Computational Linguistics: Human Language Technologies - Proceedings of the Conference*, volume 1, pages 685–696.

WCAG 2018. 2018. Web Content Accessibility Guidelines (WCAG) 2.1 – 3.1 Understanding. Standard, W3C.

Rodrigo Wilkens, David Alfter, Xiaoou Wang, Alice Pintard, Anaïs Tack, Kevin Yancey, and Thomas François. 2022. FABRA: French Aggregator-Based Readability Assessment toolkit.

Tianyi Zhang, Varsha Kishore, Felix Wu, Kilian Q. Weinberger, and Yoav Artzi. 2020. Bertscore: Evaluating Text Generation With Bert. *8th International Conference on Learning Representations, ICLR 2020.*

On Operations in Automatic Text Simplification

Rémi Cardon
CENTAL, IL&C
UCLouvain, Belgium
remi.cardon@uclouvain.be

Adrien Bibal
University of Colorado
Anschutz Medical Campus, USA
adrien.bibal@cuanschutz.edu

Abstract

This paper explores the literature of automatic text simplification (ATS) centered on the notion of operations. Operations are the processed of applying certain modifications to a given text in order to transform it. In ATS, the intent of the transformation is to simplify the text. This paper overviews and structures the domain by showing how operations are defined and how they are exploited. We extensively discuss the most recent works on this notion and perform preliminary experiments to automatize operations recognition with large language models (LLMs). Through our overview of the literature and the preliminary experiment with LLMs, this paper provides insights on the topic that can help lead to new directions in ATS research.

1 Introduction

Automatic Text Simplification (ATS) is a natural language processing (NLP) task that consists in modifying a text in order to make it more readable or understandable. Generally, ATS systems work at the sentence leval. They take a sentence as an input and produce a modified version of it, with the objective of making it simpler for a given audience. To characterize the modifications that are performed or aimed at, a lot of different works established various sets of operations. For a broad definition, an operation is a change performed on a textual unit, for example the deletion of a clause or the reformulation of a complex expression with simpler terms. Simplifying sentences or documents typically involves more than one operation.

In this work, we investigate the ATS literature to gather what it says about operations. Indeed, while it is always present at every level of works on ATS, since the task appeared, operation as a concept has received little attention. Our first intention is to provide the community with a structured review of the literature centered on operations, in particular how and why they are used. We also hope to bring a new perspective to feed the current reflection on evaluation in ATS and ultimately on the definition of the task. We intend this paper to benefit both newcomers to the field – as we summarize elements from a large number of works of the domain – and active members of the community – as our observations enable new insights.

The contributions of this paper are the following:

- a detailed history and discussion of the role of operations in ATS;
- an overview of recently proposed typologies, along with a comparison and a discussion of the current role of operations in ATS;
- a review of the current means and goals to automate the annotation of operations;
- a preliminary experiment on the automation of linguistic operations identification using large language models.

In order to develop these contributions, the paper is organized as follows. We first report the definition of the different types of operations in the literature and how they are exploited (Section 2). Then we look closely at three recent papers that focus on typologies (Section 3). After that we address the question of automatic operation identification – why and how it is performed – and propose a preliminary experiment for the task with large language models (Section 4). We finally discuss our insights in Section 5 and the limitations of our work in Section 6, to finally conclude in Section 7.

2 Categorizing Operations in ATS

This section aims at giving a clear and detailed categorization of what is called "simplification operations" in the ATS literature (Section 2.1), and how they have been operationalized (Section 2.2).

Proceedings of the Second Workshop on Text Simplification, Accessibility and Readability associated with RANLP-2023, pages 116–130,
held in Varna Bulgaria, Sept 7, 2023.
https://doi.org/10.26615/978-954-452-086-1_012

2.1 What Operations Are

This section reports on the operations that are found in the literature. While surveying the literature, we did not find two identical sets of operations. In consequence, we do not attempt at producing an exhaustive catalogue of individual operations. There are two main objectives here: one is to clarify the principles that guide how operation sets can be put together, and the other one is to give a good view on what nuances can exist in the analysis and annotation of operations.

We divide the presentation using two broad types of operations: linguistically-based operations and string edits. In order to introduce the distinction between the two, consider Example (1) below, taken from the ASSET corpus (Alva-Manchego et al., 2020):

(1) Original: *Despite this, Farrenc was paid less than her male counterparts for nearly a decade.*
Simple: *Farrenc was paid less than her male co-workers for almost ten years.*

One operation in this example can intuitively be described as the deletion of the segment "*Despite this,*". The distinction between operation types depends on how this segment is characterized. On the one hand, linguistically-based operation types characterize the segment as a single linguistic unit. In this example, the operation may be described as the deletion of a sentence complement (its grammatical function) or of an adverbial phrase (its grammatical nature). On the other hand, string edits consider textual units as strings of individual tokens. In this example, most approaches that use string edits in fact describe this segment deletion as three operations: deletion of the token "*Despite*", deletion of the token "*this*" and deletion of the token ",".

ATS is largely focused on sentences, we mainly report on operations occurring within that level. As they appeared first in the literature, we start with linguistically-based operations (Section 2.1.1). We then move on to string edits (Section 2.1.2). We then report on operations described above the sentence level (section 2.1.3). Note: throughout this paper, we call linguistically-based operations "linguistic operations", operations on strings of tokens "edits", and we use "operations" to refer to any type of operation.

2.1.1 Linguistically-Based Operations

The very first works on ATS aimed at simplifying text as an input for other systems. In consequence, they were focused on the sentence structure, i.e. syntactic simplification (Siddharthan, 2014). The goal of these works was to reduce sentence complexity for downstream natural language processing (NLP) tasks, such as machine translation or information retrieval. Those approaches consist in manually designing simplification rules that modify constituency or dependency trees. An example of rule is the extraction of appositives (Chandrasekar et al., 1996), which is used to create two simple sentences from a complex one. In fact, this work concentrates on presenting two methods to only perform this specific operation. As syntactic operations can be the result of dependency or constituency trees, the linguistic elements they address can be denoted by their grammatical function (e.g., appositive, modifier, etc.) or their grammatical nature (e.g., relative clause, noun phrase, adjective, etc.).

With the appearance of works that focus on text simplification for human readers (which aim at improving readability or understandability), the scope of considered operations expanded. The operations can be syntactic and similar to the works mentioned above, such as recognizing a type of clause to delete or to extract in order to form a new simple sentence or to reorder sentence elements (Zhu et al., 2010). They can also be lexical, such as paraphrase or synonymy (lexical simplification has become a specific line of research and its details are out of scope of this paper, see Saggion et al. (2022) for more details). Operations can also occur at the morphological level, such as changing the mood or tense of a verb (Gala et al., 2020).

2.1.2 String Edits

The second type of operations is composed of operations applied to sentences considered as sequences of tokens. These operations are usually referred to in the literature as edits or string edits. They are considered at the token level and their name is self-explanatory. The operations that are always present in typologies of this kind are DELETE and ADD (also called INSERT). In order to account for all the token changes between two sentences, a (non-) operation is needed: KEEP. Depending on the goal for the operations in a given context, the list is adjusted. For instance, Alva-Manchego et al. (2017) introduce an operation called REWRITE, which they define as "a special case of REPLACE where the words involved are isolated (not in a group of same operation labels) and belong to a list of non-content words". On occasions they can be considered at the n-gram level. It is the case in the calculation of SARI (Xu et al., 2016), for example. Contrarily to the linguistic type, these basic operations can be combined to form new operations. An example of this is REPLACE, which is sometimes described as an operation in itself, and sometimes as a combination of DELETE and ADD. Another one is MOVE, which is sometimes considered as a REPLACE where the deleted token is the same as the added one.

2.1.3 Operations Above the Sentence Level

At this time, there are not many works that address simplification above the sentence level in the literature. We report our findings for discourse, paragraph and document levels here.

Discourse A few works focus on simpflification at the discourse level. Wilkens et al. (2020) propose text simplification through coreference resolution. In their typology of operations, Gonzalez-Dios et al. (2018) introduce discourse-level operations: coreference resolution and change of discourse markers.

Paragraph-level Only one work can be found on paragraph simplification that mentions broad operation types (Devaraj et al., 2021). The operations described in this work are paraphrasing, word/sentence deletion, and summarization.

Document-level Sun et al. (2021) propose six operations, following Alva-Manchego et al. (2019b): sentence joining, sentence splitting, sentence deletion, sentence reordering, sentence addition, and anaphora resolution. In another work, Cripwell et al. (2023) mention copy, rephrase, split and delete as document-level operations. Laban et al. (2023) propose a dataset for document-level simplification where they also establish a typology of operations. Most of the operations of this typology are common sentence-level operations. They characterize the operations that involve adding or removing sentences under the "Semantic edits" category. Those three works have three very different approaches to describing operations related to document-level simplification.

2.2 How Operations Are Used

We now describe the operationalization of the operation types we identified in the previous section. We divide the presentation into four stages that usually occur in research works on ATS: data analysis or creation, system design, automatic evaluation and human evaluation.

2.2.1 Data Analysis and Creation

Often in the literature, researchers have analyzed the corpus they created or collected to indicate what they contain in terms of linguistic operations. This has been made for a variety of languages: Spanish (Bott and Saggion, 2014), Italian (Brunato et al., 2014, 2022), French (Koptient et al., 2019), German (Stodden et al., 2023), Brazilian Portuguese (Caseli et al., 2009), Basque (Gonzalez-Dios et al., 2018) and English (Amancio and Specia, 2014). In order to facilitate the annotation of operations, Stodden and Kallmeyer (2022) have proposed a dedicated tool. The transformation labels can be customized in the tool, with the default labels being *delete*, *insert*, *merge*, *reorder*, *split* and *lexical simplification*. The creators of the French corpus ALECTOR (Gala et al., 2020) used linguistic operations as guidelines for annotators to manually simplify texts. The result is a parallel document-level corpus. Cardon et al. (2022) built on existing typologies in order to study the ASSET test set (Alva-Manchego et al., 2020), a corpus made for the test and validation of ATS systems. They released the corpus with the annotated operations, called ASSET_{ann}. Several evaluation corpora (WikiSmall and WikiLarge (Zhang and Lapata, 2017), TurkCorpus, TurkCorpus (Xu et al., 2015), MSD (Cao et al., 2020), ASSET (Alva-Manchego et al., 2020) and WikiManual (Jiang et al., 2020)) have been analyzed in terms of string edits (Vásquez-Rodríguez et al., 2021b). While considering different types of operations, in their respective conclusions both Cardon et al. (2022) and Vásquez-Rodríguez et al. (2021b) make the case for caring about the distribution of operations in the datasets used in ATS.

2.2.2 System Design

Historically, linguistic operations were used as rules, as we mentioned in Section 2.1.1. In consequence, they were the heart of the definition of the task and the system design, i.e. ATS consisted in the application of precisely pre-defined operations. A lot of different rule-based approaches have been proposed to do so, we refer the reader to Siddharthan (2014) and Saggion (2017) for more information. Rule-based approaches are still being explored today (Todirascu et al., 2022; Chatterjee and Agarwal, 2021; Evans and Orasan, 2019).

As manually crafting rules could be costly, another approach is to build a system that will learn operations on a corpus. A famous work using this approach is Woodsend and Lapata (2011). Their method, applied to Wikipedia data, uses a quasi-synchronous grammar to learn three types of rules based on constituency trees: syntactic rules, lexical rules and sentence splitting. Comparing their work to Zhu et al. (2010), they state that their model is "a more general model not restricted to specific rewrite operations" as an explanation of why it reaches better performance. We believe this statement epitomizes a turn in ATS research, where the presence of operations shift from the definition of the task (including system design) to the output of a model. The difference between this type of approach and the more recent neural approaches is that it produced explicit operations or rules, interpretable by humans. Neural models are expected to learn rules during training and apply them during inference (Nisioi et al., 2017; Štajner et al., 2022), but there is currently no identified way of accessing the operations that were learned.

Opaque neural models do not mark the complete disappearance of operations in task definition and system design in all ATS works. Some systems incorporate edits within a neural architecture (Alva-Manchego et al., 2017; Dong et al., 2019). More recently, a line of research has been focused on what has been called "controllable" text simplification (Martin et al., 2020; Maddela et al., 2021; Sheang and Saggion, 2021). The general idea is to prepend "control tokens" to the inputs to gain control on the ratio between the input and the output for a selection of attributes. Those attributes can be, for instance, sentence length, word frequency or syntactic tree depth. With this type of approach, operations are not made explicit, but the attributes influence their amount. For instance, variations to the sentence length ratio will have an impact on the amount of deletions.

2.2.3 Automatic Evaluation

Edits are present in the broadly used evaluation metric SARI (Xu et al., 2016). It counts the n-grams that were kept, added or deleted between the input and the reference(s) and between the output and the reference(s). An F1 score is calculated for each of the edits and each of the n-grams size (usually from 1 to 4) and the final score is the average of those scores. EASSE, the commonly used evaluation suite for ATS (Alva-Manchego et al., 2019a), reports the amounts of additions and deletions. Cardon et al. (2022) used linguistic operations to analyze the behavior of automatic metrics. SAMSA (Sulem et al., 2018) is an evaluation metric that evaluates the semantics of sentences that are the result of a split operation. More recently, Heineman et al. (2023) incorporate operation annotations in the training of a recent ATS metric, LENS (Maddela et al., 2023), and show that the metric gets more sensitive to their edit ratings. Automatic evaluation is a part of ATS that has started exhibiting promising perspectives for putting more thought on the integration of operations in ATS works.

2.2.4 Human Evaluation

The typical framework for the human evaluation of ATS outputs is to ask human judges to rate them according to three criteria, using 5-point Likert scales (Stodden, 2021). Yamaguchi et al. (2023) offer a method for analyzing ATS systems' outputs, according to simplification strategies and simplification errors. Cumbicus-Pineda et al. (2021) propose a structured framework for manually evaluating outputs according to the changes that were performed. Nisioi et al. (2017) asked two annotators to count the number of changes and state whether they are correct. In case of disagreement, a third annotator was asked to take a side. The type of change that was considered is not specified, the only information is that it can be applied at the phrase level and not only at the token level. Cooper and Shardlow (2020) established a 6-category typology of changes, some of them include both linguistic operations and edits.

3 Recent Advances on Simplification Typologies

In this section, we discuss in details the recent papers that are anchored in ATS and that focus mainly on observing the changes from an original sentence to its (attempted) simplification. We identified three such papers that we present chronologically in Section 3.1. After their presentation, we compare the three typologies in Section 3.2.

3.1 Typology Description

For each of the typologies we describe, we report the following information: the goal of the typology, the type of operations it contains and how many there are, the way it was built, the structure, the reasoning followed for annotation (if present in the original paper), the amount of inter-rater agreement, and finally the availability of guidelines and data.

Cardon et al. (2022). The main goal of the typology is to assess the content of a corpus. The authors explicitly mention that they cannot assess simplicity without the participation of members of a target audience, and that a detailed analysis of resources with linguistic operations can be used to select adequate data regarding the targeted application of a system. As stated in Section 2.2.1, this typology is composed of linguistic operations, which are inherited from past works on ATS corpora manual analysis in different languages. The authors added an "error" label to discard sentence pairs where the simplification is not grammatical or not semantically related to the original sentence. If used, no further annotation is performed. The authors present a structure for the rest of the operations (26 items), by mapping subsets to edits, namely deletions, additions and replacements. Other operations are described as too inconsistent to be mapped to edits, such as verbal voice change or transition from impersonal form to personal form. The authors also organize subsets that correspond to lexical and syntactic operations. A substantial inter-rater agreement is reported, with a trade-off between granularity and agreement. The annotation guide and the annotated data are available.

Yamaguchi et al. (2023). The main goal is the evaluation of ATS systems' outputs. the authors propose three different typologies: one for errors (4 items), one for content strategy (30 items), and one for surface strategy (22 items). The error set is composed of four labels "inappropriate deletion", "inappropriate addition", "inappropriate paraphrase" and "non-sentence". The other operation sets are built by the authors according to manual observations made in two stages. First they analyzed Newsela complex-simple sentence pairs (obtained after a manual alignment, as Newsela is not aligned at the sentence level) to produce a set of operations. Then, they added new operations by analyzing ATS systems' outputs. There are operations above the sentence level in this typology, such as "move a sentence" (within a document). During annotation, the first decision was to identify whether the operation under consideration is an error. If it is not, then a detailed decision tree is available for content and surface strategies. The decision trees were built by trial and error by two authors, and applied by the third one as a means of validation. The authors report a very high inter-rater agreement. The decision trees for content and surface strategies are available. As they used Newsela, the authors specify that the annotated data cannot be shared due to the terms of use.

Heineman et al. (2023). The main goal is the evaluation of ATS systems' outputs. This typology is structured in four parts: edit selection, information change, edit type classification and edit efficacy/severity rating. The first part is to identify whether the operation is an insertion, a deletion, a substitution, a reorder, a split or a structure change. The second part concerns the degree of semantic change divided into three categories: conceptual, syntactic and lexical. The authors present one category separately: grammar error, arguing that grammar and semantics are independent. For conceptual changes, there is a distinction between the operations that add information or the ones that remove information. Insertion is mapped to conceptual with more information, deletion is mapped to conceptual with less information. Reorder, split and structure change are mapped to syntax, and substitution can be mapped to three categories: conceptual with more information, conceptual with less information, and lexical. For each of these subcategories, a list of specific characterizations (there are 21 across all subcategories) is provided, which indicate a success (e.g., "elaboration" for a good insertion, or "generalization" for a good deletion), a failure (e.g., "bad deletion" for deletions, "information rewrite" or "complex wording" for a bad lexical edit). Some of these characterizations have the same name as a failure and as a success (e.g., "structure change" can be both). The authors report a general low inter-rater agreement that is broken down by edit type. It appears that the agreement is rather high for deletions and splits, and low for the other types. Examples are given for each individual fine-grained category. The authors state that they plan on releasing the data in the future, the paper being currently under review and available as a pre-print only.

3.2 Typology Comparison

For readability purposes, in this section we refer to the typologies as the first letter of the first author's name: C for Cardon et al. (2022)'s typology, Y for Yamaguchi et al. (2023)'s typology and H for Heineman et al. (2023)'s typology.

The three works use very different approaches for annotating the content of complex-simple sentence pairs. C adopts a classical approach based on existing works while Y and H propose a new framework. Y is the one with the most operations, and two detailed decision trees for annotation. The decision trees may explain the very high inter-rater agreement they obtained. Besides, Y is the most analytical and does not seem to leave much room for subjectivity, except for error characterization, while H states that instances could be annotated with several operations, as such they can be ambiguous. Error identification is the first step of C and Y, while H performs this characterization last. Y and H analyze errors at the operation level while C applies it to the whole sentence. The choice for a specific framework between those three should be driven by the type and granularity of information that is considered useful. H is the one with the least operations, the annotation process is clear and appears that it can be made quickly while giving an overview of what the differences are in complex-simple pairs. The room for ambiguity or subjectivity may impair reproductibility, while allowing for adaptation to different use cases. C is more detailed and clearly oriented towards linguistic operations. It can be adapted at different levels of granularity (e.g. grouping synonym, hyperonym and hyponym to one paraphrasing category). Y is the one that yields the more information, but also seems to be the most time-consuming.

All three works report different obstacles and limitations in the operation annotation task. Automating the task would facilitate this process of knowledge acquisition. In the next section, we propose to discuss the review the automation of operation annotation, as well as a preliminary experiment with large language models.

4 Automation of Operations Annotation

One interest of simplification typologies is to help understand and annotate the operations used to transform a complex sentence into one or more simpler sentences. In case of large corpora, it may be difficult to ask experts to annotate the operations involved in each transformation in the corpus. In such a case, it may be useful to automatically annotate the operations involved in all simplifications in the corpus.

This section proposes an overview of the current automation possibilities for the annotation of operations. Section 4.1 starts by presenting the currently used methods. Section 4.2 shows how large language models (LLMs) currently perform in this automation task.

4.1 Methods for Automatic Operation Annotation

As presented in Section 2.2, edits are now part of neural architectures and have been used to produce automated analyses of corpora. To achieve this, these edits need to be automatically identified. We report here how this is done in the literature, as the methods are varied. They often rely on the automatic alignment of tokens between two sentences.

Alva-Manchego et al. (2017) use the tool proposed by Sultan et al. (2014). Based on the alignments, they use heuristics to assign edit labels. To detect edits, Vásquez-Rodríguez et al. (2021a) and Vásquez-Rodríguez et al. (2021b) adapt the Wagner-Fischer algorithm – so that it can work at the token level instead of the character level – for alignment, and use heuristics to characterize the edits. EASSE (Alva-Manchego et al., 2019a) relies on MASSAlign (Paetzold et al., 2017) for alignment (or SimAlign (Jalili Sabet et al., 2020) as indicated in Alva-Manchego et al. (2021)), and heuristics for characterization. In EditNTS, Dong et al. (2019) implement their own neural-programmer interpreter to identify the edits.

Narayan and Gardent (2016) propose an approach that learns sentence splitting and phrase deletion. To do so, they rely on DRS (discourse representation structure (Kamp, 1984)) and graphs, using Boxer 1.00 (Curran et al., 2007), to produce those representations.

For linguistic operations, to the best of our knowledge nothing exists in the literature. One attempt at characterizing translation operations can be found in Zhai et al. (2019), which can be considered as a related task.

4.2 Prospect of Automation using LLMs

To the best of our knowledge, no work attempted to automatically annotate operations using large language models (LLMs). LLMs are not new in the literature. Indeed, first LLMs like GPT-1 (Radford et al., 2018) and T5 (Raffel et al., 2020) have been present for a few years. In the scientific literature, the number of papers about large language models started to exponentially grow with the release of InstructGPT and ChatGPT (Zhao et al., 2023). Due to their ever increasing performance, LLMs offer a new avenue to solve machine learning and natural language processing problems.

4.2.1 Experimental Setup

In order to test the ability of LLMs to perform the task of annotating operations, we performed preliminary experiments with BLOOM (Scao et al., 2022), BLOOMchat (SambaNova Systems and Together Computer, 2023), GPT-2 (Radford et al., 2019), GPT-3.5 (OpenAI, 2022) and Bard (Manyika, 2023). It appeared that GPT-3.5 was the only LLM capable of providing outputs that were making sense for our task. Indeed, all other LLMs provided outputs that are not worth reporting here. The remainder of this section will therefore focus on the use of GPT-3.5 (more specifically GPT-3.5-turbo) with temperature frequency and presence penalties at 0.

The goal of the LLM is to annotate the operations used in a transformation using each of the three typologies presented in Section 3.1. In order to obtain appropriate results, many different prompts have been tried, with different formulations of the problem.

4.2.2 Prompts and Results

The question we explore in this work is: can the LLM annotate pairs of sentence with operations when a typology of operations is provided as a list? In the prompt, we sometimes included or excluded the mention that the sentences were in English, and included or excluded the explicit mention of "simplification". Concerning the formulation of the problem, we provide the full description of each typology and a complex-simple pair and ask the model to identify the corresponding operations. We show here the final prompt pattern that was used[1]:

> You are an expert in linguistics. I will provide you with a taxonomy of operations that can be performed on sentences. The taxonomy is composed of C categories: [list of categories].
>
> Here are the operations contained in the [1st category]:
> [list of operations]
>
> Here are the operations contained in the [2nd category]:
> [list of operations]
>
> [...]
>
> Here are the operations contained in the [Cth category]:
> [list of operations]
>
> Given the above taxonomy, what are the operations used to transform [sentence 1] into [sentence 2]?

Without annotated data from all taxonomies (see Section 3.1), we used examples provided in the papers to check if the LLM could reproduce the annotations provided as examples. Due to space constraints, we only show examples that we think are representative of the LLM behavior on this task.

In all cases, the LLM always uses the operations in the provided taxonomy. However, very often the operations proposed by the LLM differ from the ones provided as examples in the papers. It is worth noting that while some operations proposed by the LLM are different from typology's papers are undoubtedly incorrect, others are interesting and worth considering.

An example with both correct and incorrect annotations is in the following example (from Cardon et al. (2022)):

> From: "Meteora earned the band multiple awards and honors."
>
> To: "Meteora won the band awards."

The output provided by the LLM is

> [...][2]
> 1. (C3) Delete proposition: Remove the proposition "earned" from the sentence.
> 2. (C4) Insert modifier: Add the modifier "the band" to specify which awards are being referred to.
> 3. (C5) Delete modifier: Remove the modifier "multiple" from the sentence.
> 4. (C7) Delete for consistency: Remove the word "and" to maintain consistency with the desired sentence structure.
> 5. (C9) Delete other: Remove the word "honors" as it is not mentioned in the desired sentence.
> 6. (C10) Replace with synonym: Replace the word "earned" with the synonym "won" to convey the same meaning.
> 7. (C14) Replace plural with singular: Change the word "awards" to its singular form "award" to match the desired sentence.
> 8. (C15) Replace segment with a pronoun: Replace the segment "Meteora" with the pronoun "it" to refer to the band.
> [...]

While indeed, some operations are correct (e.g., operation 3, as provided in example by Cardon et al.

[1]See Appendix A for the three complete prompts.

[2]In all reported outputs, we cut the introductory paragraph that rephrases the question that was asked and the final paragraph that summarizes the answer.

(2022)), others are undoubtedly incorrect (e.g., operation 7, as "awards" is plural in both sentences).

In other examples, some incorrect annotations are more subject to interpretation. This is the case, for instance, of the following example from Heineman et al. (2023) for Heineman et al.'s typology:

> From: "Éric Gauthier is also a novella author."
>
> To: "Éric Gauthier, famous for his soloist dancing career, is also a novella author."

The output provided by the LLM is

> [...]
> Conceptual Operation:
> (C1) Elaboration - Adding the information "famous for his soloist dancing career" to elaborate on Éric Gauthier.
>
> Syntax Operation:
> (S1) Word-level Reorder - Reordering the words "famous for his soloist dancing career" to come before "is also a novella author."
>
> Lexical Operation:
> No lexical operations are performed in this transformation.
> [...]

While the elaboration was indeed detected, considering the addition of "famous for his soloist dancing career" in the sentence as a word-level reorder and not as a lexical addition can be questioned.

In some cases, LLM's outputs are different from the examples provided in the typology's papers, but seem correct nonetheless. This is the case of the following example from Yamaguchi et al. (2023) for Yamaguchi et al.'s typology:

> From: "It shows you that hard work will help you reach your goals"
>
> To: "They show you that hard work will help you reach your goals"

The output provided by the LLM is

> [...]
> Surface Strategies:
> - Replacement:
>   - (S2) Replace at word level: Replace "It" with "They"
>
> Content Strategies:
> - No content change:
>   - (C5) Remain unchanged: No changes to the content of the sentence are required.
> [...]

While there is indeed a replace operation at the word level, the LLM also considers that no change in content is induced by the change of "It" by "They", while Yamaguchi et al. (2023) consider on their end that a change in content occurred through a paraphrase for adjustment.

While some of the operations in our experiments have correctly been identified, it is worth noting that a larger portion of operations were incorrectly annotated. A particular issue that was common to all the LLMs tested is their lack of stability. Indeed, it was often witnessed that trivial changes (e.g., adding a comma or removing an irrelevant word in the prompt) could lead to important changes in the LLM's output (i.e. a different annotation), even with temperature set to 0. This shows how difficult, but very important, prompt engineering is.

Based on our review and analysis of the recent typologies, their automation and the prospect of the use of LLMs for this automation, the next section proposes some elements of discussions that can open the literature to new directions.

5 Discussion and Perspectives

Shardlow (2014) wrote that "Simplicity is intuitively obvious, yet hard to define." This also seems to be true for simplification. Recent works on ATS evaluation (Cardon et al., 2022; Stodden, 2021; Alva-Manchego et al., 2021) show the community's perplexity as to how to assess successful simplifications. After the exploration of the literature presented in this paper, we would like to highlight an important observation: we did not find two works using the exact same set of operations. This is true for both linguistic operations and string edits. While we may have left out relevant papers, we are confident that finding identical typologies would be more of a coincidence than an indication of stability. This finding sheds light on the fact that there is no prototypical and consensual view on ATS as an NLP task, from which specific use cases would derive.

We believe that ATS could benefit from a structured framework for thinking of and manipulating operations. There are several perspectives we identified that could help build such a framework. First, operations typologies are mostly built on observations made on corpora. Those corpora are rarely produced by experts in simple writing or experts of potential target audiences. In consequence, what is called "simplification operation" is often an operation observed in a corpus that is used in a way or another for ATS. In their annotation framework, Heineman et al. (2023) ask humans to judge whether operations are relevant for simplification.

We think more work is needed for defining the criteria to distinguish between an operation that actually simplifies a text, and one that does not. Ultimately, while useful, operation sets are mostly built without a clearly defined grounding. Identifying operations that are relevant for a given target audience is a line of research that would be beneficial for making ATS systems available to end users. Rennes et al. (2022) show that while some concrete insights exist, little is still known in that area.

Another part of building a set of operations is the level of analysis. As we have seen in section 2, some operations can be described as belonging to different categories. This is for example the case of coreference/anaphora resolution, which has been positioned at the discourse level (Wilkens et al., 2020), the document level (Laban et al., 2023) or the sentence level (Cardon et al., 2022). Besides this specific example, other decisions can be whether to mix different operation types (linguistic and edits, categorizing grammatical function or nature), or whether considering different paradigms in which operations can overlap (e.g. syntax, discourse, semantics). We argue that those choices should be made knowingly.

On a more practical level, we believe that extending automatic operation annotation to all operation types would be beneficial to the domain. As we have seen, both edit-based and controllable architectures mark the return of operations in the system design. Current evaluation practices also leverage the automatic identification of string edits. Those uses of edits yielded improvements at several levels. However, linguistic operations are more akin to how humans conceive simplification. For example, when deleting a segment, humans do not work token by token but identify a segment and delete it at once. Enabling a reasoning on operation that is closer to the human one, on large amounts of data, would help interpretation of ATS systems' decisions and ATS evaluation metrics' scorings. Efforts towards automated linguistic operations could also help in data curation. It could expand the possibility of exploiting knowledge from experts of specific audiences' needs, as those are formulated as linguistic operations (Siddharthan, 2014; Rennes et al., 2022).

Another perspective is to analyze and structure in more depth the operations at levels above the sentence. As we saw in section 2, there are only a few works that present typologies at that level, yet they already exhibit great disparities.

6 Limitations of this Study

Our study comes with a set of limitations that are mostly focused on our preliminary experiments using LLMs.

First of all, while we experimented with 5 LLMs (BLOOM, BLOOMchat, GPT-2, GPT-3.5 and Bard), many other exist in the literature. For instance, every month, new LLMs appear in the top of the Hugging Face leaderboard [3].Determining if the task is completely solvable using LLMs therefore requires a thorough investigation of many of the existing LLMs.

Second, the lack of stability mentioned in Section 4.2 stresses the importance of prompt engineering to solve the task. While we tested many different prompts in several different configurations, one can never be sure that another untested prompt would not solve the task at hand.

Finally, the lack of access to the annotated corpora of the studied typologies made it difficult to evaluate the LLM on many examples and to provide quantitative results. A corpus containing ground truth annotations for all typologies on the same examples would allow to quantitatively evaluate the performance of LLMs.

7 Conclusion

This paper structured the ATS literature around the question of operations. Indeed, this overlooked angle led us to analyze recent typologies that have been proposed and to highlight their particular features, as well as the differences between them. We described what operations are found in the literature, how they are used and identified (manually and automatically) and provided insights that we hope can help spur new directions for research. In addition to a structured approach of the literature, we also proposed a preliminary experiment investigating the potential of large language models (LLMs) in the automatic annotation of operations. We show that albeit the new opportunities offered by LLMs, linguistic operations identification does not seem to be a trivial task.

We believe that this task may be an important one to address so as to have a better definition of the task, which would facilitate the implementation in real-world settings.

[3]https://huggingface.co/spaces/HuggingFaceH4/open_llm_leaderboard

8 Lay Summary

Automatic text simplification (ATS) systems take a text as an input and the output is expected to be a text with the same meaning, that is easier to read. Any change that is performed to transform the input into the output is called an operation. Operations are therefore the core of the simplification process. "Operation" is a generic term that can cover a variety of different phenomena. Some examples of linguistic operations are clause deletion, replacing a word by a more frequent one, or splitting a complex sentence into two simple ones. Operations can also be considered from the perspective of tokens. In that case token deletion, insertion and preservation are considered operations. Operations have been present in all the stages of ATS works, such as corpus creation and analysis, system design and system evaluation (human or automatic).

In this paper, we explore the literature in automatic text simplification from the perspective of operations. While they are always present in works on ATS, operations have rarely been the main focus of scrutiny by the community. Research on evaluation for ATS has gained traction recently, which involves the manual annotation of operations in ATS corpora or system outputs. We compare three different typologies produced in works on ATS evaluation and contrast them. We also perform preliminary experiments in order to check whether annotating with those three typologies is an easy task to automate, with LLMs.

Our findings expose an absence of stability in the sets of operations that are used in ATS, as there are no two identical ones in the papers we surveyed. Our comparison of the three recent typologies illustrates this absence of a common reference, in terms of defining, structuring and using operations. We find that automating linguistic operation annotation is not a trivial task. However, we believe facilitating the integration of such operations in system design and evaluation would enable new perspectives for ATS.

Our paper is intended for newcomers to the field, as a point of reference to have a better understanding of what operations are, how they have been used throughout ATS research. We believe that active members of the community can also find interesting insights, as the perspective of operations can bring interesting elements to the current reflection around ATS evaluation and how to tailor systems for end users.

Acknowledgments

We thank the anonymous reviewers for their valuable comments and suggestions. Rémi Cardon is supported by the UCLouvain through the FSR Incoming Fellowship Postdoc program. Adrien Bibal is supported by a Belgian American Educational Foundation (BAEF) grant.

References

Fernando Alva-Manchego, Joachim Bingel, Gustavo Paetzold, Carolina Scarton, and Lucia Specia. 2017. Learning how to simplify from explicit labeling of complex-simplified text pairs. In *Proceedings of the Eighth International Joint Conference on Natural Language Processing (Volume 1: Long Papers)*, pages 295–305, Taipei, Taiwan. Asian Federation of Natural Language Processing.

Fernando Alva-Manchego, Louis Martin, Antoine Bordes, Carolina Scarton, Benoît Sagot, and Lucia Specia. 2020. ASSET: A dataset for tuning and evaluation of sentence simplification models with multiple rewriting transformations. In *Proceedings of the Annual Meeting of the Association for Computational Linguistics*, pages 4668–4679.

Fernando Alva-Manchego, Louis Martin, Carolina Scarton, and Lucia Specia. 2019a. EASSE: Easier automatic sentence simplification evaluation. In *Proceedings of the Conference on Empirical Methods in Natural Language Processing and the International Joint Conference on Natural Language Processing (EMNLP-IJCNLP): System Demonstrations*, pages 49–54.

Fernando Alva-Manchego, Carolina Scarton, and Lucia Specia. 2019b. Cross-sentence transformations in text simplification. In *Proceedings of the Workshop on Widening NLP*, pages 181–184.

Fernando Alva-Manchego, Carolina Scarton, and Lucia Specia. 2021. The (un)suitability of automatic evaluation metrics for text simplification. *Computational Linguistics*, 47(4):861–889.

Marcelo Amancio and Lucia Specia. 2014. An analysis of crowdsourced text simplifications. In *Proceedings of the 3rd Workshop on Predicting and Improving Text Readability for Target Reader Populations (PITR)*, pages 123–130, Gothenburg, Sweden. Association for Computational Linguistics.

Stefan Bott and Horacio Saggion. 2014. Text simplification resources for Spanish. *Language Resources and Evaluation*, 48:93–120.

Dominique Brunato, Felice Dell'Orletta, and Giulia Venturi. 2022. Linguistically-based comparison of different approaches to building corpora for text simplification: A case study on italian. *Frontiers in Psychology*, 13.

Dominique Brunato, Felice Dell'Orletta, Giulia Venturi, and Simonetta Montemagni. 2014. Defining an annotation scheme with a view to automatic text simplification. In *Proceedings of the Italian Conference on Computational Linguistics and of the International Workshop EVALITA*, pages 87–92.

Yixin Cao, Ruihao Shui, Liangming Pan, Min-Yen Kan, Zhiyuan Liu, and Tat-Seng Chua. 2020. Expertise style transfer: A new task towards better communication between experts and laymen. In *Proceedings of the 58th Annual Meeting of the Association for Computational Linguistics*, pages 1061–1071, Online. Association for Computational Linguistics.

Rémi Cardon, Adrien Bibal, Rodrigo Wilkens, David Alfter, Magali Norré, Adeline Müller, Watrin Patrick, and Thomas François. 2022. Linguistic corpus annotation for automatic text simplification evaluation. In *Proceedings of the Conference on Empirical Methods in Natural Language Processing*, pages 1842–1866.

Helena M Caseli, Tiago F Pereira, Lucia Specia, Thiago AS Pardo, Caroline Gasperin, and Sandra Maria Aluísio. 2009. Building a brazilian portuguese parallel corpus of original and simplified texts. *Advances in Computational Linguistics, Research in Computer Science*, 41:59–70.

R. Chandrasekar, Christine Doran, and B. Srinivas. 1996. Motivations and methods for text simplification. In *COLING 1996 Volume 2: The 16th International Conference on Computational Linguistics*.

Niladri Chatterjee and Raksha Agarwal. 2021. Depsym: A lightweight syntactic text simplification approach using dependency trees. In *Proceedings of the SEPLN Workshop on Current Trends in Text Simplification*.

Michael Cooper and Matthew Shardlow. 2020. CombiNMT: An exploration into neural text simplification models. In *Proceedings of the Language Resources and Evaluation Conference*, pages 5588–5594.

Liam Cripwell, Joël Legrand, and Claire Gardent. 2023. Document-level planning for text simplification. In *Proceedings of the Conference of the European Chapter of the Association for Computational Linguistics*, pages 993–1006. Association for Computational Linguistics.

Oscar M Cumbicus-Pineda, Itziar Gonzalez-Dios, and Aitor Soroa. 2021. Linguistic capabilities for a checklist-based evaluation in automatic text simplification. In *Proceedings of the SEPLN Workshop on Current Trends in Text Simplification*.

James Curran, Stephen Clark, and Johan Bos. 2007. Linguistically motivated large-scale NLP with C&C and boxer. In *Proceedings of the 45th Annual Meeting of the Association for Computational Linguistics Companion Volume Proceedings of the Demo and Poster Sessions*, pages 33–36, Prague, Czech Republic. Association for Computational Linguistics.

Ashwin Devaraj, Iain Marshall, Byron Wallace, and Junyi Jessy Li. 2021. Paragraph-level simplification of medical texts. In *Proceedings of the Conference of the North American Chapter of the Association for Computational Linguistics: Human Language Technologies*, pages 4972–4984.

Yue Dong, Zichao Li, Mehdi Rezagholizadeh, and Jackie Chi Kit Cheung. 2019. EditNTS: An neural programmer-interpreter model for sentence simplification through explicit editing. In *Proceedings of the Annual Meeting of the Association for Computational Linguistics*, pages 3393–3402.

Richard Evans and Constantin Orasan. 2019. Sentence simplification for semantic role labelling and information extraction. In *Proceedings of the International Conference on Recent Advances in Natural Language Processing (RANLP 2019)*, pages 285–294, Varna, Bulgaria. INCOMA Ltd.

Núria Gala, Anaïs Tack, Ludivine Javourey-Drevet, Thomas François, and Johannes C. Ziegler. 2020. Alector: A parallel corpus of simplified French texts with alignments of misreadings by poor and dyslexic readers. In *Proceedings of the Twelfth Language Resources and Evaluation Conference*, pages 1353–1361, Marseille, France. European Language Resources Association.

Itziar Gonzalez-Dios, María Jesús Aranzabe, and Arantza Díaz de Ilarraza. 2018. The corpus of Basque simplified texts (CBST). *Language Resources and Evaluation*, 52(1):217–247.

David Heineman, Yao Dou, Mounica Maddela, and Wei Xu. 2023. Dancing between success and failure: Edit-level simplification evaluation using SALSA. In *arXiv:2305.14458*.

Masoud Jalili Sabet, Philipp Dufter, François Yvon, and Hinrich Schütze. 2020. SimAlign: High quality word alignments without parallel training data using static and contextualized embeddings. In *Findings of the Association for Computational Linguistics: EMNLP 2020*, pages 1627–1643.

Chao Jiang, Mounica Maddela, Wuwei Lan, Yang Zhong, and Wei Xu. 2020. Neural CRF model for sentence alignment in text simplification. In *Proceedings of the 58th Annual Meeting of the Association for Computational Linguistics*, pages 7943–7960, Online. Association for Computational Linguistics.

Hans Kamp. 1984. *A Theory of Truth and Semantic Representation*, pages 1–42. De Gruyter Mouton, Berlin, Boston.

Anaïs Koptient, Rémi Cardon, and Natalia Grabar. 2019. Simplification-induced transformations: typology and some characteristics. In *Proceedings of the 18th BioNLP Workshop and Shared Task*, pages 309–318, Florence, Italy. Association for Computational Linguistics.

Philippe Laban, Jesse Vig, Wojciech Kryscinski, Shafiq Joty, Caiming Xiong, and Chien-Sheng Wu. 2023. SWiPE: A dataset for document-level simplification of Wikipedia pages. In *Proceedings of the 61st Annual Meeting of the Association for Computational Linguistics (Volume 1: Long Papers)*, pages 10674–10695, Toronto, Canada. Association for Computational Linguistics.

Mounica Maddela, Fernando Alva-Manchego, and Wei Xu. 2021. Controllable text simplification with explicit paraphrasing. In *Proceedings of the 2021 Conference of the North American Chapter of the Association for Computational Linguistics: Human Language Technologies*, pages 3536–3553, Online. Association for Computational Linguistics.

Mounica Maddela, Yao Dou, David Heineman, and Wei Xu. 2023. LENS: A learnable evaluation metric for text simplification. In *Proceedings of the 61st Annual Meeting of the Association for Computational Linguistics (Volume 1: Long Papers)*, pages 16383–16408, Toronto, Canada. Association for Computational Linguistics.

James Manyika. 2023. An overview of Bard: An early experiment with generative AI.

Louis Martin, Éric de la Clergerie, Benoît Sagot, and Antoine Bordes. 2020. Controllable sentence simplification. In *Proceedings of the Language Resources and Evaluation Conference*, pages 4689–4698.

Shashi Narayan and Claire Gardent. 2016. Unsupervised sentence simplification using deep semantics. In *Proceedings of the 9th International Natural Language Generation conference*, pages 111–120, Edinburgh, UK. Association for Computational Linguistics.

Sergiu Nisioi, Sanja Štajner, Simone Paolo Ponzetto, and Liviu P. Dinu. 2017. Exploring neural text simplification models. In *Proceedings of the Annual Meeting of the Association for Computational Linguistics (Volume 2: Short Papers)*, pages 85–91.

OpenAI. 2022. Introducing ChatGPT.

Gustavo Paetzold, Fernando Alva-Manchego, and Lucia Specia. 2017. MASSAlign: Alignment and annotation of comparable documents. In *Proceedings of the International Joint Conference on Natural Language Processing: System Demonstrations*, pages 1–4.

Alec Radford, Karthik Narasimhan, Tim Salimans, Ilya Sutskever, et al. 2018. Improving language understanding by generative pre-training.

Alec Radford, Jeffrey Wu, Rewon Child, David Luan, Dario Amodei, Ilya Sutskever, et al. 2019. Language models are unsupervised multitask learners. *OpenAI blog*, 1(8):9.

Colin Raffel, Noam Shazeer, Adam Roberts, Katherine Lee, Sharan Narang, Michael Matena, Yanqi Zhou, Wei Li, and Peter J Liu. 2020. Exploring the limits of transfer learning with a unified text-to-text transformer. *The Journal of Machine Learning Research*, 21(1):5485–5551.

Evelina Rennes, Marina Santini, and Arne Jonsson. 2022. The Swedish simplification toolkit: – designed with target audiences in mind. In *Proceedings of the Workshop on Tools and Resources to Empower People with REAding DIfficulties (READI) at the Language Resources and Evaluation Conference*, pages 31–38.

Horacio Saggion. 2017. *Automatic Text Simplification*. Synthesis Lectures on Human Language Technologies. Morgan & Claypool Publishers.

Horacio Saggion, Sanja Štajner, Daniel Ferrés, Kim Cheng Sheang, Matthew Shardlow, Kai North, and Marcos Zampieri. 2022. Findings of the TSAR-2022 shared task on multilingual lexical simplification. In *Proceedings of the Workshop on Text Simplification, Accessibility, and Readability (TSAR-2022)*, pages 271–283, Abu Dhabi, United Arab Emirates (Virtual). Association for Computational Linguistics.

SambaNova Systems and Together Computer. 2023. BLOOMChat: A new open multilingual chat LLM.

Teven Le Scao, Angela Fan, Christopher Akiki, Ellie Pavlick, Suzana Ilić, Daniel Hesslow, Roman Castagné, Alexandra Sasha Luccioni, François Yvon, Matthias Gallé, et al. 2022. BLOOM: A 176b-parameter open-access multilingual language model. In *arXiv:2211.05100*.

Matthew Shardlow. 2014. A survey of automated text simplification. *International Journal of Advanced Computer Science and Applications(IJACSA), Special Issue on Natural Language Processing 2014*, 4(1).

Kim Cheng Sheang and Horacio Saggion. 2021. Controllable sentence simplification with a unified text-to-text transfer transformer. In *Proceedings of the 14th International Conference on Natural Language Generation*, pages 341–352, Aberdeen, Scotland, UK. Association for Computational Linguistics.

Advaith Siddharthan. 2014. A survey of research on text simplification. *International Journal of Applied Linguistics*, 165(2):259–298.

Regina Stodden. 2021. When the scale is unclear-analysis of the interpretation of rating scales in human evaluation of text simplification. In *Proceedings of the SEPLN Workshop on Current Trends in Text Simplification*.

Regina Stodden and Laura Kallmeyer. 2022. TS-ANNO: An annotation tool to build, annotate and evaluate text simplification corpora. In *Proceedings of the 60th Annual Meeting of the Association for Computational Linguistics: System Demonstrations*, pages 145–155, Dublin, Ireland. Association for Computational Linguistics.

Regina Stodden, Omar Momen, and Laura Kallmeyer. 2023. DEplain: A German parallel corpus with intralingual translations into plain language for sentence and document simplification. In *Proceedings of the Annual Meeting of the Association for Computational Linguistics (Volume 1: Long Papers)*, pages 16441–16463.

Elior Sulem, Omri Abend, and Ari Rappoport. 2018. Semantic structural evaluation for text simplification. In *Proceedings of the 2018 Conference of the North American Chapter of the Association for Computational Linguistics: Human Language Technologies, Volume 1 (Long Papers)*, pages 685–696, New Orleans, Louisiana. Association for Computational Linguistics.

Md Arafat Sultan, Steven Bethard, and Tamara Sumner. 2014. Back to basics for monolingual alignment: Exploiting word similarity and contextual evidence. *Transactions of the Association for Computational Linguistics*, 2:219–230.

Renliang Sun, Hanqi Jin, and Xiaojun Wan. 2021. Document-level text simplification: Dataset, criteria and baseline. In *Proceedings of the Conference on Empirical Methods in Natural Language Processing*, pages 7997–8013.

Amalia Todirascu, Rodrigo Wilkens, Eva Rolin, Thomas François, Delphine Bernhard, and Núria Gala. 2022. HECTOR: A hybrid TExt SimplifiCation TOol for raw texts in French. In *Proceedings of the Thirteenth Language Resources and Evaluation Conference*, pages 4620–4630, Marseille, France. European Language Resources Association.

Laura Vásquez-Rodríguez, Matthew Shardlow, Piotr Przybyła, and Sophia Ananiadou. 2021a. Investigating text simplification evaluation. In *Findings of the Association for Computational Linguistics: ACL-IJCNLP 2021*, pages 876–882.

Laura Vásquez-Rodríguez, Matthew Shardlow, Piotr Przybyla, and Sophia Ananiadou. 2021b. The role of text simplification operations in evaluation. In *Proceedings of the SEPLN Workshop on Current Trends in Text Simplification*, pages 57–69.

Rodrigo Wilkens, Bruno Oberle, and Amalia Todirascu. 2020. Coreference-based text simplification. In *Proceedings of the 1st Workshop on Tools and Resources to Empower People with REAding DIfficulties (READI)*, pages 93–100, Marseille, France. European Language Resources Association.

Kristian Woodsend and Mirella Lapata. 2011. Learning to simplify sentences with quasi-synchronous grammar and integer programming. In *Proceedings of the 2011 Conference on Empirical Methods in Natural Language Processing*, pages 409–420, Edinburgh, Scotland, UK. Association for Computational Linguistics.

Wei Xu, Chris Callison-Burch, and Courtney Napoles. 2015. Problems in current text simplification research: New data can help. *Transactions of the Association for Computational Linguistics*, 3:283–297.

Wei Xu, Courtney Napoles, Ellie Pavlick, Quanze Chen, and Chris Callison-Burch. 2016. Optimizing statistical machine translation for text simplification. *Transactions of the Association for Computational Linguistics*, 4:401–415.

Daichi Yamaguchi, Rei Miyata, Sayuka Shimada, and Satoshi Sato. 2023. Gauging the gap between human and machine text simplification through analytical evaluation of simplification strategies and errors. In *Findings of the Association for Computational Linguistics: EACL 2023*, pages 359–375.

Yuming Zhai, Pooyan Safari, Gabriel Illouz, Alexandre Allauzen, and Anne Vilnat. 2019. Towards recognizing phrase translation processes: Experiments on english-french. In *Proceedings of the International Conference on Computational Linguistics and Intelligent Text Processing*.

Xingxing Zhang and Mirella Lapata. 2017. Sentence simplification with deep reinforcement learning. In *Proceedings of the 2017 Conference on Empirical Methods in Natural Language Processing*, pages 584–594, Copenhagen, Denmark. Association for Computational Linguistics.

Wayne Xin Zhao, Kun Zhou, Junyi Li, Tianyi Tang, Xiaolei Wang, Yupeng Hou, Yingqian Min, Beichen Zhang, Junjie Zhang, Zican Dong, Yifan Du, Chen Yang, Yushuo Chen, Zhipeng Chen, Jinhao Jiang, Ruiyang Ren, Yifan Li, Xinyu Tang, Zikang Liu, Peiyu Liu, Jian-Yun Nie, and Ji-Rong Wen. 2023. A survey of large language models. In *arXiv:2303.18223*.

Zhemin Zhu, Delphine Bernhard, and Iryna Gurevych. 2010. A monolingual tree-based translation model for sentence simplification. In *Proceedings of the 23rd International Conference on Computational Linguistics (Coling 2010)*, pages 1353–1361, Beijing, China. Coling 2010 Organizing Committee.

Sanja Štajner, Kim Cheng Sheang, and Horacio Saggion. 2022. Sentence simplification capabilities of transfer-based models. *Proceedings of the AAAI Conference on Artificial Intelligence*, 36(11):12172–12180.

A Full Prompts for the Experiments

In this appendix, we show the prompts that we used for our experiments with gpt-3.5-turbo.

A.1 Prompt for Cardon et al.'s Taxonomy

You are an expert in linguistics. I will provide you with a taxonomy of operations that can be performed on sentences. The taxonomy is composed of two sets of operations: computational operations and computational operation combinations.

Here are the operations contained in the set of computational operations:
(C1) Move
(C2) Insert proposition
(C3) Delete proposition
(C4) Insert modifier
(C5) Delete modifier
(C6) Insert for consistency
(C7) Delete for consistency
(C8) Insert other
(C9) Delete other
(C10) Replace with synonym
(C11) Replace with hyperonym
(C12) Replace with hyponym
(C13) Replace singular with plural
(C14) Replace plural with singular
(C15) Replace segment with a pronoun
(C16) Replace pronoun with its antecedent
(C17) Modify verbal features

Here are the operations contained in the set of computational operation combinations: (CC1) Active to passive
(CC2) Passive to active
(CC3) Part-of-speech change
(CC4) Split
(CC5) Merge
(CC6) To impersonal form
(CC7) To personal form
(CC8) Affirmation to negation
(CC9) Negation to affirmation

Given the above taxonomy, what are the operations used to transform [sentence 1] into [sentence 2].

A.2 Prompt for SALSA's Taxonomy

You are an expert in linguistics. I will provide you with a taxonomy of operations that can be performed on sentences. The taxonomy is composed of three categories: conceptual operations, syntax operations and lexical operations.

Here are the operations contained in the category of conceptual operations:
(C1) Elaboration
(C2) Generalization

Here are the operations contained in the category of syntax operations:
(S1) Word-level Reorder
(S2) Component-level Reorder
(S3) Sentence Split

Here are the operations contained in the category of lexical operations:
(L1) Structure Change
(L2) Paraphrase
(L3) Insertion
(L4) Deletion

Given the above taxonomy, what are the operations used to transform [sentence 1] into [sentence 2].

A.3 Prompt for Yamaguchi et al.'s Taxonomy

You are an expert in linguistics. I will provide you with a taxonomy of operations that can be performed on sentences. The taxonomy is composed of two set of strategies: the first set contains the surface strategies and the second set contains the content strategies.

The surface strategies are categorized into 7 categories of operations: "replacement", "deletion", "addition", "integration", "splitting", "move" and "no transformation". Here are the operations contained in each of these 7 categories:
- Replacement:
(S1) Replace at punctuation level
(S2) Replace at word level
(S3) Replace at phrase level
(S4) Replace at clause level
(S5) Replace at sentence level

- Deletion:
(S6) Delete at punctuation level
(S7) Delete at word level
(S8) Delete at phrase level
(S9) Delete at clause level
(S10) Delete at sentence level

- Addition:
(S11) Add at punctuation level
(S12) Add at word level
(S13) Add at phrase level
(S14) Add at clause level
(S15) Add at sentence level

- Integration:
(S16) Integrate two sentences
(S17) Integrate more than two sentences

- Splitting:
(S18) Split by phrase
(S19) Split by clause

- Move:
(S20) Move constituents
(S21) Move a sentence

- No transformation:
(S22) Use an identical sentence

The content strategies are categorized into 5 categories of operations: "no content change", "content deletion", "content addition", "content change" and "document-level adjustment". Here are the operations contained in each of these 5 categories:
- No content change:
(C1) Transform syntactic structure
(C2) Paraphrase into an abbreviation
(C3) Paraphrase into a non-abbreviation
(C4) Paraphrase into standard form
(C5) Remain unchanged

- Content deletion:
(C6) Delete introduction / conclusion
(C7) Delete a parallel element
(C8) Delete information for cohesion
(C9) Delete a modifier
(C10) Delete important information
(C11) Delete detail / extra information

- Content addition:
(C12) Add introduction / conclusion
(C13) Add a parallel element
(C14) Add contextual information
(C15) Add information for cohesion
(C16) Add a modifier
(C17) Add detail / extra information

- Content change:
(C18) Change aspect
(C19) Change modality
(C20) Paraphrase into a similar phrase
(C21) Paraphrase into an explanatory expression
(C22) Paraphrase into a direct expression
(C23) Paraphrase into a brief expression
(C24) Paraphrase into a concrete expression
(C25) Paraphrase into an essential point
(C26) Paraphrase into a different view

- Document-level adjustment:
(C27) Change information flow
(C28) Delete for adjustment
(C29) Add for adjustment
(C30) Paraphrase for adjustment

Given the above taxonomy, what are the operations used to transform [sentence 1] into [sentence 2].

An automated tool with human supervision to adapt difficult texts into Plain Language

Paul Poupet
U31
https://u31.io/
paul.poupet@u31.io

Morgane Hauguel
U31
https://u31.io/
morgane.hauguel@u31.io

Erwan Boehm
U31
https://u31.io/
erwan@u31.io

Charlotte Roze
U31
https://u31.io/
charlotte.roze@u31.io

Paul Tardy
U31
https://u31.io/
pltrdy@gmail.com

Abstract

In this paper, we present an automated tool with human supervision to write in plain language or to adapt difficult texts into plain language. It can be used on a web version and as a plugin for Word/Outlook plugins. At the publication date, it is only available in the French language. This tool has been developed for 3 years and has been used by 400 users from private companies and from public administrations. Text simplification is automatically performed with the manual approval of the user, at the lexical, syntactic, and discursive levels.

Screencast of the demo can be found at the following link: https://www.youtube.com/watch?v=wXVtjfKO9FI.

Keywords : text simplification, Plain language, French, automated tool, simplification tool

1 Introduction

Understanding textual information is a societal issue. The lack of clarity in textual content is an essential dimension of the accessibility issue, in both the physical and digital worlds. It is essential for everyone's access to goods and services, assistance and rights.

1.1 Reading difficulties

16% of the population encounters difficulties to read and understand common textual information of their daily life (INSEE 2012). The right to accessible information is a fundamental right that should be granted to all people (UN, 2020). It is the key factor of personal empowerment and social inclusion. Nevertheless, textual information found on the web, in the news, health leaflets, and other sources is often so linguistically complex it can impede their active participation in the society.

1.2 Plain language

Plain Language is one of the standard standards that aims at providing texts that can be more easily understood by people, especially those who experience difficulties to read and understand. In 2023, ISO-24495 established governing principles and guidelines for developing Plain Language. Plain Language is mainly about using reduced vocabulary, simple sentences and an easy-to-understand discursive organization.

1.3 Text simplification

In order to make texts more readable while preserving their original content, text simplification operates at different linguistic levels (lexical, morphosyntactic, and discursive). Syntactic simplification consists in reducing the complexity of syntactic structures by deleting or replacing complex constructions. Discursive simplifications address phenomena, such as paragraph splitting or reordering, explicitness of coreference chains, anaphora resolution, creation of titles.

2 An automated tool with human supervision

We have developed a tool to help people create plain language texts by using different text simplification techniques. A complexity score is computed for any given text input. The score ranges from 0 to 100, with 0 meaning the text is not clear at all, and 100 meaning it is very clear. Then, the user is presented with an experience/interface similar to a spell and grammar checker: difficult words, sentences or paragraphs are underlined and linked to a suggestion. The user can ignore or accept the suggestion in order to replace the difficult element by a simpler one. Figure 1 shows the interface.

Proceedings of the Second Workshop on Text Simplification, Accessibility and Readability associated with RANLP-2023, pages 131–133,
held in Varna Bulgaria, Sept 7, 2023.
https://doi.org/10.26615/978-954-452-086-1_013

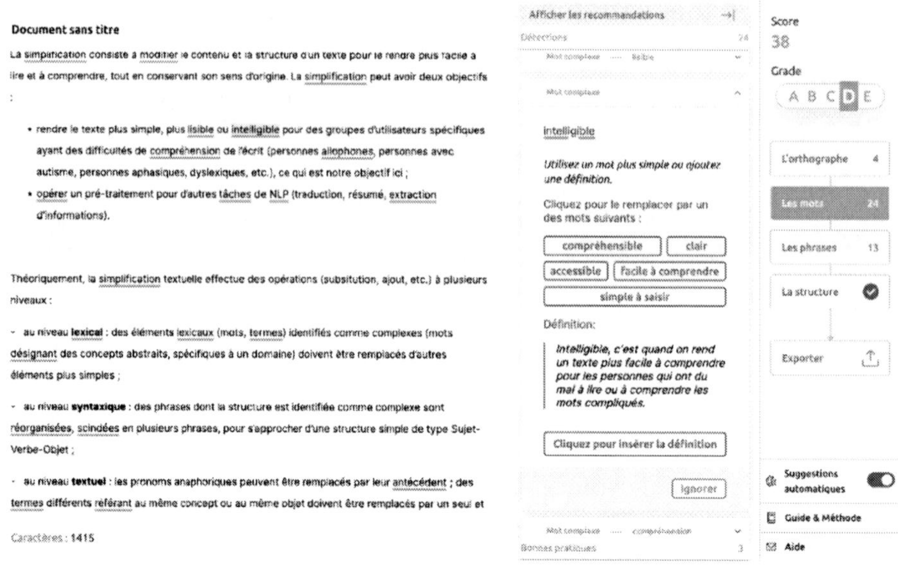

Figure 1: Tool interface

2.1 Scoring

The scoring part has been developed using two French pre-trained language models such as BARThez (Kamal Eddine et al., 2021) and CamemBERT (Martin et al., 2019). The model was then fine-tuned with a classification head as the output layer.

2.2 Complexity identification

The identification of complexity is handled at several levels. Lexical complexity takes into account several parameters: orthograph, appearance rate in a corpus, number of consonants, lists of domain-specific concepts, list of abbreviations and acronyms. At syntactic level, sentence structures are identified as complex with rule-based analysis using SpaCy pipeline based on both dependency and constituency parsing. At textual level, a ruled-base analysis is made to detect anaphora, coreference difficulties, discursive pronouns, length of paragraphs, presence of titles.

2.3 Substitution by simpler solutions

At lexical level, we use use databases of context-based synonyms with a lower difficulty score and context-based definitions with simple words. We also use a custom LLM approach for synonyms and definition generation.

At syntactic level, we both use a rule-based system and a custom LLM approach for simpler paraphrases generation. Simplification rules modify complex sentences by splitting them into several simpler ones and/or reorganizing them.

3 Conclusion and future work

An automated tool is effective to broadcast the use of Plain Language. Users of our tool are private companies and public administrations. More than 400,000 words have been analyzed at the publication date. Continuous improvements are made at each level. Moreover, federated learning allows the scoring, words difficulties and the LLM to improve themselves. At discursive level, logic or temporal reorganization will be tackled.

4 Lay Summary

We present an automated tool for writing in plain language and adapting difficult texts into plain language. It can be used on a web version and as a plugin for Word/Outlook. At the publication date, it is only available in the French language.

This tool has been developed for 3 years. It has been used by 400 users from private companies and from public administrations. Text simplification is automatic with the manual approval of the user, at word, sentence, and text levels.

Screencast of the demo can be found at the following link: `https://www.youtube.com/watch?v=wXVtjfKO9FI`.

References

INSEE 2012. 2012. Pour les générations les plus récentes, les difficultés des adultes diminuent à l'écrit, mais augmentent en calcul. Standard, INSEE.

Moussa Kamal Eddine, Antoine Tixier, and Michalis Vazirgiannis. 2021. BARThez: a skilled pretrained French sequence-to-sequence model. In *Proceedings of the 2021 Conference on Empirical Methods in Natural Language Processing*, pages 9369–9390, Online and Punta Cana, Dominican Republic. Association for Computational Linguistics.

Louis Martin, Benjamin Müller, Pedro Javier Ortiz Suárez, Yoann Dupont, Laurent Romary, Éric Villemonte de la Clergerie, Djamé Seddah, and Benoît Sagot. 2019. Camembert: a tasty french language model. *CoRR*, abs/1911.03894.

Beyond Vocabulary: Capturing Readability from Children's Difficulty

Arif Ahmed
Department of Computer Science
Boise State University
arifahmed@u.boisestate.edu

Abstract

Readability formulae targeting children have been developed, but their appropriateness can still be improved, for example by taking into account *suffixation*. Literacy research has identified the suffixation phenomenon makes children's reading difficult, so we analyze the effectiveness of suffixation within the context of readability. Our analysis finds that suffixation is potentially effective for readability assessment. Moreover, we find that existing readability formulae fail to discern lower grade levels for texts from different existing corpora.

1 Introduction

Readability is employed as a tool for various audiences, including children and second-language users, as well as diverse tasks such as web search, recommendation, selecting textbook materials, calibrating books, text summarization, machine translation, automatic text simplification, and more (Bilal and Huang, 2019; Alharthi and Inkpen, 2019; Stenner, 1996; Paul and Sumita, 2011; Štajner and Saggion, 2013). Importantly, the use of readability for such tasks becomes critical when the target users are children (grades K-6). Unlike adults, they do not (yet) have all the necessary reading skills, so children require more appropriate text according to their grade level (Rahman et al., 2020).

However, Allen et al. (2022) highlighted that the performance of traditional readability formulae greatly varies across different grade levels while estimating the readability of children's resources. Also, they proposed a lexicon-based formula named *Spache-Allen*, which could capture readability better than other traditional formulae. Generally, lexicon-based readability formulae consider sentence length and static vocabulary to determine text readability (Spache, 1968). Over the years, researchers augmented

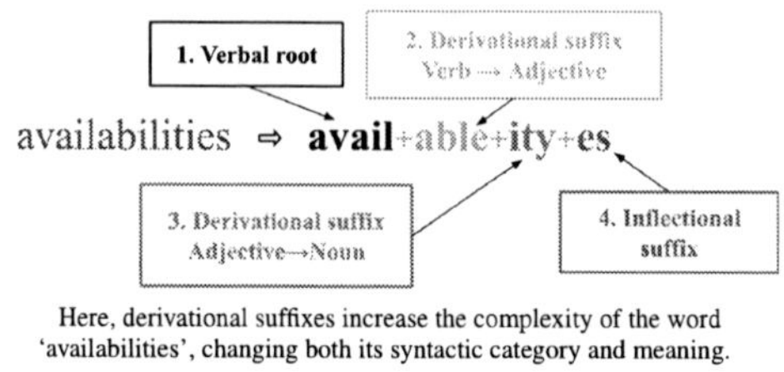

Figure 1: Suffixation in 'availabilities'

these static vocabularies (from 1064 to 65,669 words) to increase lexicon-based formula's performance (Spache, 1968; Madrazo Azpiazu et al., 2018; Allen et al., 2022). While looking up a word within the vocabulary, such formulae do not consider words' complex properties, such as inflectional endings and derivational suffixes. More recently, Allen et al. (2022) included the Age-of-Acquisition dataset (Kuperman et al., 2012) to the original Spache (1968) vocabulary in their Spache-Allen formula, because they considered children are taught these words over the years. Importantly, children learn these words in a staircased fashion from lower to more complex words across grade levels. Even though vocabulary augmentation has increased their formula's performance, it does not capture the children's staircased word learning process. Researchers on literacy identified *suffixation* as an influential factor that affects children's reading experience (Nagy et al., 1985, 1991). In Figure 1, we show how suffixation makes a word more complex. To the best of our knowledge, no readability research has taken into account the factor of suffixation carefully, which makes children's reading difficult. Instead of increasing the size of static vocabulary to push the formulas' performance digits, we should carefully understand children's vocabulary acquisition process from literacy research for the readability assessment task.

Proceedings of the Second Workshop on Text Simplification, Accessibility and Readability associated with RANLP-2023, pages 134–141,
held in Varna Bulgaria, Sept 7, 2023.
https://doi.org/10.26615/978-954-452-086-1_014

In this paper, we investigate how suffixes indicate the readability level of English text with the research question **RQ:** ***How effective are ranked suffixes from literacy research for readability assessment?*** To answer this research question, we take advantage of prior work of Jarmulowicz (2002), where they identified 43 derivational suffixes and ranked them in 25 discrete levels based on frequency. We posit that these ranks will help us capture the staircased word complexity that children learn over the grade levels. Furthermore, we have made our suffixation approach implementation publicly available on GitHub.[1]

2 Background and Related Work

2.1 Children's Reading Behaviour

As children learn to read and their vocabulary expands, derived words (e.g., inflectional morphology or compound formation) play a substantial role in text comprehension (Jarmulowicz, 2002). In fact, the knowledge of *vocabulary* children already have works as the best predictor for reading comprehension (Stahl and Nagy, 2007). Studies showed that children's knowledge of *morphology* has a significant impact on reading (Anglin et al., 1993; Carlisle, 2000, 2003). Whenever they encounter any unfamiliar morphologically complex words, they use their knowledge of root words and affixes to determine the meaning of that word. Children develop different facets of knowledge of morphology at different rates and times (Tyler and Nagy, 1989). Nagy et al. (1991) found that after the third grade, students gain knowledge of common English suffixes (e.g., '-es' in oxes), and some students face severe problems with understanding the function of suffixes. Children learn inflectional suffixes and compounding before derivational suffixation (e.g., '-able' in readable) (Derwing and Baker, 1979). Later, Nagy et al. (1993) identified one reason for that is the relative abstractness of the information conveyed in derivational suffixes.

2.2 Readability for Children

Over the past century, researchers proposed hundreds of readability assessment methods ranging from classic formulae to featureless models (Flesch, 1948; Madrazo Azpiazu et al., 2018; Filighera et al., 2019; Vajjala and Lučić, 2018; Deutsch et al., 2020; Huebner et al., 2021; Lee et al., 2021; Rao et al., 2021). Still today, traditional formulae from early periods are widely used, which consider word counts, sentence length, lexical, and syntactic features (Flesch, 1948; Dale and Chall, 1948; Flesch, 1950; Gunning et al., 1952). These readability formulae are widely used in real-world environments (Begeny and Greene, 2014; Crossley et al., 2019), as these formulae are easy to deploy. In real-world settings, children are becoming a large user group. So, it is crucial to investigate the appropriateness of the existing readability formula. Article no. 17 of United Nations' Convention on the Rights of the Child also encouraged so.[2] To support children to understand real-world text, we should develop an appropriate readability formula for them.

3 Method

3.1 Data Setup

3.1.1 Corpora

Targeting children (grades K-6), we consider the following datasets.

(a) Common Core State Standards (CCSS): We extract book excerpts from the appendices of the CCSS.[3] Targeting children (grades K-6), we consider 196 books from grades K-8, as texts from grades 6-8 are grouped under the same labeling.

(b) WeeBit: We consider this for web resources (Vajjala and Meurers, 2012). We apply the downsampling technique to the dataset and consider 629 samples from each class. This is a common approach researchers apply to this dataset (Deutsch et al., 2020; Lee et al., 2021).

(c) Science: This corpus has science-related text (i.e., informational text) for K-12 population (Nadeem and Ostendorf, 2018). However, only their publicly available test samples covering grades 3-12 are accessible. To ensure consistent comparison across the three corpora, we select 1035 samples from grades 3-8.

3.1.2 Corpus Analysis

Before we answer our research question, we conduct correlation analysis on the data (Sec. 3.1.1) to identify potential biases. For correlation analysis, we denote two variables– shallow factors (vocabulary size per text, number of words per text, average words per sentence, number of sentences per text) as X (continuous) and grade levels as Y (ordinal). Here, the Y variable is ordinal because each of the

[1] https://github.com/arif09/beyond_vocabulary

[2] https://www.unicef.org/child-rights-convention/convention-text-childrens-version

[3] http://www.corestandards.org/assets/Appendix_B.pdf

grade levels is a discrete ordinal representing the degree of text complexity. Based on the best practices (Khamis, 2008), we choose Kendall τ as the correlation metric for CCSS, and Spearman's ρ for the WeeBit and Science corpora.

3.2 Suffixation Based Text Complexity

3.2.1 Suffix Ranking for Words

The text simplification research shows that text containing a few complex words or sentences can increase overall text difficulty (Glavaš and Štajner, 2015). In Sec. 2.1, we explain that derivational suffixes make a word more complex than other affixes. To explore this direction, we take advantage of the prior work of Jarmulowicz (2002), which identified 43 derivational suffixes and ranked them from 1 to 25 based on the frequency of a child-directed corpus. We mark this *'derivational suffix rank'* as a complexity indicator that can capture children's cognitive processing effort. In this paper, we represent these 43 ranked derivational suffixes with S_{der}. To the best of our knowledge, this is the first attempt that uses the rank of derivational suffixes as a way to capture a word's complexity.

It is certain that lower grade text (e.g., K-2) may not have any or few derivational suffixes as children start learning the function of suffixes in grade 3 (Nagy et al., 1991). To thoroughly cover a broad spectrum of words, it is appropriate to consider all the derivational and inflectional suffixes (e.g., '-s', '-es') in addition to the 43 S_{der}s. Therefore, we find unique 556 inflectional suffixes and 452 derivational suffixes from UniMorph.[4] Among these 1008 suffixes, it is necessary to assign a rank to these 965 (1008−43) unranked suffixes, $S_{der+inf}$. To achieve this, we follow these three steps:

1. Create character's positional vectors $\vec{S}_{der+inf}$ and $\vec{S}_{der}$ from $S_{der+inf}$ and S_{der} respectively.
2. Derive cosine similarity, $cos(\vec{S}_{der+inf}, \vec{S}_{der})$.
3. For each *candidate* suffix in $S_{der+inf}$, identify the most similar suffix from S_{der} and assign the corresponding rank to the *candidate* suffix.

In Figure 2, we illustrate the process of ranking the suffix '-sion' through the three aforementioned steps. First, we generate positional vectors for the characters of the ranked S_{der} suffixes and the unranked '-sion' suffix. Second, we compute the

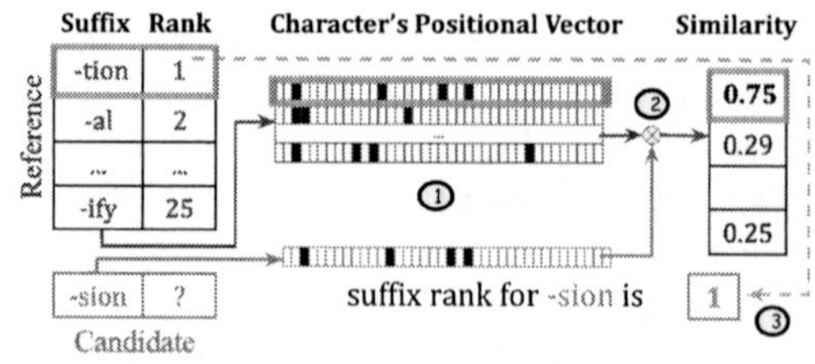

Figure 2: Suffix Ranking Example

cosine similarity scores between the vector of the unranked suffix and all other ranked suffix vectors. Third, we determine that the unranked '-sion' suffix shows the highest similarity score of 0.75 with the '-tion' suffix. Since the '-tion' suffix holds a rank value of 1, we assign the same rank value of 1 to the unranked '-sion' suffix.

3.2.2 Measuring Text Complexity

Although we have assigned rank values (1 to 25) to all the inflectional and derivational suffixes (Sec. 3.2.1), we must put more weight on derivational suffixes. This is because, derivational suffixes are more complex (e.g., changes both syntactic category and meaning of a word) than inflectional suffixes. Considering this fact, we first define word-level complexity. Using these complexity scores, we define text-level complexity.

(a) Word Level: We check a word's derivational suffix by looking it up in UniMorph and verifying if the word is in its derived form. Next, if the derived word, along with its suffix, alters the base word's syntactic category (parts of speech), we categorize that suffix as derivational; otherwise, we classify it as inflectional. We compute C_w, the complexity score of the given word w following the equation:

$$C_w = \begin{cases} rank & : w \text{ has derivational suffix} \\ 1 + \frac{rank}{n} & : w \text{ has inflectional suffix} \\ 0 & : w \text{ has no suffix} \end{cases} \quad (1)$$

Here, **Case 1**: if a word contains a derivational suffix, we directly assign its suffix rank. **Case 2**: in the case of words with an inflectional suffix, we divide the rank by $n = 10$ (randomly chosen) and then add 1. This approach limits the complexity score advancement of inflectional suffixes, thereby emphasizing the contribution of derivational suffixes to the overall complexity score. So, the complexity score of inflectional suffixes would range from 1.1 to 3.5, a considerably lower range compared to the values obtained for derivational suffixes, which span from 1 to 25. **Case 3**: if a word

[4] `https://github.com/unimorph/eng/`

is either in its base form or bears only prefixes, we consider a 0 (zero) complexity score for it.

(b) Text Level: After measuring the word complexity within a sentence, we take the maximum complexity score from a sentence. Taking the mean value from all the sentences could potentially affect the overall score, so we take the median value from all the sentences within a text.

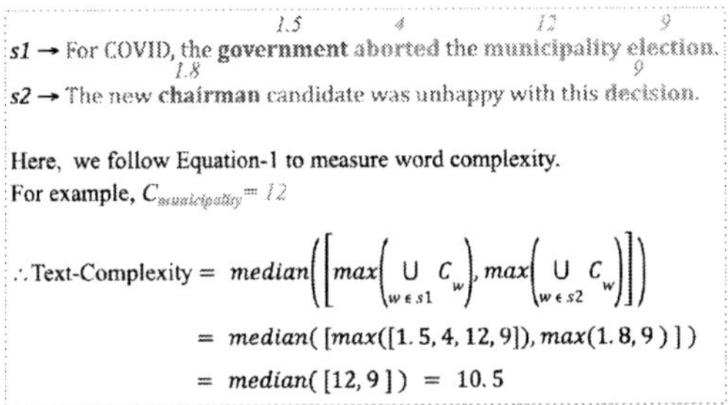

Figure 3: Suffixation-Based Text Complexity Scoring

Figure 3 illustrates our process for measuring text complexity using our novel suffixation approach for a sample text comprising two sentences.

3.2.3 Readability Analysis

To answer our research question, we first compute text complexity using our suffixation-based approach (Sec 3.2). To see how these scores indicate different reading levels for our selected corpora, we carefully conduct this analysis. Since outliers can significantly influence correlation analysis, it is important to analyze the relationship between actual scores and grade levels visually. Visual inspection can reveal unusual circumstances (e.g., flat or rise to specific grades) that might not be apparent from correlation scores alone. In order to illustrate the effectiveness of our novel suffixation-based approach, we employ a visual technique (i.e., box-and-whisker plot) as opposed to reporting only numeric correlation scores.

Now, we estimate readability levels for Spache-Allen (Allen et al., 2022) and employ the same visual technique to gain insight and compare with our proposed approach.[5] However, Allen et al. (2022) showed the performance of formulae using the Mean Error Rate (MER) metric where the error was computed by taking the absolute difference between actual grade level and predicted grade level. Thus, MER does not indicate if the formula is estimating a grade level above or below the actual grade level. So, we use the raw scores (grades) of Spache-Allen (Allen et al., 2022) for our visual inspection. To gain further insight, we also consider eight other traditional readability formulae and estimate readability levels using TextStat.[6] We are considering nine formulae: Flesch-Kincaid Grade Level (FKGL), Dale-Chall (DC), Gunning Fog Index (FOG), SMOG, Spache Readability Formula (Spache), Spache-Allen (SA), Coleman-Liau Index (COLE), RIX, and LIX (Flesch, 1950; Chall and Dale, 1995; Albright et al., 1996; Mc Laughlin, 1969; Spache, 1968; Allen et al., 2022; Coleman and Liau, 1975; Anderson, 1983).

4 Results and Discussion

4.1 Corpus Analysis

From Figure 4, we find that shallow factors of texts are not highly correlated with the grade levels for all three corpora. This finding confirms that no confounding factors impact our analysis and result.

Here, ρ: Spearman's ρ correlation, τ: Kendall τ correlation.

Figure 4: Correlation of Shallow Factors with Grades

4.2 Readability Analysis

Figure 5(a) shows how suffix-based complexity measurements indicate reading levels of different corpora. We can see a gradual increase in complexity scores across grade levels for all corpora. Specifically, the median values for each boxplot gradually increase from lower grades to upper grades except for the Science corpus. We see more longer boxes and outliers toward the upper grades. We also see that the upper whiskers are much longer than the lower whiskers. These findings indicate that suffixation increases from lower to upper grades. In particular, almost no presence of suffixes in K-1 grade levels and a very low presence of suffixes from grades 2-3, which supports the findings from literacy education research (Nagy et al., 1991). As the Science corpus represents scientific text, it contains more derived words. We find the suffixes increase very slowly across grade levels 3-6.

[5]We follow the author-provided implementation.

[6]https://pypi.org/project/textstat/

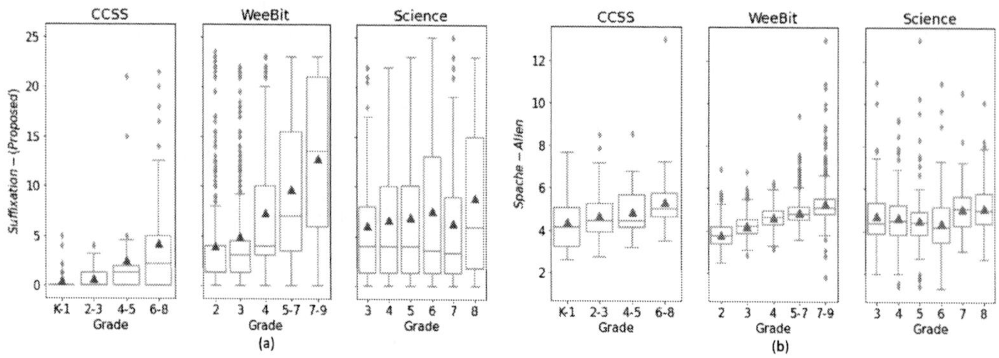

Figure 5: (a) Suffixation-Based Text Complexity Score and (b) Estimated Grades (raw) Using Spache-Allen Formula

On the contrary, Spache-Allen (Allen et al., 2022) readability formula estimated grade levels for all corpora around grade 4 [Figure 5(b)]. In the CCSS corpus, we discover nearly identical median values across grades K-5. It is a concern that this formula estimates higher complexity for texts from grades K-3 in CCSS. In fact, K-2 text contains mostly very simple words (e.g., cat, bat). In a recent study, Bettencourt et al. (2022) utilized Spache-Allen for assessing text complexity in web search results to study children's (grades 1-6) web search engagement. Here, a potential concern arises that using an appropriate readability formula might yield different results in their analysis. Hence, our analysis addresses our research question, confirming that suffixation effectively captures readability for children.

While our focus is on suffixation, we do not delve into the performance of other readability formulae; however, we provide their performance in Appendix A. Our findings indicate that traditional formulae estimate significantly higher grade levels for our chosen corpora, whereas Allen et al. (2022) discovered only an increase of 1-3 grades. For WeeBit, most of the formulae show an upward linear trend but estimated grade levels inaccurately. This observation stems from our corpus analysis, where we address that shallow factors correlate with grade levels of WeeBit corpus better than CCSS and Science corpora.

We could not access NewsELA and Reading A-Z corpora which were merged with WeeBit and CCSS in Allen et al.'s experiments. It is possible that these unavailable datasets contributed to increasing formulas' performance in their conducted experiment. Typically, children's books might not be ideal for automatic readability assessment. For example, easy words are repeated more frequently in lower-grade text. Particularly, educators and teachers increase the amount of text across grade levels, which is a very common confounding factor that can deceive readability assessment. In fact, many complex instruction texts in books are not intended for children. While working on these children's books, we must carefully consider such factors that might affect our experiment.

5 Conclusion

Our investigation shows that findings from literacy research can help us develop the appropriate readability formula for children. We also show the current state-of-the-art readability formula for children fails to discern words with complex morphological properties. Moreover, our work shows that we should consider the findings from other disciplines (e.g., Education, Literacy) to better capture readability to suggest appropriate text for children, a rapidly increasing user group accessing digital platforms. Our word-level complexity scoring can directly support lexical simplification tasks and text-level complexity scoring can enhance text accessibility for diverse user groups (e.g.,second-language learners or marginalized populations). Besides, our novel suffixation approach can serve as a versatile feature for feature-based models across various Natural Language Processing tasks, encompassing various domains such as Information Retrieval or Human-Computer Interaction.

Acknowledgements

We extend our gratitude to Dr. Sowmya Vajjala for generously sharing their WeeBit corpus. We thank the anonymous reviewers for their suggestions and Sharif Ahmed for helpful discussions.

6 Lay Summary

Children in grades K-6 are becoming a large group in online platforms, they use various applications for educational and learning purposes. Specifically, their use of such platforms becomes useful when they can understand the information, mostly text. To serve their purpose, researchers from many disciplines working towards measuring the appropriateness of the text targeting children. To measure the difficulty of any given text, researchers have proposed many methods over the last hundred years. The term 'readability' measures how easy (i.e., text from specific grade levels) any text is for a reader group (i.e., preschool, school, or college).

Most readability research introduced new datasets or increased vocabulary (i.e., word lists) size to show their formula's performance better. Instead of proposing a new readability formula, we try to understand what factors make children's (grades K-6) reading difficult by exploring literacy education research. From that exploration, we identify that 'suffixation' makes children's reading difficult. So, we fit this theory for the readability problem and propose a new approach to compute text difficulty.

Our paper uncovers the effectiveness of 'suffixation' for determining the reading level of any text. Compared to the existing readability formula, it can discern lower-grade text effectively.

References

Judith Albright, Carol de Guzman, Patrick Acebo, Dorothy Paiva, Mary Faulkner, and Janice Swanson. 1996. Readability of patient education materials: implications for clinical practice. *Applied Nursing Research*, 9(3):139–143.

Haifa Alharthi and Diana Inkpen. 2019. Study of linguistic features incorporated in a literary book recommender system. In *Proceedings of the 34th ACM/SIGAPP Symposium on Applied Computing*, pages 1027–1034.

Garrett Allen, Ashlee Milton, Katherine Landau Wright, Jerry Alan Fails, Casey Kennington, and Maria Soledad Pera. 2022. Supercalifragilisticexpialidocious: Why Using the "Right" Readability Formula in Children's Web Search Matters. In *Advances in Information Retrieval*, pages 3–18, Cham. Springer International Publishing.

Jonathan Anderson. 1983. Lix and rix: Variations on a little-known readability index. *Journal of Reading*, 26(6):490–496.

Jeremy M Anglin, George A Miller, and Pamela C Wakefield. 1993. Vocabulary development: A morphological analysis. *Monographs of the society for research in child development*, pages i–186.

John C Begeny and Diana J Greene. 2014. Can readability formulas be used to successfully gauge difficulty of reading materials? *Psychology in the Schools*, 51(2):198–215.

Benjamin Bettencourt, Arif Ahmed, Nic Way, Casey Kennington, Katherine Landau Wright, and Jerry Alan Fails. 2022. Searching for engagement: Child engagement and search engine result pages. In *Interaction Design and Children*, IDC '22, page 479–484, New York, NY, USA. Association for Computing Machinery.

Dania Bilal and Li-Min Huang. 2019. Readability and word complexity of serps snippets and web pages on children's search queries: Google vs bing. *Aslib Journal of Information Management*.

Joanne F Carlisle. 2000. Awareness of the structure and meaning of morphologically complex words: Impact on reading. *Reading and writing*, 12(3):169–190.

Joanne F Carlisle. 2003. Morphology matters in learning to read: A commentary. *Reading Psychology*, 24(3-4):291–322.

Jeanne Sternlicht Chall and Edgar Dale. 1995. *Manual for use of the new Dale-Chall readability formula*. Brookline Books.

Meri Coleman and Ta Lin Liau. 1975. A computer readability formula designed for machine scoring. *Journal of Applied Psychology*, 60(2):283.

Scott A Crossley, Stephen Skalicky, and Mihai Dascalu. 2019. Moving beyond classic readability formulas: New methods and new models. *Journal of Research in Reading*, 42(3-4):541–561.

Edgar Dale and Jeanne S Chall. 1948. A formula for predicting readability: Instructions. *Educational research bulletin*, pages 37–54.

Bruce L Derwing and William J Baker. 1979. Recent research on the acquisition of english morphology. *Language acquisition*, pages 209–223.

Tovly Deutsch, Masoud Jasbi, and Stuart Shieber. 2020. Linguistic features for readability assessment. In *Proceedings of the Fifteenth Workshop on Innovative Use of NLP for Building Educational Applications*, pages 1–17, Seattle, WA, USA → Online. Association for Computational Linguistics.

Anna Filighera, Tim Steuer, and Christoph Rensing. 2019. Automatic text difficulty estimation using embeddings and neural networks. In *European Conference on Technology Enhanced Learning*, pages 335–348. Springer.

Rudolf Flesch. 1950. Measuring the level of abstraction. *Journal of Applied Psychology*, 34(6):384.

Rudolph Flesch. 1948. A new readability yardstick. *Journal of applied psychology*, 32(3):221.

Goran Glavaš and Sanja Štajner. 2015. Simplifying lexical simplification: Do we need simplified corpora? In *Proceedings of the 53rd Annual Meeting of the Association for Computational Linguistics and the 7th International Joint Conference on Natural Language Processing (Volume 2: Short Papers)*, pages 63–68, Beijing, China. Association for Computational Linguistics.

Robert Gunning et al. 1952. Technique of clear writing.

Philip A. Huebner, Elior Sulem, Fisher Cynthia, and Dan Roth. 2021. BabyBERTa: Learning more grammar with small-scale child-directed language. In *Proceedings of the 25th Conference on Computational Natural Language Learning*, pages 624–646, Online. Association for Computational Linguistics.

Linda D. Jarmulowicz. 2002. English derivational suffix frequency and children's stress judgments. *Brain and Language*, 81(1):192–204.

Harry Khamis. 2008. Measures of association: How to choose? *Journal of Diagnostic Medical Sonography*, 24(3):155–162.

Victor Kuperman, Hans Stadthagen-Gonzalez, and Marc Brysbaert. 2012. Age-of-acquisition ratings for 30,000 english words. *Behavior research methods*, 44(4):978–990.

Bruce W. Lee, Yoo Sung Jang, and Jason Lee. 2021. Pushing on text readability assessment: A transformer meets handcrafted linguistic features. In *Proceedings of the 2021 Conference on Empirical Methods in Natural Language Processing*, pages 10669–10686, Online and Punta Cana, Dominican Republic. Association for Computational Linguistics.

Ion Madrazo Azpiazu, Nevena Dragovic, Oghenemaro Anuyah, and Maria Soledad Pera. 2018. Looking for the movie seven or sven from the movie frozen? a multi-perspective strategy for recommending queries for children. In *Proceedings of the 2018 Conference on Human Information Interaction amp; Retrieval*, CHIIR '18, page 92–101, New York, NY, USA. Association for Computing Machinery.

G Harry Mc Laughlin. 1969. Smog grading-a new readability formula. *Journal of reading*, 12(8):639–646.

Farah Nadeem and Mari Ostendorf. 2018. Estimating linguistic complexity for science texts. In *Proceedings of the Thirteenth Workshop on Innovative Use of NLP for Building Educational Applications*, pages 45–55, New Orleans, Louisiana. Association for Computational Linguistics.

William Nagy, Irene-Anna Diakidoy, and Richard C. Anderson. 1991. The development of knowledge of derivational suffixes.

William E Nagy, Irene-Anna N Diakidoy, and Richard C Anderson. 1993. The acquisition of morphology: Learning the contribution of suffixes to the meanings of derivatives. *Journal of reading Behavior*, 25(2):155–170.

William E. Nagy, Patricia A. Herman, and Richard C. Anderson. 1985. Learning words from context. *Reading Research Quarterly*, 20(2):233–253.

Michael Paul and Eiichiro Sumita. 2011. Translation quality indicators for pivot-based statistical MT. In *Proceedings of 5th International Joint Conference on Natural Language Processing*, pages 811–818, Chiang Mai, Thailand. Asian Federation of Natural Language Processing.

Rashedur Rahman, Gwénolé Lecorvé, Aline Étienne, Delphine Battistelli, Nicolas Béchet, and Jonathan Chevelu. 2020. Mama/papa, is this text for me? In *Proceedings of the 28th International Conference on Computational Linguistics*, pages 6296–6301, Barcelona, Spain (Online). International Committee on Computational Linguistics.

Simin Rao, Hua Zheng, and Sujian Li. 2021. Cross-lingual leveled reading based on language-invariant features. In *Findings of the Association for Computational Linguistics: EMNLP 2021*, pages 2677–2682, Punta Cana, Dominican Republic. Association for Computational Linguistics.

George D Spache. 1968. Good reading for poor readers.

Steven A Stahl and William E Nagy. 2007. *Teaching word meanings*. Routledge.

Sanja Štajner and Horacio Saggion. 2013. Readability indices for automatic evaluation of text simplification systems: A feasibility study for Spanish. In *Proceedings of the Sixth International Joint Conference on Natural Language Processing*, pages 374–382, Nagoya, Japan. Asian Federation of Natural Language Processing.

A Jackson Stenner. 1996. Measuring reading comprehension with the lexile framework.

Andrea Tyler and William Nagy. 1989. The acquisition of english derivational morphology. *Journal of memory and language*, 28(6):649–667.

Sowmya Vajjala and Ivana Lučić. 2018. OneStopEnglish corpus: A new corpus for automatic readability assessment and text simplification. In *Proceedings of the Thirteenth Workshop on Innovative Use of NLP for Building Educational Applications*, pages 297–304, New Orleans, Louisiana. Association for Computational Linguistics.

Sowmya Vajjala and Detmar Meurers. 2012. On Improving the Accuracy of Readability Classification using Insights from Second Language Acquisition. In *Proceedings of the Seventh Workshop on Building Educational Applications Using NLP*, pages 163–173, Montréal, Canada. Association for Computational Linguistics.

A Appendix

Because of limitations in scope and page count, we include Figure 6 in this section, illustrating the efficacy of readability formulae on our selected corpora. For better visualization, any estimated grade levels exceeding 13 were adjusted to 13 for visualization purposes.

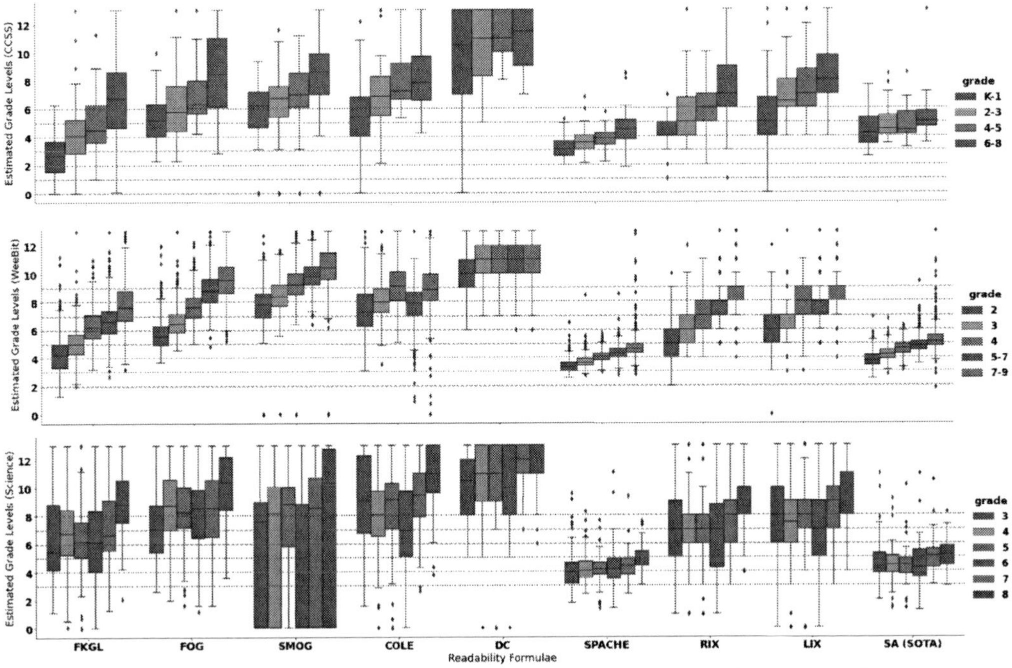

Here, each colored dashed horizontal line represents the actual grade level for that corpus, with the boxes indicating the estimated grade levels.

Figure 6: Estimation of Text Readability Using Traditional Readability Formulae

Author Index